Ethiopia
Social Sector Report

The World Bank
Washington, D.C.

Cover photo: "Ethiopia: Mother, child, coffee. Coffee was boiled in a clay pot over coals and ceremonially poured into small china cups." Photo taken by Ian Newport, chief counsel for the Europe and Central Asia Region of the World Bank, during his one week in Afgol Kebele in Tigray, Ethiopia, in May 1998, as part of the Grassroots Immersion Program under the World Bank Executive Development Program.

ISSN: 0253-2123

Library of Congress Cataloging-in-Publication Data

Ethiopia : social sector report.
       p. cm. — (A World Bank country study)
   ISBN 0-8213-4314-9
   1. Ethiopia—Social conditions—1974– 2. Ethiopia—Social policy.
3. Education—Ethiopia. I. World Bank. II. Series.
HN789.A8E87 1998
306'.0963—dc21
                                      98-34326
                                       CIP

CONTENTS

ABSTRACT x

PREFACE xi

ACKNOWLEDGMENTS xii

ACRONYMS AND ABBREVIATIONS xiv

EXECUTIVE SUMMARY xv

1   BACKGROUND 1

Objectives of This Report 1
Using a Life Cycle Approach to Social Sector Strategy Formulation 2
Data Sources 3

**2   CONTEXTUAL FACTORS INFLUENCING ETHIOPIA'S
     SOCIAL SECTORS** 7

Social Sector Performance and the Economy 7
Policy and Economic Environment 9
    Economic Growth 10
    Fiscal Policy Reform 11
Institutional Context 12
    Regionalization 12
    Private Sector Role 13
    Community Involvement 14
Population Projections and Implications 14

3   THE ETHIOPIAN HOUSEHOLD 19

Income and Sources of Income 19
Household Expenditure Patterns 20
Impact of Community Level Infrastructure and Services 21

4   HEALTH **23**

Indicators of Health Status 23
Burden of Disease 24
Demand for Health 26
      Incidence and Duration of Illness 26
      Utilization Rates 27
      Choice of Provider 29
      Health Expenditure at the Household Level 30
Supply of Health Services 32
      Health Services and Utilization 32
      Availability of Facilities 33
      Staffing and Inputs 35
      Medical Supplies and Pharmaceuticals 37
Policy and Institutional Framework 38
Decentralization: Managerial and Institutional Framework 39
      Government Agencies 39
      Private Sector 40
      Community Participation 40
      Nongovernmental Organizations 41
Costs and Financing 41
      Levels and Composition of Financing 41
      Sources of Financing 43
      Cost Recovery 44
      Adequacy and Sustainability of Financing 46
      Future Options for Financing 46
Program Implications for the Health Sector 50

5   NUTRITION **53**

Malnutrition in Ethiopia 53
      Child Malnutrition 53
      Other Nutrition Problems 56
Poverty and Malnutrition 57
Programs and Policies 61
Program Implications for Nutrition 64

6   POPULATION **65**

Outcomes 65
      Population Growth and Structure 65
      Fertility 66
      Mortality 67
      STDs and HIV/AIDS 68

Demand for Services 69
    Preference for Children 69
    Knowledge and Use of Contraceptives 70
    Other Determinants of Demand 72
Programs and Policies 72
    Program Coverage and Finance 72
    Population Policy 73
Program Implications of Projected Population Changes 74
    Projected Population Changes 74
    Integrating Services 75
    Elimination of Harmful Practices 76
    Improvement in the Socioeconomic Status of the Population, Especially of Women . . 76

7   EDUCATION 77

General Structure and Performance of the Education Sector 78
    Primary School 78
    Urban-Rural Differences 79
    Regional Differences 80
    Gender Differences 81
    Secondary School 81
    Tertiary Schooling 82
    Technical and Vocational Education 82
Household Demand for Education 82
    Attitudes toward Schooling 83
    Household Education Expenditures 84
    Opportunity Costs of Schooling 85
    Perceived Returns to Schooling 86
    Other Factors That Affect Household Demand for Schooling 88
Supply-Side Assessment 88
    Provision of Educational Facilities and Services 91
    Teaching and Administrative Staff 92
Cost and Financing of Education 94
    Sources and Uses of Funds 94
    Public Spending on Education 95
    Stability of Funding Sources 98
    Alternative Domestic Sources of Funding 99
    Cost Efficiency 101
Program Implications in the Education Sector 104

8   IMPLICATIONS OF FINDINGS ON THE PROPOSED HEALTH
    AND EDUCATION SECTOR DEVELOPMENT PROGRAMS 107

Overall Assessment 108

Issues for Education and Health Sector Development Programs 108
    Demand Side Constraints 108
    Financial and Organizational Sustainability 110
    Flexible Service Delivery 112
    The Social Sector Strategic Vision 113
    Monitoring and Evaluating Progress 114

ANNEX 1. List of PHRD Social Sector Studies and Authors **115**

ANNEX 2. Population Projections **117**

ANNEX 3. Statistical Appendix **119**

BIBLIOGRAPHY **133**

TABLES

BACKGROUND
    Table 1.1   Situation of Ethiopians at Various Stages of the Life Cycle 4

CONTEXT OF THE SOCIAL SECTORS
    Table 2.1   Demographic and Economic Indicators 8
    Table 2.2   Other Social Welfare Indicators 9
    Table 2.3   Age Distribution of Population 16

THE ETHIOPIAN HOUSEHOLD
    Table 3.1   Household and Community Characteristics in Rural Ethiopia 21

HEALTH
    Table 4.1   Basic Health Status Indicators 23
    Table 4.2   Burden of Disease for Ethiopia 25
    Table 4.3   Percent of Life Years Lost by Region and Cause 26
    Table 4.4   Illness Episodes and Source of Treatment 28
    Table 4.5   Proportion of Children Immunized for Measles, BCG, and DPT 29
    Table 4.6   Type of Provider Utilized by Expenditure Group 30
    Table 4.7   Expenditure per Treatment By Expenditure Group 31
    Table 4.8   Annual Household per Capita Health Expenditures 32
    Table 4.9   Supply of Health Facilities 34
    Table 4.10 Summary of Health Facilities-to-Population Ratio in All Regions
      by Type of Facility 35
    Table 4.11 Health Sector Staffing and Distribution 36
    Table 4.12 Availability of Basic Drugs 38
    Table 4.13 Financing the Health Sector in Ethiopia 45

NUTRITION

    Table 5.1 Prevalence of Stunting and Wasting for Children Under 6 Years, 1983–86 . 54

    Table 5.2 Prevalence of Malnutrition by Age and Sex, 1992 and 1995 54

    Table 5.3 Average Weight Increase between Rounds for Children under 6,
    by Consumption Group, 1994/95 55

    Table 5.4 Prevalence of Malnutrition by Household Per Capita
    Expenditure Group, 1995/96 55

    Table 5.5 Prevalence of Malnutrition in Rural Areas by Mother's Education,
    1994/95 56

    Table 5.6 Regional Changes in Malnutrition, 1983–92 56

    Table 5.7 Malnutrition of Adults by Consumption Group in Rural Areas,
    1994/95 56

    Table 5.8 Changes in the Incidence and Severity of Poverty and
    Malnutrition in Selected Regions 61

POPULATION

    Table 6.1 Age and Sex Distribution of the Population, 1995 and 2020 66

    Table 6.2 Reported AIDS Cases, 1991–95 68

    Table 6.3 HIV/AIDS Projections, 1995–2020 69

    Table 6.4 Current and Projected Use of Family Planning, 1995–2020 71

    Table 6.5 Coverage of Selected Reproductive Health Programs by Region 73

EDUCATION

    Table 7.1 Major Education Statistics, 1995 79

    Table 7.2 Net Enrollment Ratios by Schooling Level, Urban/Rural,
    and Gender 80

    Table 7.3 Promotion Rates by Grade 80

    Table 7.4 Enrollment by Gender, 1995 81

    Table 7.5 Household Heads' Attitudes toward Schooling 83

    Table 7.6 Regression Results: Socioeconomic Determinants of Enrollment,
    School Performance, and Education Expenditures 88

    Table 7.7 Responsibilities for Education Management 90

    Table 7.8 Unavailability of Teaching Materials in Schools 92

    Table 7.9 Training Levels of Primary and Secondary School Teachers,
    1993/94 93

    Table 7.10 Sources of Financing for Education in Government Schools,
    1995/96 95

    Table 7.11 Total Education Budget as a Share of GDP and
    Total Public Budget, 1990/91–1995/96 95

    Table 7.12 Allocation of Government Recurrent and Capital Budget for Education
    by Region, 1994/95 97

    Table 7.13 Sources of Finances as Reported by Schools 99

    Table 7.14 Breakdown of Fees Collected from Households by
    Government and Nongovernment Schools 99

Table 7.15   Percentage of Different Income Groups Benefiting from Education 100
Table 7.16   Comparison of Reported School Running Costs, Government
and Nongovernment 102

FIGURES AND BOXES

EXECUTIVE SUMMARY
Figure 1   Peace Dividend: Allocation of Government Expenditures, 1989–1995 xvi

BACKGROUND
Figure 1.1   Ethiopia: Human Capital Development throughout the Life Cycle 2

CONTEXT OF THE SOCIAL SECTORS
Figure 2.1   GNP Per Capita, 1994 7
Figure 2.2   Change in Infant Mortality, 1980–94 9
Figure 2.3   Trends in GDP and Main Sectors, 1985–94 10
Figure 2.4   Government Revenues and Expenditures as Share of GDP, 1990–95 11
Figure 2.5   Budgetary Allocations to the Social Sector, 1987–89 and 1993–95 11
Figure 2.6   Population Projections, 1995–2020 15
Figure 2.7   Age and Sex Distribution of the Population, 1995 and 2020 16

THE ETHIOPIAN HOUSEHOLD
Figure 3.1   Allocation of Rural Household Expenditures 20

HEALTH
Figure 4.1   Burden of Disease in Eastern Africa 25
Figure 4.2   Percent of Total Deaths and Life Years Lost by Cause 26
Figure 4.3   Reported Illness Episodes during Last Two Months
by Age Group 27
Figure 4.4   Utilization of Health Facilities by Expenditure Group 28
Figure 4.5   Health Services and Utilization Rates 33
Figure 4.6   Per Capita Health Budget by Region 43
Figure 4.7   Sources of Financing in the Health Sector, 1986 and 1996 44

NUTRITION
Figure 5.1   Foodgrain Production and Population Affected
by Drought, 1985–96 57
Figure 5.2.a   Actual and Predicted Dietary Supply by PPP-
Corrected Mean Consumption per Month 59
Figure 5.2.b   Actual and Predicted Prevalence of Undernutrition by PPP-
Corrected Mean Consumption per Month 59
Figure 5.3.a   Actual and Predicted Dietary Energy Supply by PPP-
Corrected Mean Consumption per Month 60
Figure 5.3.b   Actual and Predicted Prevalence of Undernutrition by PPP-
Corrected Mean Consumption per Month 60

Figure 5.4 Actual and Predicted Underweight and Health Expenditures
(including nutrition) by Selected Low-Income African Countries 62

POPULATION
Figure 6.1 Population Growth (1980–90) and Total Fertility (1994) Rates 66
Figure 6.2 Percent of Women Desiring More Children, by Number
of Surviving Children 70
Figure 6.3 Use of Family Planning Methods by Educational Experience
of Women   71
Box 6.1   Experience in Raising Contraceptive Prevalence Rates
in Three Countries 75

EDUCATION
Figure 7.1 Gross Primary Enrollment Rates in the World 77
Figure 7.2 Primary Gross Enrollment Trends for Ethiopia and
Sub-Saharan Africa 79
Figure 7.3 Average Monthly Household Education Expenditures by Monthly
Household Total Expenditure Quartile 84
Figure 7.4a Why Children Never Attend School in Ethiopia: First Reason 86
Figure 7.4b Why Children Never Attend School in Ethiopia: Second Reason 86
Figure 7.5 Comparison of Earnings by Educational Attainment in Ethiopia 87
Figure 7.6 Sources of Funds for the Education Sector, 1994/95 94
Figure 7.7 Allocation of Primary School Recurrent Expenditures 96
Figure 7.8 Allocation of Recurrent Budget by Education Level 96
Figure 7.9 Trends in Sources of Government Capital Expenditures
on Education 100
Figure 7.10 International Comparison of Education Expenditures and Primary
School Enrollments 101

IMPLICATIONS OF FINDINGS FOR THE SECTOR DEVELOPMENT PROGRAMS
Box 8.1 Goals of the Education Sector Development Program, 1997–2001 107
Box 8.2 Goals of the Health Sector Development Program, 1997–2001 108

ABSTRACT

This report was prepared by the World Bank to provide a comprehensive review of Ethiopia's social sectors covering education, health, nutrition and population. It contributes to the ongoing social sector policy dialogue with the Government. The report is based on eighteen individual sub-sectoral studies and household surveys carried out from 1995 to 1997 by the Government of the Federal Democratic Republic of Ethiopia and the World Bank.

The analytical work contained in this report contributed to the identification and preparation of four key social sector programs for the next decade and supported by IDA credit, namely: the Education Sector Development Program, the Health Sector Development Program, the Population and HIV/AIDS Project, and the Early Child Development Project.

The report begins with a description of the trends in the social sectors and an analysis of the factors that influence these trends including the performance of the economy, government social expenditures, changes in household incomes and poverty, population trends, and the regionalization policy. Ethiopia's dismal social indicators reflect the stress from the twenty years of civil war which ended in 1991, and the devastation from two of the biggest droughts this century. Important shifts in government expenditures toward the social sectors away from defense expenditures have been noted in the first half of the 1990s, which somewhat improved enrollments and increased health care coverage. However, literacy, nutritional and health status still remain amongst the poorest in the region.

Findings from the household surveys, participatory assessments, school and health facility surveys, the 1994 Population Census, and public expenditure reviews are synthesized to provide a comprehensive picture of the demand for and supply of education and health services. The report presents issues, trends, and government policies in education, health, nutrition and population and provides a framework for the implementation of a coherent social sector strategy for the next decade.

PREFACE

After being immersed in almost three decades of civil conflict, the prevailing peace and political stability in Ethiopia allowed its government to focus on rebuilding its economy. As an integral part of this undertaking, the Federal Democratic Republic of Ethiopia (FDRE) is seeking to overhaul the landscape of human capital development in the country. By launching two sector-wide reforms in education and health through its education sector development and health development programs in July, 1997, the government has demonstrated its commitment to improve the lives of Ethiopians, particularly those in poor and underserved areas.

This report aims to assist the government in achieving its goal to improve the quality and accessibility of social services by providing the most recent information on the social sectors in Ethiopia and by raising issues for further consideration and discussion. Earlier versions of this report have provided inputs towards the preparation of the two sector-wide programs in education and health, as well as in shaping the World Bank's country assistance strategy for Ethiopia.

The core material of this report is drawn from eighteen social sector studies managed by the government of the Federal Democractic Republic of Ethiopia together with the World Bank, with assistance from international experts. Fifteen studies were undertaken by local Ethiopian consultants and three studies by consultants from Oxford University's Center for the Study of African Economies, based on a survey done in collaboration with Addis Ababa University. The process of developing the studies was initiated in early 1996 by the FDRE's Social Sector Steering Committee, Office of the Prime Minister. A PHRD Social Sector Project Office in Addis Ababa coordinated the recruitment and supervision of local consultants for the studies and prepared two sectoral syntheses reports on education and health. A nutrition synthesis study was prepared by Bank staff.

The report discusses the situation and trends in education, health, nutrition, and population, and the barriers to improvement from the points of view of Ethiopian households, public and private suppliers of services. It also attempts to identify the means by which the government can use public resources more effectively.

Chapter 1 provides background information on the preparation of this report and lays out a conceptual framework for the formulation of a social sector analysis. Chapter 2 discusses the contextual factors that influence the social sectors such as the performance of the economy, relevant macroeconomic policies, regionalization policy, and population trends. Chapter 3 presents the key characteristics of Ethiopian households including their income and expenditure patterns and community characteristics. Chapter 4 presents the analysis of the situation, trends, issues, and strategy for the Health Sector, followed by Nutrition (Chapter 5), Population (Chapter 6), and Education Sector (Chapter 7). Finally, Chapter 8 discusses some implications of the findings on the design of the Health Sector Development Program and the Education Sector Development Program.

ACKNOWLEDGMENTS

This report was prepared by the Bank social sector team for Ethiopia following a mission to review the Social Sector Studies conducted by the Government of the Federal Democratic Republic of Ethiopia with assistance from the World Bank. The studies were funded by the Japanese Government through a Policy and Human Resource Development (PHRD) Grant to support lending operations in health, education and the social sectors. The review mission included Marito Garcia (mission leader), David Dunlop, Young Hoy Kimaro, Christine Pena, Kaori Miyamoto, Yang-ro Yoon, Anil Deolalikar and Jacob van Lutsenburg Maas (AFTH1); Gebreselassie Okubaghzi (AFMET); Adam Lagerstedt, Helen Craig, Carlos Gargiulo and Dayl Donaldson (consultants). Additional analyses and subsequent revisions (based on comments from the Government of Ethiopia and other reviewers) were done after the mission by Christine Pena (AFTH4), Frank Riely (consultant), K. Subbarao, Kalpana Mehra (PRMPO), Khadija Hashi (consultant), Gurushri Swamy (EAHD), Gita Gopal (AFTH4), Larry Forgy (IENTI), Meera Shekar (UNICEF Addis Ababa), and Carlos Gargiulo (consultant). Arvil Van Adams, David Dunlop, and Young Hoy Kimaro provided additional information on education and health sectors.

This report was prepared by a task team led by Marito Garcia (AFTH1), supervised by Ruth Kagia, Sector Manager of Africa Human Development I (AFTH1), Arvil Van Adams, Sector Manager of Africa Human Development IV (AFTH4), and Oey Astra Meesook, Country Director for Ethiopia (AFCO6). The Resident Mission, especially Fayez Omar, Resident Representative, and Dr. Gebreselassie Okubaghzi, social sector specialist, provided technical and administrative support in the implementation of the studies. Peer reviewers are William McGreevey (HDDHE) and Maris O'Rourke and Eluned Roberts-Schweitzer (HDDED). Jacob van Lutsenburg Maas (CTETE) was the lead sector specialist.

The authors of the PHRD Ethiopian Social Sector Studies are listed in Annex I. Fifteen of the eighteen PHRD Ethiopian Social Sector Studies were conducted by private Ethiopian consultants in Addis Ababa who were selected through a competitive and nationally advertised process. Three of the studies were prepared by the Oxford University Center for the Study of African Economies based on a survey done jointly with Addis Ababa University (AAU). The TORs are available at this Web site:

http://www.ari.net/sojourners/ethiopia/index.html

The work was coordinated by the Government of Ethiopia through the PHRD Project Office in Addis Ababa under the supervision of the Government Social Sector Steering Committee, chaired by Dr. Kebede Taddese of the Office of the Prime Minister. The PHRD Study Project Office was managed by Ato Shimeles Worku and assisted by Dr. Gebremeskel Habtemariam (seconded from the Ministry of Health) and Ato Hailu Sime (seconded from the Ministry of Education). We would like to especially commend the PHRD Office for its superb management of all of the studies.

International consultants who provided guidance in methodology and review include: Maureen Woodhall, Anil Deolalikar (University of Washington), Margaret Grieco (Oxford CSAE), Carlos Gargiulo (RTI North Carolina), Dayl Donaldson (Harvard University), Tony Reed, and Dr. Birger Forsberg (Indevelop Sweden). We acknowledge the assistance provided by Paul Collier, John Knight and the research staff of the Oxford University Centre for the Study of African Economies for their assistance in the use of the longitudinal Ethiopian Rural Household Surveys 1989-1995 conducted with Addis Ababa University Department of Economics and the International Food Policy Research Institute (IFPRI) of Washington DC. Pammi Sachdeva (CGIAR) provided guidance in the development of the study TORs at the early stages of the study formulation. Reviews were received from Ruth Kagia (AFTH1), Oey Astra Meesook, Harry Patrinos (HHDED), Marlaine Lockheed (MNHSD), Mariam Claeson (HDDHE), Gita Gopal, Young Kimaro (AFTH1), Andrew Mason (PRMGE), Robert Mattson (HDNVP), Hailu Mekonnen (LATAD), and Don Holsinger (USAID/WB).

We would like to express our appreciation to the Ethiopian Government's Social Sector Steering Committee of the Prime Minister's Office, including: Dr. Kebede Taddese (Chairman), Ato Neway Gebreab (Economic Advisor in the Prime Minister's Office), Wzo. Genet Zewdie (Minister of Education), Dr. Adem Ibrahim (Minister of Health); and Ato Girma Birru (Minister of Economic Development and External Cooperation) for providing overall guidance in the execution, review and dissemination of the PHRD Ethiopian Social Sector Studies. We also wish to acknowledge the cooperation of the regional governments in the collection of baseline data. Dr. Abdulahi and the Central Statistical Authority, Tim Marchant (AFTK3), Saji Thomas (AFTI1) and NORAD were particularly helpful in providing the 1995/96 National Household Income, Consumption and Expenditure Survey and preliminary estimates from the 1994 Population Census. We would also like to acknowledge the excellent support provided by Heidi Fritschel, Suzanne Gnaegy, Gaudencio Dizon, Dora Hollister, Vanessa Saldanha, Lydia Tabi, Yordi Seium, Lourdes Cuadro-Meliotes, and Farida Reza at the World Bank Headquarters.

ACRONYMS AND ABBREVIATIONS

CAS	Country assistance strategy
CDD	Control of diarrhoeal diseases
EIC	Ethiopian Insurance Corporation
EMPDA	Ethiopia Materials Production and Distribution Agency
ESDP	Education Sector Development Program
ENI	Ethiopia Nutrition Institute
FDRE	Federal Democratic Republic of Ethiopia
GER	Gross Enrollment Rate
HICE	Household Income, Consumption, and Expenditure Survey
HIV	Human Immunodeficiency Virus
HSDP	Health Sector Development Programme
IEC	Information, education, and communication
IDD	Iodine deficiency disorder
IMR	Infant mortality rate
MEDAC	Ministry of Economic Development and Cooperation
MOA	Ministry of Agriculture
MOH	Ministry of Health
MWR	Ministry of Water Resources
NER	Net enrollment rate
NFFS	National Family Fertility Survey
NOP	National Office of Population
NRIH	National Research Institute of Health
PEM	Protein-energy malnutrition
PER	Public expenditure review
PHRD	Policy and Human Resource Development
SDP	Sector Development Program
SNNP	Southern Nations, Nationalities, and People's Region
TFR	Total fertility rate
TGE	Transitional Government of Ethiopia
TTI	Teacher training institutes
UNESCO	United Nations Education, Science and Culture Organization
UNICEF	United Nations Children's Fund
UNFPA	United Nations Fund for Population Activities
WB	World Bank
WFP	World Food Programme
WHO	World Health Organization
WMS	Welfare Monitoring Survey

GOVERNMENT FISCAL YEAR
July 1 - June 30

CURRENCY EQUIVALENTS
Currency Unit = Ethiopian Birr (ETB)
US$1= Ethiopian Birr 6.80

Vice-President:	Callisto E. Madavo
Country Director:	Oey Astra Meesook
Sector Director:	Birger Fredriksen
Sector Managers:	Ruth Kagia and Arvil Van Adams
Task Team Leader:	Marito Garcia

EXECUTIVE SUMMARY

STATE OF THE SOCIAL SECTORS

Ethiopia is the second most populous country in Sub-Saharan Africa (SSA), with about 54 million people, based on the 1994 census. The country, with a long and rich history, is just about the poorest in the world, impoverished by two of the biggest droughts this century and by its recently ended civil war, which caused resources to be siphoned away from social sectors. Ethiopia's per capita income of US$100 in 1995 reported in the World Development Report 1997 (US$450 in terms of PPP estimates) is one of the lowest in the world. During the twenty years of civil war until 1991, GDP grew at an average of less than 2 percent per year, and per capita income declined to about one-half of the levels in the late 1970s. This decline in income also contributed to the poor social indicators that characterize Ethiopia today. In 1995 gross primary school enrollment was 29 percent of school-aged children (compared with 72 percent for all of SSA), life expectancy was 49 years (compared with an average of 52 years in SSA), and infant mortality was 112 out of 1,000 live births (compared with 92 for SSA) in 1995. Close to 60 percent of children under 5 years of age are shorter than normal for their age, compared with 30 percent in neighboring Kenya. This is due to the frequency of early childhood malnutrition in Ethiopia. About 11 percent of the children are wasted, that is, have lower than normal weight for height; this rate is high compared with other African countries.

Living conditions have improved since the civil war ended in 1991. Annual GDP growth in the period 1991–96 averaged 5.4 percent, despite annual fluctuations due to weather. The return of peace and better economic management have contributed to improved conditions. It is estimated that the incidence of poverty in rural areas declined from 63 percent in 1989 to 48 percent in 1994, and perhaps further in the last three years. Usually, with improved incomes, the health, educational and nutritional status of a population improves. However, in Ethiopia, the recent prosperity is only partly reflected in improved social indicators. Gross primary school enrollment increased to 29 percent in 1995 but is still well below the peak of 38 percent reached in the mid-1980s. Infant mortality has fallen from 159 per thousand live births in the mid-1980s to 112 in recent years mainly as a result of immunization campaigns, but children who survive are not thriving, as shown by the poor child nutritional indicators cited. In fact, these indicators worsened over the period 1982–1995.

What were the trends in investments in social sectors in Ethiopia? Sustained economic growth usually results in significant improvements in social indicators since households have more income to spend on social services. But cross-country evidence suggests that the impact of public expenditure on social indicators (particularly health) is usually stronger than that of an increase in household per capita income. Further, two other factors underscore the role of public ex-

penditures in Ethiopia. First, the country's social indicators are among the lowest in the world and, in
some cases, lower than what might be expected for
a country at this level of income. Second, social sector spending is lower than in most other countries
in the region, both in absolute terms and as a percentage of gross domestic product (GDP). Government health care expenditures remained at US$1.50
per capita per year, significantly lower than the SSA
average of $14 per capita. Total public expenditure
on education was only 2.6 percent of GDP in 1991,
increasing to 3.8 percent in 1995/96.

The good news is the "peace dividend" in
Ethiopia. With the end of civil unrest, the government reduced military and defense spending and
increased social sector spending to 19 percent of
the government budget in 1996 from 9.8 percent
in 1989. Military spending fell from 24 percent
in 1989 to 7 percent in 1995 (Figure 1).

However, further increases in the medium
term will be difficult to achieve. To illustrate: even
under optimistic assumptions—that GDP increases at 8 percent per year up to 2020, that government expenditures as a share of GDP remain
at the 1994 levels, that the share of social sector
spending in the budget increases from current 23
percent to 34 percent of the government budget—
it would take Ethiopia 25 years to reach the per
capita expenditure level of SSA (which itself is
not high by developing-country standards).

Figure 1   Peace Dividend: Allocation of Government Expenditures, 1989-1995

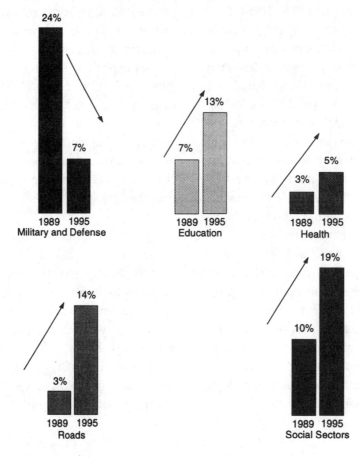

Source: WB Public Expenditure Review (1996).

It is critical therefore:

- that given limited resources, the government encourage increased private sector and community participation rather than trying to provide all services;
- that every Birr spent by the government on health, education, population, and nutrition be allocated to interventions with the greatest public impact; and
- that the interventions be well designed for maximum efficiency.

These three principles underlie the recommendations in this report.

The most recent trends in the economy have given us plenty of reason to hope. The liberalization of the economy in the past four years was met with a strong supply response, including a moderate expansion in agricultural output—the country even managed to export maize in the 1996/97 cropping season. Improved economic performance enhances the government's ability to spend for social services and increases household capacity to spend for health and education. A major turnaround is taking place in schools after a long period of decline—primary school enrollment showed a remarkable increase between 1992/93 and 1995/96. Moreover, the government's commitment to improve the social sectors by recently embarking on comprehensive education and health sector development programs is highly commendable.

This report takes stock of the present conditions of human resources in Ethiopia in terms of outcomes in health, nutrition, population and education; describes the trends and barriers in investments in human capital development; and outlines strategies to address the medium- and long-term development of the country's human resources. This report is based primarily on the findings of the Ethiopian Social Sector Studies (18 stand-alone studies together with two synthesis reports on health and education that are all available upon request) conducted by the Government of Ethiopia, together with the World Bank, Oxford University, and Addis Ababa University, and with assistance from international experts and private Ethiopian consultants in Addis Ababa.

CHARACTERISTICS OF THE ETHIOPIAN HOUSEHOLD

Poverty and extreme difficulties emanating from years of internal conflict characterize the Ethiopian household today:

- There are 10.2 million households (54 million people) based on the 1994 population census, with average household size of 5.2.
- About 2.5 million of these households (25 percent) are female headed, and 45 percent are in urban areas.
- Household surveys show annual expenditures (as proxy for income) at US$150 to US$175 per capita per day—this range is substantially higher than the accepted figure of US$100 based on the national income accounts (World Bank 1997a) but still quite low.
- About 5.3 million out of the 10.2 million households earn less than US$1 a day.
- Income is so low in rural areas that households spend most of their resources on food; rural household expenditures are allocated as follows:
    - 75 percent on food (45 percent of this comes from subsistence production, the rest from market purchases)
    - 2 percent on medical, health care
    - Less than 1 percent on schooling
    - 8 percent on clothing
    - 2 percent on transport
    - 6 percent on ceremonials and contributions
    - 2 percent on durables and building materials
    - 4 percent on other expenditures
- Only 8 percent (445,000) of households send children to school.

- Only 10 percent sought treatment in a clinic in the two months prior to the surveys, or about half of the 20 percent who reported having fallen ill in that period.
- The rural poor live far from infrastructure. Average distance to the nearest all-weather road is 3.6 kilometers, for the poorest income quartile, it is about 6 kilometers and for the richest quartile it is less than 2 kilometers.
- Only half (54 percent) of the rural population have an all-weather road in their village.
- Only about 28 percent of households have access to clean piped water.

EDUCATION

Main Findings

Low enrollment and low coverage, high opportunity costs, and poor efficiency characterize the education sector:

- The gross enrollment ratio is 29 percent at the primary level (less than half of the Sub-Saharan average of 72 percent), 19 percent at the junior secondary level, 9 percent at the senior secondary level, and less than 1 percent at the tertiary level.
- The net enrollment ratio is 16 percent at the primary level, 5 percent at the junior secondary level, 5 percent at the senior secondary level, and below 1 percent at the tertiary level.
- Only 2.1 million children out of 12.3 million children age 7–14 years are in school; another 1.0 million children in primary school are overage, or above 14 years.
- There are significant rural and urban differences: primary education is almost universal in Addis Ababa and other urban areas while gross primary enrollment in rural areas is only 18 percent.
- Regional disparities in enrollment are extremely wide. Gross primary enrollment in Afar region is 9.1 percent. In the other extreme, it is 53 percent in Tigray (greater in its cities) and 90 percent in Addis Ababa.
- Gender bias is marked. Only 24 percent of girls are at primary school level compared with 33 percent of boys.
- Adult illiteracy is very high at approximately 65 percent of adults above 15 years, compared with 53 percent for all of Sub-Saharan Africa.
- Household expenditures on education have very low elasticity, ranging between 0.1 and 0.4 (compared with 1.1 in South Korea, for example).
- The age of entry for primary school is very late: it averages 11 years old and, in rural areas, closer to 12, compared with 6–7 years old in most parts of the world. Thus, for the first decade of their lives, most Ethiopian children are likely to have little formal stimulation or formal learning.
- There are 10,503 primary schools in the country; only 38 percent of the 27,000 villages in the country have schools.
- Schools serve more than a single village; more than 94,600 primary school teachers are employed; on average therefore, each primary school has about 9 teachers to serve 3 to 4 villages.
- Villages are too far from each other for primary school children to travel between villages to go to school; villages typically cover 45 square kilometers of land, or slightly less than 7 kilometers from one side to another. In many countries, primary school children walk less than 3 kilometers to school.
- Internal efficiency of the educational system is low; the drop-out rate between grades 1 and 3 is 22 percent; the average repetition rate for all primary grades is 11 percent.
- The teacher-student ratio is low at 1:33, but varies substantially by region, ranging from 1:21 in the Somali region to 1:51 in Addis Ababa.
- Facilities and equipment in surveyed schools are in poor condition or nonexistent; only 24 percent of surveyed schools have desks in good condition; only half have library facilities.

• Textbook ratios are low; the average is 1 textbook to 3 students in primary schools and 1 textbook to 4 students in secondary schools.

Household responses in a subsample survey conducted by Addis Ababa University/Oxford University revealed that:

• The primary reason (46 percent of respondents) for not enrolling rural children 6–12 years old is that parents and teachers consider them "too young." Since age in years is not a commonly used concept in rural areas, this response probably means that children are considered too small to walk to the nearest school, reflecting the stunted physical stature of more than 60 percent of Ethiopia's children caused by malnutrition in early childhood;

• The second most important reason given (nearly 30 percent) for not enrolling children 6–12 years of age was that children are needed for farm work (for boys) or housework (for girls). This was the primary reason given by 55 percent of respondents concerning children 13–18 years old.

• Education is perceived to be worthwhile only if the child can go to secondary school and ultimately gain formal sector employment in a city. The value of education in the traditional farm setting is not high, since less than half of the respondents agreed that boys who go to school are better farmers than boys who do not.

• There is mixed evidence on the impact of the direct cost of education and of distance to school on enrollment. Respondents did not list either as a primary reason. However, when combined with other determinants of schooling in the statistical analysis, distance to school is correlated with low enrollment in rural areas (where the average distance to a primary school is 2 kilometers and to a secondary school is 20 kilometers). Long distances also cut into the time that children are required to spend on house and farm work. Also, although government schools do not charge tuition fees, parents spent, on average, Birr 24 ($3.6) per year per child (excluding clothing) in rural areas. While this is not high compared with other countries in the region, many low-income families with an average of 4–5 children in each household may find it difficult if not impossible to send all of their children to school at the same time.

Main Recommendations on Education

In sum, while there is a strong case to be made for increasing the availability of schools, particularly primary schools, it will be necessary to focus also on programs that minimize the opportunity costs of education. There is also an overriding need to keep unit costs low. The following recommendations are made. Most of these are now being considered by the Government and are being incorporated in its education sector development program.

• Build smaller schools closer to the communities. This will put schools within reach of younger children and reduce travel time.

• Reduce the opportunity cost of schooling by adjusting the school calendar, making it more compatible with the peak agricultural season.

• Establish double shifts as the norm, so that instead of having to spend the whole day in school, children can choose to come to school either in the morning or in the afternoon. This would accommodate more children, reducing unit costs. In Zambia, Jamaica, and Malaysia, for example, costs were reduced by 25 to 50 percent. Double shifts also reduce the number of hours away from the home or farm, helping reduce the opportunity cost of schooling.

• Provide distance learning opportunities, which may be a better option for teaching older children and adults and for upgrading teacher skills. More intensive use of modern communications technology should be explored to break the barrier of remoteness. The use of mass media has considerable potential but can only work with sufficient access to electricity and radio.

- Increase opportunities for literacy programs to address the high adult illiteracy rates. This could be developed also through distance learning.
- Provide integrated early childhood intervention programs as essential complements to education. As opportunity costs are lowered, households are more likely to send their younger children to school, thereby allowing older girls (who are often at home to provide child care) to go to school. Evidence from such programs in other countries also shows that children participating in early developmental programs are more likely to stay in school and perform better. A strong nutritional component may be built into the early childhood programs to reduce the high levels of child undernutrition.
- Promote early attendance in school, including a major promotional campaign to encourage parents to enroll children at an early age, as a strategy to achieve the government's goal of 50 percent gross primary enrollment rate in 5 years. It is likely that the biggest gains in enrollment can be attained from enrollment in the younger children because their opportunity cost is lower than those of the older children. For the 11 to 18-year-old children, part of the solution involves adjusting the school calendar to avoid the agricultural peak demand season. Some innovations that have worked in other countries could be developed. Examples of these are: the highly participatory community-oriented approach used by Escuela Nueva in Colombia and the scholarships for girls in Bangladesh and Pakistan. Earlier attendance in primary school will produce multiple effects. It will (a) increase children's chances of getting at least 4 years of primary schooling before they become more valuable on the farm; (b) provide girls with basic education before they get married (35 percent of Ethiopian girls are married by age 15; 70 percent are married by age 17); (c) likely reduce fertility since educated girls are likely to marry late or more likely to use contraceptives; (d) allow girls to become literate

before early marriage; (e) likely free the time of mothers (and elder sisters) from looking after young children at home; thus, they can work, go to school and have more leisure time.

HEALTH

Main Findings

Ethiopia has a heavy burden of disease but a low rate of self-reported illness and low health facility coverage and utilization.

- Of 1.90 million children born each year, 230,000 (12 percent) die before reaching their first birthday; another 160,000 (8 percent) die before their fifth birthday.
- Major causes of death in infancy and early childhood are acute respiratory infection (ARI), diarrhea, nutritional deficiencies, and measles. These account for 80 percent of deaths of children under age 5.
- The total burden of disease in Ethiopia is 350 discounted life years (DLYs) lost per 1,000 people, compared with 170 in Kenya and 230 in Tanzania.
- The top 10 killers, which account for 75 percent of all deaths, include perinatal-maternal conditions (17 percent), ARI (14 percent), malaria (10 percent), (14 percent), nutritional deficiency for children under 5 (8 percent), diarrhea (8 percent), AIDS (7 percent), and tuberculosis (5 percent).
- There is wide regional variation in the burden of disease: AIDS accounts for 18 percent of DLYs lost in Addis Ababa but only 6 percent in Amhara region; ARI accounts for 17 percent of DLYs lost in Oromia but only 6 percent in Dire Dawa; malaria accounts for 11 percent in Benishangul but only 3 percent in Dire Dawa.
- ARI, diarrhea, measles, and nutritional deficiencies are the major childhood diseases, while malaria, tuberculosis, and AIDS are the

major adult diseases. Nearly 17 percent of deaths are women who die from pregnancy and childbirth related complications. In rural areas, for every three people who report illness, five people report chronic disability.

- The expenditure elasticity of demand for health care is relatively low.
- The rate of self-reported illness ranges between 18 days per year per person (episodic illness only) and 40 days per year per person (including chronic disability). The rate of episodic illness is low not only in comparison with other countries, but also in comparison to the situation in Ethiopia about 15 years ago, when, on average, reported illness was 30 days per person per year. It is highly unlikely that health status has improved in the last 15 years; this apparent decline may therefore be attributed to a phenomenon often observed—that in poor countries people tend to report less sickness because, unfortunately, they are used to being sick.
- Of those reporting illnesses, only about 50 percent seek treatment. The rural surveys cited high cost of treatment, distance to health providers, and poor quality and unavailability of drugs and trained providers as the most common reasons for not seeking treatment. The average number of visits to government health facilities is low: 0.25 per person per year compared with 1.0 for Sub-Saharan Africa.
- A statistical analysis of the factors that determine whether a person seeks treatment or not indicates strongly that distance to a facility is an important factor, particularly in rural areas. A reduction of 1 kilometer in the distance to a facility would increase the probability of treatment by 2 percent. In rural areas, nearly 80 percent of the population lives more than 4 kilometers from a health facility; about 50 percent lives more than 11 kilometers away. Much of Ethiopia is characterized by rugged terrain and little or no public transportation, and therefore even a relatively short distance can be difficult to traverse.

- There is only one health station for every 23,000 people (compared with 1 for every 8,000 for Sub-Saharan Africa) and one health center for nearly 300,000 people.
- There is one doctor for every 35,000 people (compared with 1 for every 10,000 in Sub-Saharan Africa), 63 percent of all doctors are located in Addis Ababa.
- Poor facilities characterize the public health system. There is 1 hospital bed for every 5,000 people, 1 x-ray machine for every 500,000 people, and 1 HIV screening center for every 800,000 people. Of 89 hospitals only 41 have operating theaters, to serve a population of 54 million people.
- The quality of services offered is poor. Surveys showed that about half the facilities had no supply of antibiotics (this is a measure of quality).
- With distance and income being held constant in regression analysis, an individual's educational status has a strong influence on whether he or she seeks treatment. Both primary schooling and post primary education increase the probability of seeking treatment.
- Overall, females tend to report a higher incidence of illnesses than did men, particularly those over 10 years of age. At the same time, however, mothers' education has a strong impact on whether treatment is sought. It also has a strong impact on whether a child is immunized and on the nutritional status of young children in general.
- Ethiopians use a wide variety of health service providers, across income groups. Pharmacies and drug vendors, both predominantly privately owned, are utilized by 25 percent of the poor and 11 to 18 percent of the other income groups. Health posts, centers, stations, and hospitals, mostly government owned, are used by 52 percent of the poor and about 50 percent of the other income groups, Richer households tend to use hospitals more, while the poor use the lower-level facilities. About 14 percent of the health stations are owned by NGOs, mainly

religious missions, and about 5 percent by other private owners.

- Until recently, government health expenditures were biased toward hospital-based curative services in urban areas. Curative services constituted almost 80 percent of total government health expenditures in 1994. As a result, coverage rates for most disease prevention and control programs have been low. In 1995, less than 20 percent of pregnant women received antenatal care (compared with over 60 percent in Sub-Saharan Africa). Only 25 to 30 percent of children were immunized. Through much of the 1980s, the share of personnel costs in health costs increased, reaching 65 percent in 1990. This increase came at the expense of spending on drugs and facility maintenance.

Since 1992 there has been a gradual but significant reorientation of the government health budget toward facilities outside of Addis Ababa, away from hospitals, and toward increased purchases of supplies. A large share of the increased spending has gone to drugs, and the proportion of salary costs has declined to 53 percent, yet, most facilities report shortages of supplies.

Main Recommendations in Health

Increased access and quality should be the main objectives for the health sector in Ethiopia today. More facilities are needed within a reasonable distance to households; at the same time, appropriate levels of funding will be needed to supply these facilities with needed equipment, drugs, and well-trained personnel. Government spending must continue to shift toward disease prevention and other basic programs. The role of the private sector needs to be strengthened. Most of the following recommendations are are now being incorporated by the government in the ongoing health sector development program.

- Increase the number of lower-level government facilities. The proposal to consolidate the three lower levels (health posts, centers,

and stations) into primary health care centers should not result in increasing distances for the households.

- Increase access to a minimal set of essential cost-effective health services with the greatest impact on the disease burden, such as integrated management of childhood illnesses (covers ARI, diarrhea, malaria, malnutrition, vitamin A supplementation) and reproductive health services, including treatment of sexually transmitted diseases (STDs) and prenatal services.
- Provide adequate drugs, medical supplies, and equipment.
- Improve the quality of services at first-level facilities through upgrading of health workers' skills, training, and improved supervision.
- User fees for curative services should continue to replace government subsidies, and facilities should be allowed to keep most of the proceeds. The tradition of *iddir*, or insurance against catastrophic illness and death, could be used as the basis of a health insurance fund to which public funds could be added.
- Engage the private sector by easing licensing requirements and offering incentives.
- Encourage the privatization of pharmaceutical production and distribution. Assist rural drug vendors whose services are used by a considerable proportion of poor rural households.
- Explore more intensive use of modern communications technology for breaking the barrier of remoteness in delivering services

NUTRITION

Main Findings

The high levels of malnutrition in Ethiopia are among the most serious detriments to the well-being of the population; poor nutrition undermines child development, the cognitive abilities of schoolchildren, and the productivity of the workforce.

- Protein-energy malnutrition measured by stunting (low height compared with standard height for age) affects 5 million children under five years old.
- Between 1983 to 1996 the rate of stunting rose from 60 percent to 64 percent.
- The number of children currently affected by wasting (very low weight for height) is estimated at 470,000 and is responsible for the high infant mortality rate.
- Nutritional deficiencies account for 7.8 percent of all deaths (50 percent under age 5), and 9.3 percent of DLYs lost. Taking into account the interaction of nutritional deficiency with other childhood diseases like measles, ARI, and diarrhea, the total and indirect contribution to mortality is 29 percent.
- In terms of micronutrient deficiencies, findings are as follows:
  - Iodine deficiency disorders (IDD) affect 10 million people: 71 percent in some regions and 31 percent among schoolchildren. The deleterious effects of IDD on pregnancy outcomes are severe: about 13,600 neonatal deaths yearly, 14,800 still births, and 20,000 miscarriages.
  - Vitamin A deficiency, manifested in blindness (Bitot spot), affects 1 percent of children under 5, compared with the 0.5 percent level maximum set by the World Health Organization. Recent survey indicates that 5 million children under age 6 show subclinical manifestations of vitamin A deficiency, which could lead to blindness.
  - Anemia affects two-thirds of women of reproductive age and is partly responsible for the very high maternal mortality, ranging from 450 to 1,540 per 100,000 births.
- The rural surveys show that protein-energy malnutrition (PEM) measured by low BMI (body mass index), affects 25 percent of the adult working population. The impact on agricultural productivity is likely to be high since agriculture in Ethiopia is based on manual labor. Loss of agricultural output due to poor nutrition in the labor force is estimated at about 10 to 15 percent of agricultural production.

Main Recommendations in Nutrition

This report recommends a nutrition lending operation to address the multisectoral origins of the nutrition problem in Ethiopia. Specific strategies are as follows:

- Children in the age group from birth to 24 months are most in need of intervention.
- Interventions should be targeted to mothers of young children to bring about changes in feeding practices and child care.
- Food supplementation should seek to address not only PEM but also micronutrient deficiencies.
- Interventions should be nationwide (covering food-deficit as well as food-surplus areas) and cut across all income (consumption) groups.
- Early-childhood development initiatives should be combined with efforts to improve mothers' education.

Other potential early-childhood development interventions include community growth monitoring and promotion, deworming, establishment of child development centers run by communities and parents, provision of nonformal parenting classes for parents and caregivers, and national advocacy and communication strategy on care of very young children.

Interventions to combat adult malnutrition in Ethiopia fall into three major groups:
- those aimed at reducing chronic household-level food insecurity,
- those aimed at reducing temporary food insecurity from drought and other calamities, and
- those aimed at improving the biological utilization of food by focusing on improved health, water, sanitation, and nutrition.

POPULATION

Main Findings

The analysis is based on the preliminary results of the 1994 census. Expanding population creates a particular obstacle to progress in social sector development.

- The population today of 54 million will increase to 97 million in the year 2020 even using a conservative population growth rate.
- Population grew by 3.1 percent per year from 1980 to 1990 (World Bank 1996), with total fertility rate estimates ranging from 5.8 (Population Census 1994) to 7.7 (NFFS 1990). Cities grew faster—Addis Ababa grew by 4.1 percent per year from 1984 to 1994.
- Contraceptive prevalence is only 7 percent (up from 4 percent in 1991), well below the African average of over 20 percent.

Population projections have several implications for the social sectors:

- To attain universal primary education by 2015, the country will need to provide classrooms for a projected 22 million children age 7 to 14 years (from the present capacity of 3.5 million). The Education Sector Development Program (1997–2002) intends to supply capacity for 4 million (single-shift) to 7 million (double-shift) places in primary schools.
- Attempts to increase immunization coverage to 90 percent would triple the number of vaccines required.
- Increasing contraceptive prevalence to 44 percent in the year 2020 implies family planning commodity costs of US$450 million in constant 1995 dollar terms.

- Simply maintaining current coverage for maternal immunizations (estimated at 20 percent in 1995) would require a 26 percent increase in resources in the next 25 years.

Simply put, the task is big and cannot be sustained by the budget. The population projections suggest the increasing difficulty of expanding coverage of basic social services, because of the funds and number and types of staff required.

Main Recommendations in Population

It is therefore proposed that support be given to a population program that would increase contraceptive prevalence and improve the reproductive health of women of child-bearing age. In particular, the following strategies are recommended:

- Reproductive policies should be integrated with social policies that address poverty reduction and human development. Maternal and child health care, family planning, and prevention and treatment of sexually transmitted diseases need to be integrated into a comprehensive reproductive health care package.
- Adolescents need to be provided with information on family planning and reproductive health.
- Communities need to be educated about the harmful effects of practices like female genital mutilation. Because this is a cultural issue, it must be approached sensitively.
- Increased quality of service through trained personnel and enhanced availability of drugs and contraceptives is essential.
- Strong public action (such as increased female education) should be taken to make changes in the roles and status of women, which should help reduce high rates of HIV/AIDS and other sexually transmitted diseases.

MAIN RECOMMENDATIONS
OF THE REPORT

Ethiopia is one of the poorest countries in the world. Low income and poor social indicators characterize the typical Ethiopian household, impoverished by 30 years of civil conflict, devastating droughts, and the previous government's economic mismanagement. Households cannot readily invest in either education or health care as they struggle with scarcity on a daily basis. The new government is increasing investment in human capital as one of its principal strategies for getting households out of poverty. The present capacity of the government to ameliorate the identified problems is limited. Given that local resources are limited and that existing implementation is low, goals set should be realistic and sequencing and prioritization of investments is clearly necessary.

- First, support the drive to enroll half of all primary school-aged children in the next five years (from today's 29 percent enrollment) through a school rebuilding and quality enhancement program and through a strategy to reduce the high opportunity cost of schooling in rural areas.
- Second, increase primary health care coverage to 70 percent within the first five years of the Health Sector Development Program, focusing on the rural population. Alleviate the heavy burden of disease by rebuilding the health care delivery system and increasing the share of the budget spent on drugs, medical supplies, and well-trained health staff.
- Third, improve the nutrition of children and women to improve the quality of the next cohort of primary schoolers, who would lead toward the goal of universal primary education by 2015.
- Fourth, reduce population growth by taking action to increase contraceptive prevalence and improve family planning education.

There is a strong political will to address these problems in Ethiopia, as shown by the FDRE's comprehensive Health Sector Development Programme (HSDP) and Education Sector Development Programme (ESDP) proposals presented and discussed at the Meetings of Donors and FDRE in Addis Ababa in December 1996 and in Debre Zeit in March 1997. The FDRE has continued to demonstrate its commitment to improving its sector development programs, which were launched in July 1997, by engaging in further discussions with joint donor technical assistance teams for education and health (ESDP has already benefited from three multidonor missions, and HSDP has had two). In these discussions, the FDRE has become more cognizant of the fact that the tasks at hand are enormous and that, therefore, government should not do it alone. It aims to actively re-engage the private sector and mobilize communities and NGOs to participate in moving both ESDP and HSDP forward.

Sector Assistance Strategy
in the Immediate Term

- Support the government's proposal for a massive reform and expansion of the education system through the Education Sector Development Program I. This program aims to increase the gross primary enrollment from 29 percent today to 50 percent by the year 2002, based on the premise that basic education is essential to Ethiopia's human capital development. Increased attention to demand side problems must be an essential element of the strategy, primarily to address the high opportunity cost of schooling in rural areas.
- Support the government's proposal for reform and expansion of the health sector through the Health Sector Development Program I. This program aims to achieve 70 percent primary health care coverage by the year 2002 (from 45 percent today) and reduce the burden of disease that hinder economic development.

- Arrest the deterioration of the country's nutritional status, particularly of children and women, through policy reforms and lending operations for nutrition that would aim to reduce the level of child malnutrition from its present level of 60 percent to at least 30 percent by 2004. Because child nutrition is inextricably tied to farm output and output prices, a comprehensive policy is required.
- Support targeted initiatives for integrated early childhood intervention programs to improve primary schooling and health outcomes of the coming generation of primary schoolers.
- Reduce the rate of population growth by supporting a population and reproductive health program to reduce the high fertility rate.
- Reduce adult malnutrition by supporting agricultural development and nutrition programs.

- Support initiatives to empower women through the elimination of legal and other barriers to access to economic resources. Build institutional capacity in the regions to develop gender-balanced development planning.

Sector Assistance Strategy in the Medium Term

- Support the drive for universal primary education by 2015 through an Education Sector Development Program II lending operation that would follow up on and consolidate the gains from Education SDP I.
- Support a Health Sector Development Program II lending operation with the goal of achieving 90 percent coverage of primary health care.

1

BACKGROUND

OBJECTIVES OF THIS REPORT

This report has four main objectives:

- to present the current condition of human resources in Ethiopia and its implications for health, nutrition, population, and education;
- to describe the level and trends in investment in human capital by households, communities, the private sector, NGOs, the government, and donor agencies;
- to describe barriers to human capital development at the household level and from the points of view of the government sector, the private sector, NGOs, and communities;
- to discuss the implications of its findings for the implementation of sectoral interventions for the immediate and medium term.

The report presents the findings of the Ethiopian Social Sector Studies conducted by the Federal Democratic Republic of Ethiopia, together with the World Bank with assistance from international experts and private Ethiopian consultants in Addis Ababa. The process of developing the studies was initiated in early 1996 by the government's Social Sector Steering Committee, based in the Office of the Prime Minister. A Policy and Human Resource Development (PHRD) Social Sector Project Office in Addis Ababa composed of three professionals in health, education, and planning was established. This office coordinated the recruitment and supervision of local consultants for the studies and prepared two sectoral synthesis reports on education and health.

Eighteen studies in health, population, nutrition, education, and household behavior were completed, 15 studies by local Ethiopian consultants and three studies by consultants from Oxford University's Center for the Study of African Economies. Three synthesis documents were written, those on health and education by the PHRD project office in Addis Ababa, and the nutrition synthesis study by Bank staff. Initial findings were discussed in a technical review workshop attended by local, regional and international participants, and donors, held in Ethiopia in June 1996. The results from the PHRD Social Sector Studies, along with other sources of information, are being used as baseline information for the government's proposals for a Health Sector Development Program (1997–2002) and an Education Sector Development Program (1997–2002), both of which the government presented to donors at the Consultative Group Meeting held in Addis Ababa in December 1996 and at the Social Sector Donor-Government Workshop held in Debre Zeit, Ethiopia, in March 1997. These programs were launched in July 1997. Discussions between the government and multidonor teams have since been held on how to improve the programs and prepare them for donor financing.

The core material of this report, drawn from the 18 sector studies, provides information for the development of programs and policies in the social sectors. We report on the situation and trends in education, health, nutrition, and population, and the barriers to improvement from the point of view of Ethiopian households and of public and private suppliers of the services. We refer to the specific PHRD studies from which further detail can be obtained on a particular topic. We have also attempted to identify the means by which the government can use public resources more effectively.

The findings of this report contributed to the development of a World Bank social sector assistance strategy for Ethiopia. It helped shape the World Bank's lending in the immediate term, and we anticipate that it will also influence lending in the next 10 years. The report also identifies the activities that will be required to rebuild Ethiopia's human capital.

USING A LIFE CYCLE APPROACH TO SOCIAL SECTOR STRATEGY FORMULATION

Extensive analytical work was undertaken for this report. Three elements in our approach deserve to be highlighted: (1) listening to people; (2) considering both demand-side and supply-side issues;

and (3) building a bridge from strategic analysis to the design of the social sector programs in Ethiopia.

The analytical work started with listening to people. This helps us focus on the often neglected area of demand analysis. Two large-scale national household surveys gathered detailed information on the profile of the Ethiopian people, their incomes and sources of incomes, their expenditure patterns, their needs and preferences, and difficulties they face in daily life, including constraints of time, money and access to infrastructure and services. Access to the preliminary results of the 1994 Population Census enriched our understanding of Ethiopian households. Community participatory assessments further verified findings on the ground. In addition, interviews were conducted with the central government agencies, all regional government bureaus in health and education in the 11 regions, private sector representatives, health and education service providers, and NGOs. Finally, national macro-

Figure 1.1   Ethiopia: Human Capital Development throughout the Life Cycle

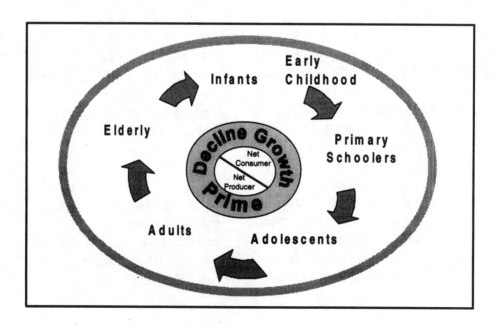

level information was gathered from public expenditure reviews.

From these facts and findings, we are building a bridge to action—with recommendations and sequencing of activities to improve the social sector. What is the government planning to do? How can the international donor community help? What should be the Bank's social sector investment strategy in the near term and in the medium term?

The recommendations for future actions and sequencing are based on a dialogue with the government and strategic thinking grounded in empirical findings and demand projections. This report suggests a new way of thinking about how to address the problems of the social sector: a broader understanding of the intergenerational life-cycle aspects of human capital development. At which stage of the human life cycle can public action best achieve the maximum benefit with least cost? How will this achieve the maximum effect on the schooling and health of the people?

Interventions at each stage in the life cycle are, in fact, investments in the next stage and thereby achieve cumulative effects on human capital development. This framework gives a better perspective than others on how to prioritize actions to achieve maximum benefit. For example, nutrition and health interventions in early childhood produce better outcomes in learning for children entering primary school, increasing the likelihood of completion of primary schooling. Interventions addressing adolescent health, nutrition, and education of girls will produce a healthier next generation, with higher birth weights and better nutrition. Better education results in more productive adults. And so on.

This framework builds upon the general ideas developed in the *Approach Paper for the*

Health, Nutrition, and Population Sector (World Bank 1996c) and can be summarized as follows:

> *Human capital development is a process that begins with life itself, at birth, and can either occur or not occur at any stage through life, depending on the investments made. In infancy, childhood, and adolescence, humans are essentially consumers of resources, but only if investments are made in those children can they be expected to be productive contributors to society through the rest of their lives.*

When children, especially in their early years of development, are afflicted with hunger, disease, illiteracy, and lack of mental stimulation from education, they are deprived of the opportunity to develop as productive citizens contributing to society's growth. When girls marry early in life, they are exposed to potential hardships as they are not given the chance to go to school. Or in adulthood, when women are exposed to malnutrition, they bear children who are also likely to have low birth weight, which is a risk factor for childhood malnutrition.

The sector strategy proposes near-term investments to address the kinds of problems of the stage of the life cycle. This is illustrated by examples in Table 1.1 using data from the surveys.

DATA SOURCES

Primary data sources were the preliminary estimates of the Population Census of 1994, two large-scale national household surveys, two separate facility-based surveys of health and educational institutions, a community-level social assessment, and a survey of NGO and other providers of health and education services. In ad-

Table 1.1 Situation of Ethiopians at Various Stages of the Life Cycle

Stage in the Life Cycle	Population Based on the 1994 Census	Situation, Problems, and Constraints
Infants (Birth to 1 year)	1.8 million	• 15% born with low birth weight (less than 1 kg.) • 120,000 wasted (low weight for height) • 12% (216,000) die before first birthday from ARI, malnutrition, diarrhea, measles
Early Childhood (1–5 years)	8.4 million	• 25% report illness episodes in past 2 months • 60% stunted (low height for age), 11% wasted
Primary School Age (7–14 years)	12.0 million	• Only 8% (120,000) of 7-year-olds are enrolled in grade 1 • 17% (2.1 million) enrolled in primary school (29% enrollment if older children included); majority of children are out of school • Average age of grade 1 pupil: 11 years old • 31% suffer from iodine deficiency disorders
Adolescents (11–14 years)	4.8 million	• Early marriage—35% of girls married by age 15 • 70% of girls married by age 17 • 90% female genital mutilation • 43% participate in labor force (18% for females)
Adults (15–64 years)	27.5 million	• 25% are malnourished or have low body mass index • Sick 18–40 days in a year • Total fertility rate of 6.1 • 7% contraceptive prevalence • Maternal mortality rate of 540–1,500 per 100,000 births • 16% of all deaths due to perinatal-maternal problems • Life expectancy is 49 years
Elderly (above 64 years)	1.9 million	• 35% report illness in past 2 months

Source: PHRD HICE/WMS 1995/96 Survey; AAU-Oxford Survey; Population Census of 1994.

dition, secondary data were utilized, including public financial statistics and regional education and health bureau data.

The household surveys used included the Central Statistical Authority's 1995/96 National Household Income, Consumption, and Expenditure Surveys (HICES)/Welfare Monitoring Survey (WMS) (a nationally representative survey with a sample size of 12,000 households), and the Rural Household Survey of 1994/95 (1,500 households) by the Department of Economics of Addis Ababa University in cooperation with Oxford University's Center for the Study of African Economies. For the returns to schooling analysis, household surveys utilized the 1990 Survey of Adolescent Fertility, Reproductive Behavior, and Employment Status of the Youth Population in Ethiopia.

The community social assessment survey gathered information on the health and education needs and priorities of sample communities. Data were also collected on the existing capacities and roles of various service providers, as well as regulatory or other constraining factors that inhibit the participation of communities in the planning and implementation of education and health programs and services. These data should also help identify specific community institutions useful in providing health and education services.

Information from two nationally representative service provider/institutional surveys have also been used in the analysis. The educational survey covered primary, secondary and tertiary educational institutions to obtain information on unit costs and quality of instruction. The health provider survey obtained information on unit costs and quality of health services. The survey of the private sector and NGO service providers was conducted separately.

Data on government expenditures come from the PHRD studies on costs and financing, and three Public Expenditure Reviews undertaken jointly with the World Bank in 1994 and 1997 and with the European Union in 1996.

2

CONTEXTUAL FACTORS INFLUENCING ETHIOPIA'S SOCIAL SECTORS

The success of any investment in the social sectors in Ethiopia will be strongly influenced by external factors. Progress in social sector and human resource development will depend largely on linkages to the overall government policy and reform framework and, in particular, on the perceived priority of the social sector in the overall growth strategy of the government. Performance may also be influenced by the extent to which outcomes in infrastructure development and the productive sectors are complementary to social sector objectives. The policy and economic environment as well as public and private sector institutions within the social sector, have important implications for the resources available to the social sector and the efficiency with which those resources can be used to deliver social services in Ethiopia. Underlying all these issues is the country's continued population growth and urbanization, which have important implications for economic growth and human resource development in Ethiopia.

SOCIAL SECTOR PERFORMANCE AND THE ECONOMY

Ethiopia's deep-rooted poverty is perhaps the greatest obstacle in its efforts to address the pressing needs of its social sector. With per capita GNP of $100 in 1994, Ethiopia ranks as one of the poorest countries in the world and certainly within Sub-Saharan Africa. In contrast, per capita GNP in other East African countries ranges from $140 in Tanzania to $250 in Kenya (Figure 2.1).

In 1994 per capita incomes in Ethiopia were less than half of those in Sub-Saharan Africa as a whole, where per capita GNP was approximately $259, and less than one-third of those in low-income countries (LICs), which reported per capita GNP of $360 on average in the same year.

Along with very low per capita income, the number of people falling into poverty in Ethiopia is also very high. It is estimated that nearly 52 percent of the population is poor. Poverty in urban areas was estimated at 58 percent, while rural poverty was approximately 48 percent (World Bank 1993b).

Income is highly variable from year to year. Long-term variability is partly due to frequent and severe droughts, which have plagued the rural population. The country is largely de-

Figure 2.1 GNP per Capita, 1994

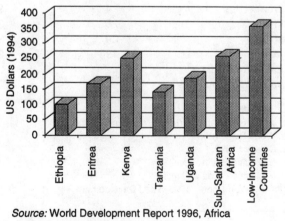

Source: World Development Report 1996, Africa Development Indicators, 1995.

pendent on the agriculture sector, which provides 86 percent of employment and 57 percent of GDP.

In 1991, the transitional government launched macroeconomic reforms that stabilized the economy, dismantled the centrally planned economy of the previous regime, and restored the country's competitive position through a devaluation of the exchange rate and opening of private investment. The GDP responded with double-digit growth of 12 percent in 1992 and nominal growth of 18 percent and 8.9 percent in 1994/95 and 1995/96.

With 54 million people in 1994, Ethiopia is the second most populated country in Sub-Saharan Africa. An important cause of Ethiopia's low per capita income growth and a major obstacle in social sector development has been the population growth of the 1980s and early 1990s. Annual population growth was 3.1 percent between 1980 and 1990, although it is estimated to have declined somewhat during the 1990–94 period (Table 2.1). By comparison, annual population growth in Sub-Saharan Africa was 3.0 percent

through the 1980s, declining to 2.7 percent more recently. Fertility remains quite high in Ethiopia, even by African standards. The total fertility rate (TFR) estimates for women between the ages of 15 and 49 years vary between 5.8 (PHRD Study No. 4, 1996)[1] and 7.5 (World Bank 1996a) in 1994. These rates compare with a fertility rate of 5.8 for Sub-Saharan Africa as a whole.

The consequences of Ethiopia's poverty and the magnitude of the challenge ahead in the social sectors are outlined in Table 2.2. For example, with an average life expectancy at birth of 49 years, Ethiopia ranks among the middle of other counties in East Africa and only slightly below Sub-Saharan Africa as a whole. However, Ethiopia again ranks well below other low-income countries, where the average life expectancy at birth is 56 years.

As indicated in Figure 2.2, Ethiopia has made important reductions in its infant mortality rate, although it still records among the highest in Sub-Saharan Africa and other low-income developing countries. Between 1980 and 1994, the in-

Table 2.1 Demographic and Economic Indicators

	Population, 1994 (millions)	Population Growth, 1980-90 (%)	Per Capita GNP, 1994 Dollars	Per Capita GNP Growth, 1985–94 (%)
Ethiopia	54	3.1	100	-0.7[a]
Eritrea	4	3.3[b]	169[c]	-0.6[b]
Kenya	26	3.4	250	0.0
Tanzania	29	3.2	140	0.8
Uganda	19	2.4	190	2.3
Sub-Saharan Africa[d]	...	3.0	259[a]	-1.0[a]
Low-Income Countries[e]	...	2.7	360	-1.1

... no data.
a. World Bank: African Development Indicators 1996.
b. World Bank 1993a.
c. Data for 1993.
d. Excluding South Africa.
e. Excluding China and India.
Source: World Bank: 1996 World Development Report.

---

[1] All PHRD Studies will be cited this way. For a complete list, see Annex 1.

Table 2.2 Other Social Welfare Indicators

	Life Expectancy at Birth, 1994	Infant Mortality Rate (per 1,000 Live Births), 1994	Total Fertility Rate, 1994	Adult Illiteracy, 1994 (%)
Ethiopia	49	120	7.5	65
Eritrea[a]	46	135	6.8	...
Kenya	59	59	4.9	22
Tanzania	51	84	5.8	32
Uganda	42	122	7.1	38
Sub-Saharan Africa[b]	52	92	5.9	43
Low-Income Countries[c]	56	86	5.1	46

... no data.
a. World Bank 1993a (data reported are for 1993).
b. Data reported include South Africa.
c. Excluding China and India.
Source: World Bank 1996a, World Development Report.

fant mortality rate dropped from 155 deaths per 1,000 lives births to 120. In 1995, it dropped further to 112 (World Bank 1997a). However, within the Eastern Africa region, only Eritrea and Uganda currently have comparably high rates. Overall, the infant mortality rate is equal to 92 deaths per 1,000 live births in Sub-Saharan Africa and 86 deaths per 1,000 live births for all low-income countries. Similarly, child and maternal mortality in Ethiopia also rank within the high extremes for the region and low-income countries in general. Access to clean water and adequate sanitation are particular concerns in Ethiopia. Approximately 19 percent of the Ethiopian population has access to a clean water supply, while only 7 percent has access to adequate sanitation facilities.

Finally, the literacy rate of Ethiopians is among the lowest in the world, representing perhaps a significant constraint to improvements in health and other measures of social welfare in the country. Sixty-five percent of adults in Ethiopia were estimated to be illiterate in 1995, an illiteracy rate nearly three times higher than in neighboring Kenya and more than double that of Tanzania. Primary school enrollment rates also remain quite low, at under 30 percent, suggesting that the problems of illiteracy and lack of educa-

tion are likely to complicate efforts in human and economic development over the long term.

POLICY AND ECONOMIC ENVIRONMENT

Ethiopia has made remarkable progress in stabilizing and invigorating the national economy, which was devastated after the long civil war and

Figure 2.2 Change in Infant Mortality, 1980–94

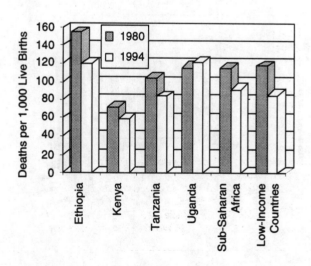

Source: World Bank 1996a.

which suffered from major macroeconomic imbalances and structural distortions under the previous government's centrally planned economy. Early in the recovery period, the transitional government adopted a series of reform measures to scale back state intervention and establish a strong market-based economy.

The government has also taken important steps to dismantle parastatal control in key productive sectors of the economy. Within the context of its reform efforts, the government will continue to reduce its role in the productive sectors in order to promote increased private sector participation, and will instead expand its role in the social and infrastructure sectors. In addition, the transitional government made efforts to decentralize decision-making to regional and local government authorities to ensure greater autonomy in both the economic and political spheres.

Because of the importance of agriculture in the economy of Ethiopia, and its particular importance to the livelihoods of the rural poor, the government has based its long-term development strategy on a process of "agriculture-development-

led-industrialization." This strategy views agriculture as the primary stimulus to generate employment and income for the poor and as a springboard for growth in other areas of the economy, particularly in the small-scale manufacturing and service sectors. Although the strategy also sets objectives in infrastructure, environment, manufacturing, and services, large-scale investments in the social sectors are seen as critical to the overall strategy's success by ensuring a more healthy, educated, and therefore more productive workforce. The requirements of the agricultural-led development strategy suggest a particular emphasis on investments in primary education and health care, literacy and numeracy training for the working-age population, vocational and technical training, and improved water and sanitation.

Economic Growth

The levels of both public and private spending on social services in Ethiopia will ultimately depend on levels of economic output, as measured by annual changes in GDP. Over the past decade, as indicated in Figure 2.3, GDP levels have fluctuated considerably, although the trend is upward. Between 1985 and 1989, average annual growth in real GDP was approximately 4.2 percent, a rate that slightly exceeded the rate of population growth.

The pattern of overall GDP growth since the mid-1980s largely parallels changes in output in the agricultural sector, which accounted for 57 percent of GDP in 1994. The most dynamic segment of the economy over the past decade has been the services sector, however, which accounts for approximately 32 percent of GDP. Between 1985 and 1989, the services sector grew by an average of 5.8 percent annually, slowing somewhat to 3.7 percent between 1990 and 1994. In contrast, growth in the industrial sector was fairly stagnant between 1985 and 1989, with an average annual increase of only 2.3 percent. Since 1990, conditions in the industrial sector have declined, as

Figure 2.3   Trends in GDP and Main Sectors, 1985–94

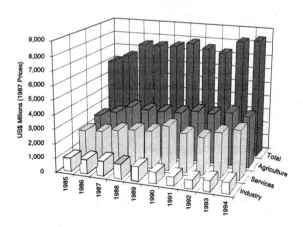

Source: WB, CAS, 1995.

indicated by an average annual growth rate of –3.8 percent (World Bank 1995a).

Fiscal Policy Reform

Since the war, the government has undertaken a significant reform of tax policy and fiscal management practices. Among other things, it has introduced income and sales tax policy reforms, measures to improve the management of counterpart funds, and fiscal decentralization and civil service reforms. Figure 2.4 shows that domestic revenues have begun to expand as a result of those measures (World Bank 1994b; CSAE 1996).

Overall government spending has also increased as a proportion of GDP in recent years. After a decline in the early 1990s, total expenditures rose sharply, from 23 percent of GDP in 1993 to 30 percent in 1994, leveling off at 29 percent in 1995. This increase in expenditure share is partly due to improved implementation capacity and partly due to the impact of the substantial devaluation. Since the end of the war, there has also been a significant reallocation of the national budget away from spending on defense and public enterprises, including parastatal trading enterprises, and toward road construction, education

Figure 2.4 Government Revenues and Expenditures as Share of GDP, 1990–95

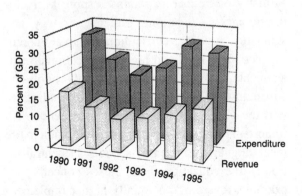

Source: CSAE 1996.

Figure 2.5 Budgetary Allocations to the Social Sector, 1987–89 and 1993–95

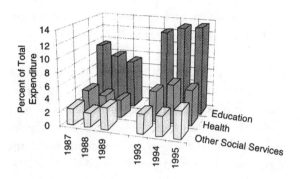

Source: World Bank 1995a.

and health. Military expenditures were sharply reduced from 24 percent of total budget in 1989 to 7.1 percent in 1995. In contrast, while spending on the social sector fell as a share of the total budget in the late 1980s, it has substantially increased in the postwar period (Figure 2.5). Spending on education increased from 7.1 to 13.4 percent of the total budget from 1989 to 1995, while health expenditures increased from 2.8 to 5.4 percent (World Bank 1995a).

Overall government spending on the social sectors amounted to approximately 6.8 percent of GDP in 1994, up from 4.5 percent in 1993. Spending on education amounted to just over 4 percent of GDP in 1994, compared with 2.8 percent in 1993. However, education spending as a share of GDP slightly declined in 1995/96 and 1996/97 to 3.7 percent and 3.8 percent, respectively. Health expenditures rose from 1.1 percent of GDP in 1993 to nearly 1.8 percent in 1994. Estimates of health spending as a share of GDP shows a slight decline to 1.6 percent in 1995/96 and 1.7 percent in 1996/97 (World Bank 1997b). On a per capita basis, total government spending on the social sectors was a relatively low US$5.60 in 1994, as measured in current prices. As an indication of the low levels of government support to the social sectors in Ethiopia, health expenditures were just under US$1.50 per capita in 1994, compared with an average of approximately US$14.00 per capita for Sub-Saharan Africa as a whole and the US$12.00 per capita that the World Bank estimates is necessary to provide essential primary health services (World Bank 1995a).

Given projected rates of population growth (see Annex 2), growth in GDP, and budget shares, it is possible to estimate the level of government resources that will be available to the social sector in the future. For example, assuming 8 percent real annual growth in GDP from 1994 to 2020 and further assuming that government expenditures as a percentage of GDP and social sector budget shares remain at 1994 levels, per capita expenditure on the social sectors would increase to US$23 in 2020. Under this scenario, government health spending would rise somewhat to US$5.50 per capita. Assuming instead that government expenditures expand to 34 percent of GDP, and that actual spending on social services increases from the current 23 percent of the budget to 35 percent, per capita expenditures would increase to US$39 by 2020. With spending on health assumed itself to be 10 percent of the budget in 2020, this latter scenario implies that it would take 25 years for per capita health expenditures to reach US$11.

INSTITUTIONAL CONTEXT

Regionalization

Among the first policies articulated by the transitional government was a strong political commitment to transfer significant autonomy and responsibilities to regional government authorities. The objectives of this decentralization and regionalization policy are to promote the democratic process and self-government at the local level, to encourage popular participation in regional development activities, and to ensure a responsive political and administrative system. To be successful, however, this policy must address the need for more skilled personnel and other inputs to improve existing implementation capacity, some inherent difficulties in raising revenue at the regional level, and the limited infrastructure, communications and other resources at the disposal of regional authorities. There is an additional concern regarding the implications of this policy for macroeconomic stabilization and fiscal control given the enormous outlay required to build capacity in the regions.

The government has also articulated policies that define the respective powers and duties of central and regional governments. Central ministries are obliged to "give assistance and advice to Regional Self-Governments" and have authority to set policies and responsibility to enforce laws and regulations. In addition to developing their own budgets and raising revenues, regional authorities are responsible for the planning and implementation of regional development programs. However, given the lack of capacity in some regions, the central government continues to provide technical assistance to these regions to help them fulfill some functions such as procurement.

The regionalization policy will have important implications for social sector development. In education, for example, the central Ministry of Education retains responsibility for the country's educational policies, strategy, and standards, as well as curriculum design at the senior secondary level and higher. Educational management, including the supervision of schools and curriculum development, will be decentralized, as will the training of primary school teachers. An important result of the policy is the decision to use local languages in primary schools. Decentralization in the education sector raises concerns, for example, regarding potentially higher implementation costs and the wide differences in the amounts allocated to education across regions.

However, these steps are seen as necessary to make the curriculum more relevant to local students and to obtain wider participation in decision-making, more responsive administration and supervision, and improved quality and more effective learning. To meet these expanded local responsibilities between 75 and 83 percent of the education budget was transferred to the regional governments in fiscal 1994.

In the health sector, the key responsibility of the central government will be to formulate public health policies and strategies, as well as to support and supervise their implementation. Government health policy will be implemented primarily through the regional governments. In fact, the decentralization policy has been implemented rapidly in the health sector. Regional governments are now responsible for nearly all health facilities and health personnel training centers in the country and have been given considerable financial authority. In fiscal 1994, between 83 and 88 percent of the total budget was allocated to regional governments. The policy of decentralization has already led to the reassignment of personnel and personnel decision-making responsibilities to the regions. Significant efforts at local capacity-building in the health sector are still required and are currently being addressed by the FDRE. The potential benefits of decentralization are more responsive planning and implementation and increased cost recovery, since local institutions will have a greater stake in the collection and use of resources.

Private Sector Role

A number of government actions have promoted greater private sector involvement in the Ethiopian economy. For example, prudent monetary policy, which has begun to reign in inflationary pressures, and the withdrawal of government intervention in the productive sectors have created a climate more conducive to private sector participation in the provision of consumer and intermediate goods.

The availability of foreign exchange has also been increased for business and other uses as well.

Although the private sector remains relatively small and undeveloped, it already plays a critical role in some aspects of the provision of social services in Ethiopia. Indeed, given Ethiopia's extremely low rates of school enrollment and the poor coverage of health facilities, even a large-scale reorientation of government resources to the social sectors is unlikely to sufficiently expand access to services for the bulk of the population without rapidly expanding private sector involvement.

In education, communities and NGOs play an important role at the kindergarten and primary school levels, the latter primarily in urban areas. Although the current government's privatization program permits the establishment of private, for-profit schools, relatively few are operating currently. In health, practically all drug vendors and drug stores are privately owned, as are more than 70 percent of pharmacies. These facilities are an important dimension of Ethiopia's health care delivery system, particularly for the rural poor. Visits to the homes of health workers or to private health clinics and health centers are also important components of the system and are used more by the wealthier individuals. There are also just under 200 NGO health clinics and 8 NGO hospitals operating throughout the country, particularly in rural areas.

While private sector participation in the social services has been facilitated by many of the reforms already described, the government is only just beginning to recognize the potential of the private sector in this area. With continued economic growth, demand for privately provided social services, particularly in health, is likely to grow. In that light, a number of actions are required to support further private sector involvement in social sector development. In the health sector, the privatization of government hospitals, the rationalization of the national pharmaceuticals distribution system, and the training of private drug vendors and pharmacists to improve the quality of care they provide are other important measures proposed to make better use of private sector resources in delivering social services throughout the country.

Community Involvement

Community participation is envisioned as a key element in the provision of social services in Ethiopia. In addition to the financial resources obtained from community members through cost-recovery efforts, local involvement in planning and implementation is intended to stimulate new initiatives at the grass-roots level, improve project management, and reduce the costs of implementation while increasing the efficiency of resource use. In the health sector, the recruitment of community health agents and traditional birth attendants has been an important component of the government's health policy since the mid-1980s. Strong community involvement in local health councils has been mandated by more recent government policies (TGE 1993).

In education, a fairly large number of kindergartens and primary schools, primarily in urban areas, are run by the communities themselves or by local private organizations that make considerable use of community resources. Within the public education sector, community involvement in government School Committees has also been an important element of policy since the mid-1980s. More recently, a number of government documents have reemphasized the importance of community financial, labor, and materials resources in supporting local educational institutions. In many areas, community members have made substantial contributions to public school construction and maintenance, the procurement of equipment and materials, and the employment of teachers. Indeed, over the past two decades, the construction of most new primary schools has been a joint venture between government and the community (PHRD Study Number 12, 1996).

In addition to the resources that communities can contribute to both public and private sector efforts in the delivery of social services, traditional community self-help mechanisms—such as savings and insurance associations or cooperative labor arrangements—may provide models for more effective ways to organize both private and public resources to improve social service delivery at the local level. For example, mutual assistance funds, or *iddirs*, which are common throughout much of Ethiopia and are used to provide resources for funerals and other family emergencies, have been proposed as a model for rural health insurance schemes, as a means to increase individual access and overall community financial contributions to health services.

POPULATION PROJECTIONS AND IMPLICATIONS

As stated, Ethiopia's large and expanding population creates a particular obstacle to rapid progress in social sector development. Because it can dampen per capita income growth and undermine the ability of the economy to absorb an expanding labor force, rapid population growth may eventually minimize potential growth in the demand for social services at the household level. On the supply side, because an expanding population base will require more and more resources simply to maintain the existing quality of, and access to, social services, rapid population growth also has important implications on the ability of public and private institutions to expand access to adequate services.

Again, between the 1984 and 1994 censuses, the population of Ethiopia is estimated to have grown by 2.6 percent annually. The population of urban centers has grown relatively more rapidly than that of the rural areas. According to preliminary census reports, Addis Ababa recorded 3.8 percent annual growth in the intercensal period, while other urban centers recorded 4.1 percent annual growth. In rural areas, the population is estimated to have grown at an annual rate of 2.2 percent.

Any future changes in the rate of population growth in Ethiopia will depend on changes in mortality levels on the one hand and, on the other, the country's ability to address economic and social factors that influence women's status and the demand for children, the use of family planning services, and a range of other factors that determine fertility. As a background to this report, a number of scenarios for population growth and its distribution have been produced, based on a range of assumptions regarding likely changes in mortality, fertility, and rural-urban migration. This exercise, the results of which can only be viewed as preliminary given the fact that they are based on the unadjusted census data that are currently available, is detailed in Annex 2.[2]

As indicated in Figure 2.6, even the most optimistic scenarios for declining fertility in Ethiopia imply a substantial increase in its population base over the next 25 years, from the current estimate of 54 million to approximately 92 million. At the other extreme, assuming no dec- line in fertility over the next 25 years, Ethiopia's populations would grow to more than 113 million. However, the scenario considered most plausible places the population at 98 million by 2020.

In addition to continued population growth and increasing urbanization, changes in the age structure of the population are also likely to occur in the future. Because of past high levels

Figure 2.6   Population Projections, 1995–2020

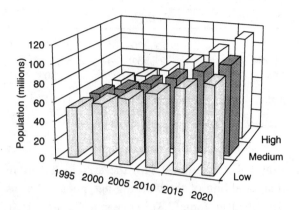

Source: PHRD Study Number 4, 1996.

of fertility, the population structure has been heavily weighted toward the young. However, because fertility is anticipated to decline over time, the median age of the population is expected to rise substantially. The magnitude of the shift in the age profile, based on the medium-level population growth scenario described, is shown in Table 2.3. By far the largest increase in population is the more than doubling of persons aged 15–64. By contrast, the population of children is expected to grow by less than 60 percent. As indicated in Figure 2.7, the proportion of the population under 20 years of age is expected to decline sharply between 1995 and 2020.

Even under moderate assumptions regarding future changes in fertility and mortality, projected population growth will present an enormous obstacle to improvements in basic social outcome variables in Ethiopia, as the population burden on the economy and social services con-

---

[2] Projections presented in this section are based on an adjusted total fertility rate (TFR) of 6.1 in 1994, as derived from the 1994 census. The · high-level scenario assumes constant fertility through 2020, while the medium-level scenario assumes a steady decline in the TFR to 3.55 by 2020. The low-level scenario assumes a more precipitous decline in TFR to 2.90 by 2020. Annex 2 also presents a series of scenarios based on an initial adjusted TFR of 7.7, as derived from the 1990 National Family and Fertility Survey. Assumptions on improvements in life expectancy vary by region, with yearly increments of between 0.3 to 0.5 percent. At this point, assumptions on life expectancy do not fully account for likely age-specific variation, due to the likely impact of HIV/AIDS, for example. Finally, net international migration was expected to be negligible.

Table 2.3   Age Distribution of Population (millions)

Age Group	1995	2020
0–14	23,820	37,094
15–64	27,531	57,850
65+	1,926	3,003
Total	53,277	97,947

Source: PHRD Study Number 4, 1996.

tinues. For example, with the anticipated more than doubling of the working age population (as described in Table 2.3) between 1995 and 2020, over 1.2 million additional workers are expected to enter the labor market each year on average. In the absence of an even more rapid economic expansion, sufficient not only to absorb new workers but to expand overall rates of employment as well, the tremendous growth in the working age population is also likely to place an overwhelming burden on Ethiopia's various safety net programs.

In general, the population projections suggest it will be increasingly difficult to expand coverage of basic social services, particularly given the numbers and types of facilities and staff that will be needed to provide services to an expanding, aging and increasingly urban-based population. More specific implications for the health sector include the following:

Figure 2.7   Age and Sex Distribution of the Population, 1995 and 2020

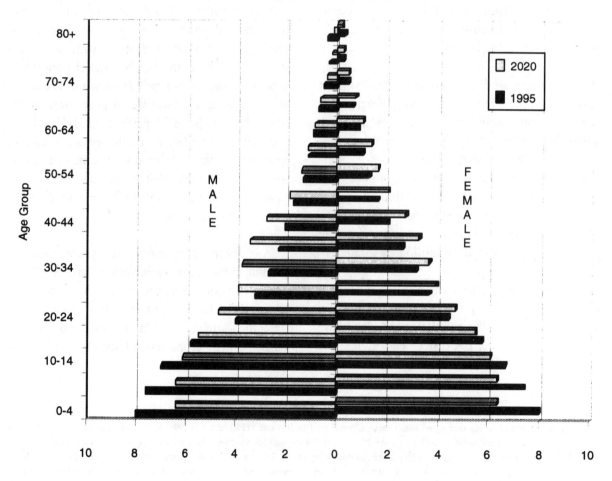

Percent of Total Population

Source: PHRD Study Number 4, 1996.

- With the number of children under one year of age expected to increase from 1.8 to 2.5 million over the next 25 years, even maintaining current EPI coverage rates of 47 percent would require a 41 percent increase in resources. Doubling the Expanded Program on Immunisation coverage to 94 percent would nearly triple the current number of vaccines required.
- To simply maintain current coverage for maternal immunizations (estimated to be nearly 20 percent in 1995) would require a more than 26 percent increase in resources over the next 25 years. A doubling of coverage would expand resource requirements by as much as 152 percent between 1995 and 2020.
- With the projected change in the population of women aged 15–49, meeting the government's goal of raising contraceptive use from 7 percent in 1995 to 44 percent in 2020 would increase family planning commodity costs from US$64 million to US$457 million in constant 1995 dollar terms, an annual increase of just under 8 percent.
- Projected increases in the population aged 15–49 years (which accounted for 93 percent of those infected with AIDS in 1995), along with the expansion of the urban population and other factors, are expected to influence the spread of HIV/AIDS in Ethiopia. The number of HIV-positive in Ethiopia is expected to more than double between 1995 and 2020, from 1.5 to 3.9 million. The number of new AIDS cases is

expected to rise from 171,000 to 551,000 in the same period. Given the high cost of treating AIDS patients, which has been estimated to range from US$85 to US$628 per patient in Ethiopia (Abdulhamid 1994), the anticipated increase in AIDS cases is likely to have significant budgetary implications apart from the physical strain on the health care delivery system.

In the education sector, the implications of even moderate population growth over the next 25 years are similarly large and suggest the difficulty of substantially increasing enrollment rates. A review of statistical figures from the Ministry of Education revealed that the estimated average annual growth rate of enrollment at the primary school level was 4.3 percent between the year 1977/78 and 1993/94. Maintaining that trend over the next 25 years would imply that the number of school children actually enrolled would increase from the present 2.7 million to approximately 7.6 million. Given the anticipated growth of the primary school-aged population, that continued rapid increase in enrollment would imply that the share of school-aged children actually attending would rise from 29 to 56 percent between 1995 and 2020. Given projections of population changes in the 15–18 age group, senior secondary school enrollment would have to increase by 72 percent over that period, simply to maintain constant enrollment rates, or by more than 244 percent if enrollment rates are doubled.

3

THE ETHIOPIAN HOUSEHOLD

An understanding of household behavior is key to the approach in this report. In order to define how human resources can be developed in Ethiopia, we must know what these human resources consist of, their constraints, their values, and their expectations. This chapter will lay out the key demographic characteristics and income and expenditure patterns of the population. Extreme poverty in the majority of Ethiopian households severely limits their ability to pay for social services, and their willingness to invest in better health and child education. This willingness will very much depend on their perceptions of the value to them, and to their children, of the returns on these investments.

Preliminary estimates from the 1994 Population Census indicate that Ethiopia has approximately 10.2 million households, with about 5.2 persons per household. Total population was estimated at 54 million in 1994, compared with 42.6 million in 1984 (the 1984 figure included Eritrea, which is now a separate country). The composition and characteristics of households have undergone major changes:
- the urban population has grown to 14 percent compared with 10 percent in 1984;
- urban households are smaller than rural households (4.9 compared with 5.2 persons);
- female-headed households now make up one-fourth of all households in Ethiopia, much more so in urban areas (44 percent of all urban households) than rural (15 percent); and
- the age dependency ratio (ratio of dependent-age—under 15 and over 64—to working-age

population) rose from 0.92 in the mid-1980s to 1.04 in 1994.

The most important conclusion from this information is that Ethiopian households are not migrating to the cities en masse as in other African or Asian countries, but the numbers are rising. Addis Ababa's population, the major urban center in Ethiopia, has grown by 3.8 percent per year since 1984. The increasing trend of female-headed households in urban areas has important implications for the development of social sectors in Ethiopia. The increasing dependency ratio is also significant, mainly because scarce resources are being subdivided simply to feed and cloth a rapidly increasing population of young.

INCOME AND SOURCES OF INCOME

On the basis of recent household income and expenditure surveys, the average income of Ethiopian households is about US$150 per capita per year in the rural areas and about US$180 for the country as a whole. In local currency this is equivalent to about Birr 78 and 85 per capita per month, respectively. The latter figure comes from the nationally representative sample of households taken by the 1995/96 Central Statistical Authority's Household Income, Consumption, and Expenditure/Welfare Monitoring Survey (HICE/WMS), while the lower figure was obtained from the 1994/95 rural household survey by Oxford University and Addis Ababa University

(Oxford-AAU). Both of these estimates are much higher than that derived from national income accounts, suggesting that the present accepted figure of US$100 per capita may underestimate the actual figure.

The main sources of livelihood of Ethiopian households are farming for men and domestic work for women. Agriculture supports 85 percent of the population but accounts for only 40 percent of the national income. An overwhelming majority of households with adult male labor have access to land, which the men farm as their primary occupation. A large proportion of children are reported to be engaged in domestic work and/or farming as well. Few adults are primarily engaged outside of farming or domestic work, with trade being the main alternative occupation for only 15 percent of adults. Off-farm activities are not lucrative enough (for households with limited amounts of capital) to encourage widespread specialization in off-farm activities. Nonagricultural manual work as a primary activity is rare for men and almost unknown for women. The industrial sector is very small and accounts for a small proportion of wage employment. It is mainly limited to Addis Ababa and the major urban centers.

HOUSEHOLD EXPENDITURE PATTERNS

Figure 3.1 summarizes the pattern of rural household expenditures in Ethiopia. The characteristic of extreme poverty is reflected in the dominant share of food, which accounts for 75 percent of all expenditures. More than half (53 percent) of food consumption was obtained by cash purchases from the local market, while about 45 percent of all food consumed came from subsistence production. These data imply that despite the overwhelming dependence on farm production for livelihood, the majority of households rely heavily

Figure 3.1 Allocation of Rural Household Expenditures

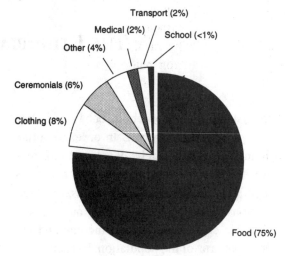

Source: Oxford-AAU Rural Household Survey, 1994/95.

on the market for the food they consume. A large proportion of own-consumption food is obtained as wage payments, or gifts or loans from friends and relatives.

The remaining 25 percent of household expenditures is spent on seven major rural household expenditure items: clothing expenses (8 percent), ceremonials and contributions (6 percent), medical expenses (2 percent), schooling (less than 1 percent), transport (2 percent), household durables and building materials (2 percent) and other expenditures (4 percent). Ethiopian households are remarkably resilient in surviving expenditure shocks such as a major health problem in the family. At the same time, spending on ceremonies appears disproportionately large. This is probably an overestimate, however, since the period of recall of these surveys covered Christmas and other important Ethiopian holidays corresponding to the season when marriages in many parts of the country are arranged. Clearly, households are severely constrained in their ability to pay for the health or education of their children.

There are significant differences between urban and rural expenditure patterns. This is also true across regions. Such differences are reflected most clearly in a breakdown by expenditure groups (expenditure quartiles). Some of the important household characteristics are presented by expenditure quartiles in Table 3.1. These data show that consumption patterns are affected by the size of households, age composition of households, and the educational levels of mothers and fathers. Regional differences are very strong. In drought-prone areas such as Gamo Gofa, the absolute expenditure for food of about Birr 45 per household per month is only a third of that of the Kedida Gamela area (Taddesse and Ghebre 1995).

IMPACT OF COMMUNITY LEVEL INFRASTRUCTURE AND SERVICES

The infrastructure and services available in communities determine, to a considerable degree, the health-seeking behavior and schooling patterns of households. Some of these important characteristics are captured in Table 3.1, given by expenditure groups. About one-half of the villages have an all-weather road nearby. The better-off households live close to these all-weather roads. Clinics, the most important facility in the primary health care system, are on average about 7 kilo-

Table 3.1 Household and Community Characteristics in Rural Ethiopia

	All Households	Poorest 25 Percent	Lower Middle	Higher Middle	Richest 25 Percent
Household Characteristics					
Household Size	6.6	7.4	6.9	6.5	5.8
Number of Adults (15 years)	4.1	4.3	4.1	4.0	4.0
Age of the Household Head	47	49	47	47	47
Percent Female-Headed	17	24	15	14	16
Consumption per Month (Birr per capita)	78	22	45	75	170
Food Consumption per Month (Birr per capita)	58	17	34	55	125
Percent of Household Heads Who Completed Primary School	8	3	9	9	13
Percent of Fathers Who Completed Primary School	12	4	13	13	18
Percent of Mothers Completed Primary School	2	1	2	3	4
Highest Grade Attained by Father	1.4	0.6	1.4	1.5	2.1
Highest Grade Obtained by Mother	0.5	0.2	0.4	0.5	0.7
Community Characteristics					
Percent of People with All-Weather Road in Village	54	22	54	65	75
Distance to Nearest All-Weather Road (km)	3.6	6.3	3.5	2.6	1.9
Distance to Nearest Clinic (km)	6.8	6.7	6.6	6.5	7.4
Distance to Nearest Hospital (km)	34	38	33	32	31
Percent of Clinics with Regular Supply of Antibiotics	50	43	48	50	75
Distance to Primary School (km)	2.1	2.7	2.3	1.9	1.7
Distance to Nearest High School (km)	20	27	22	17	15
Percent of Households with Access to Piped Water	28	13	26	34	40

Sample Size: 1,500 Rural Households

Source: Oxford-AAU Rural Household Survey, 1994/95, as reported in PHRD Study Number 2.a, 1996.

meters from the households surveyed, and only one-half of these clinics have a regular supply of antibiotics (a proxy for the measure of quality of care provided). The nearest hospital is about 40 ilometers away on average. Primary schools are, on average, only about 2 kilometers away, but secondary schools average more than 8 kilometers away. Less than one-third of the households have access to piped or pumped water (PHRD Study Number 2.a, 1996).

4

HEALTH

INDICATORS OF HEALTH STATUS

The health status of Ethiopians is extremely poor, even in comparison with the Sub-Saharan Africa region and other low-income countries. In general, the poor health status of Ethiopians can be characterized by vulnerability to largely preventable infectious diseases and nutritional deficiencies, including micronutrient deficiencies. Ethiopia's historically high rate of population growth, the low-income status of much of its population, their low education levels and high rates of illiteracy, inadequate access to clean water and sanitation facilities, and poor access to health services have all contributed to this burden of ill-health. The country's long civil war has not only exacerbated problems of poor health and low incomes among

the war's victims, but also led to the deterioration of the health infrastructure and, until recently, diverted resources away from investments in the health sector.

Table 4.1 documents the burden of ill health in Ethiopia relative to its neighbors. For example, the crude death rate in Ethiopia is approximately 18 per 1,000 population, more than double that of neighboring Kenya and second only to Uganda in Eastern Africa. Life expectancy at birth is 49 years. Although Ethiopia has made significant progress in reducing mortality rates since 1980, both infant and child mortality remain substantially higher than those of the Sub-Saharan Africa region as a whole. Infant mortality in 1994 was approximately 120 deaths per 1,000 live births, while the child mortality rate was 204

Table 4.1 Basic Health Status Indicators

	Ethiopia	Eritrea	Kenya	Tanzania	Uganda	Africa
Crude Death Rate (per 1,000)	18	15	9	14	19	15
Life Expectancy (years)	49	46	59	51	42	52
Infant Mortality (per 1,000)	120	135	59	84	122	92
Child Mortality (per 1,000)	204	204	94	167	185	172
Maternal Mortality (per 100,000)	452–1528[b]	...	510–646	200–748	550	573– ...
Immunization Coverage (percent)						
Diphtheria, Pertussis, and Tetanus	28	...	85	82	73	50
Polio	28	...	85	81	74	50
Measles	22	...	76	79	73	51
Access to Proper Sanitation (percent)	10	...	49	86	67	26[a]
Access to Safe Water (percent)	18-26	...	...	52	...	37[a]
Access to Health care (percent)	55	...	...	93	...	54[a]
Attended Births (percent)	10	...	...	60	...	34[a]

... no data.
[a] Excludes South Africa.
[b] Maternal mortality estimates for Ethiopia vary widely depending on source used.
Source: World Bank 1996a, 1996b, 1994a; PHRD Study Number 4, 1996.

deaths per 1,000. In general, high infant mortality is partly attributable to high prenatal (28 weeks of gestation to first week of life) and neonatal (birth to one month) deaths. These deaths in turn are often due to poor maternal health. The deaths of children older than one month are generally caused by disease and malnutrition (WHO 1986). Estimates of maternal mortality vary widely between 452 and 1,528 deaths per 100,000 live births in Ethiopia.[1] While the lower end of that range is comparable to maternal mortality in neighboring countries, the upper limit is more than double the high-end estimates of other countries in Eastern Africa.

As will be discussed in greater detail, coverage of basic health services and infrastructure is remarkably low in Ethiopia. Table 4.1 indicates that child immunization rates in Ethiopia are 28 percent each for DPT and polio and 22 percent for measles. Only 10 percent of Ethiopians have access to proper sanitation facilities, and 18 to 26 percent to safe water. The availability of both is highly skewed toward urban areas. In contrast, 26 percent of the population of Sub-Saharan Africa as a whole has access to sanitation. Finally, it is estimated that only 10 percent of all births in Ethiopia are attended by trained health personnel, compared with approximately 60 percent in Tanzania and 34 percent in Sub-Saharan Africa overall.

The major causes of morbidity among patients seeking treatment in health facilities include respiratory infections, malaria, skin infections, diarrheal diseases, and intestinal parasitic infections. For children, these five illnesses accounted for over 63 percent of all reported cases of child morbidity. Among those receiving in-patient care

in hospitals, tuberculosis and malaria account for 30 percent of all in-patient deaths. Other important diseases leading to premature death include perinatal and maternal complications, AIDS, and nutritional deficiencies. Some of these health problems have become more prominent in recent years, most notably malaria, TB and HIV/AIDS. In particular, HIV/AIDS is becoming an increasing threat to the population of Ethiopia. The capital city, Addis Ababa appears to be affected by the epidemic more than other regions.

BURDEN OF DISEASE

The analysis in Table 4.2 presents discounted life years (DLYs) lost owing to premature death from a variety of diseases. Conceptually, a comprehensive measurement of the burden of disease should capture all possible short- and long-term consequences of disease and injury which could be classified as acute or chronic disability as well as death. While the exclusion of disability impacts in this analysis may lead to a slight reordering of the actual results and prevents a thorough analysis of the economic implications of disease, an advantage of using only death to measure the burden of disease is that death is an unambiguous event and availability of data is better than for a wide spectrum of possible disabilities.

The total burden of disease in Ethiopia is approximately 350 DLYs lost per 1,000 people (PHRD Study Number 3, 1996). Ethiopia's burden of disease is significantly higher than in neighboring Kenya, which is estimated to be approximately 170 DLYs lost per 1,000 people. It is also much higher than Eastern Africa as a

---

[1] A number of hospital-based studies on maternal mortality carried out in Ethiopia since 1980 gave a wide range of rates from as low as 452 to as high as 1,528 maternal deaths per 100,000 live births. The World Bank's Health, Nutrition, and Population Sector Strategy estimated maternal mortality at 1,528 per 100,000 live births in 1995. Cities like Addis Ababa, Dire Dawa, and Harar have lower rates because of their higher contraceptive usage and deliveries at health institutions (MOH 1995b). However, maternal mortality rates for the majority of mothers who deliver at home could not be extrapolated from these studies. Not more than 10 percent of deliveries occur at health facilities.

Table 4.2 Burden of Disease for Ethiopia

Causes/Conditions	Population Group	Deaths (percent)	DLYs Lost (percent)	Mortality Rate per 1,000	Untreated CFR (percent)	Average Age at Death	Lost if Die
AIDS	All	7.7	8.1	1.32	100.0	27.0	26.2
ARI	Under 5	14.4	17.1	13.33	15.4	2.0	29.9
Cardiovascular	15 +	0.9	0.8	0.27	45.0	40.0	22.9
Diarrhea	Under 5	7.6	9.0	7.03	0.4	2.0	29.9
Injury/ Trauma	All	0.9	0.8	0.15	—	34.0	24.5
Malaria	All	10.0	10.9	1.71	10.0	20.0	27.5
Measles	Under 5	3.5	4.1	3.22	3.0	1.5	30.0
Nutritional Deficiency	Under 5	7.8	9.3	7.20	12.0	2.0	29.9
Perinatal-Maternal	Preg. Women + Births	16.8	16.3	—	—	25.0	26.6
Tuberculosis	All	4.8	4.8	0.82	44.6	30.0	25.5
Total Target Diseases		74.3	81.3				
All Other Diseases	All	25.7	18.7			53.0	18.3
TOTAL	All	100.0	100.0				

Source: PHRD Study Number 3, 1996.

whole, which has a burden of disease of 280 DLYs lost per 1,000 people (see Figure 4.1).

Ethiopia's burden of disease is dominated by acute respiratory infection and perinatal and maternal conditions, followed by malaria, nutritional deficiency, diarrhea, and AIDS. Indeed, the

Figure 4.1 Burden of Disease in Eastern Africa

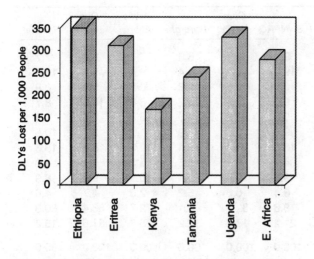

Source: PHRD Study Number 3, 1996.

top 10 causes of mortality account for 74 percent of all deaths and 81 percent of DLYs lost. Diseases that affect children under the age of 5 years (ARI, diarrhea, nutritional deficiencies, and measles) account for 33 percent of deaths and 40 percent of DLYs lost, although children under 5 represent well under 20 percent of the population. When perinatal and maternal conditions are added, the health problems of mothers and children combined account for 50 percent of all deaths and 56 percent of DLYs lost. Although largely preventable, childhood and maternal illnesses and communicable diseases are the major causes of death in Ethiopia.

Given the nature of the data available, a comprehen- sive breakdown of the relative burden of disease across regions of Ethiopia was not possible, although differences in the pattern of deaths and DLYs lost could be examined. In Addis Ababa, for example, the contribution of AIDS and injury/trauma to DLYs lost is well above the national average, while the contributions of ARI, diarrhea, and tuberculosis are well below the average. In Dire Dawa and Hararghe, the contribution of injury/trauma to DLYs lost is also well

Figure 4.2   Percent of Total Deaths and Life Years Lost by Cause

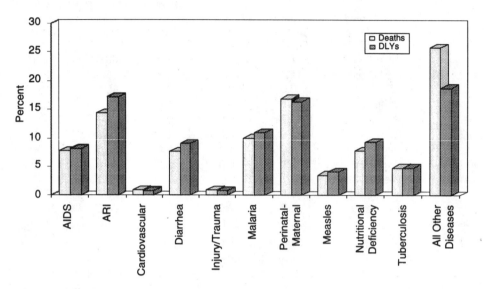

Source: PHRD Study Number 3, 1996.

above the national average. In contrast, the impact of both ARI and malaria on the burden of disease in those regions is well below the national average. Malaria appears to be significantly less of a problem in Tigray than across the remainder of the country, while the incidence of measles in Dire Dawa is also particularly low. In Benishangul, the impact of tuberculosis is significantly higher than for the rest of the country.

DEMAND FOR HEALTH

Incidence and Duration of Illness

According to the 1995/96 Household Income, Consumption, and Expenditure and Welfare Monitoring Survey (HICE-WMS, PHRD Study Number 2.b, 1996), 19 percent of the population

Table 4.3   Percent of Life Years Lost by Region and Cause

	Tigray	Amhara	Oromia	Beni-shangul	SNNPRG	Gam-bella	Hararghe	Addis Ababa	Dire Dawa	National
AIDS	5.4	6.4	5.0	7.3	2.6	5.7	8.3	17.7	8.0	7.7
ARI	17.7	19.5	17.2	16.5	19.7	15.8	9.4	9.4	5.6	16.4
Cardiovascular	0.7	0.6	1.0	0.7	0.6	0.6	0.8	0.8	0.8	0.9
Diarrhea	9.0	9.0	9.5	10.2	9.5	9.5	11.2	3.8	10.9	8.7
Injury/Trauma	1.3	0.5	0.7	1.0	0.6	1.9	14.0	5.3	8.6	0.8
Malaria	4.9	10.3	9.6	11.0	9.6	10.3	2.9	...	3.5	10.5
Perinatal-Maternal	18.4	18.3	18.6	17.9	18.6	18.4	18.4	19.9	15.7	18.3
Measles	3.3	4.0	3.8	5.4	4.2	4.5	3.5	3.3	0.7	4.0
Nutritional Deficiency	10.7	9.6	9.0	8.6	9.8	8.9	9.4	10.5	9.9	8.9
Tuberculosis	5.3	6.7	4.9	12.2	3.4	6.5	5.2	2.0	4.7	4.6
Total Target Diseases	76.7	84.9	79.3	90.8	78.6	82.1	83.1	72.7	68.4	80.8
All Other Diseases	22.9	14.8	20.5	9.1	21.2	17.6	17.2	25.7	31.6	19.2
TOTAL	100.0	100.0	100.0	100.0	100.0	100.0	100.0	100.0	100.0	100.0

... no data.
Source: PHRD Study Number 3, 1996.

Figure 4.3 Reported Illness Episodes during Last Two Months by Age Group

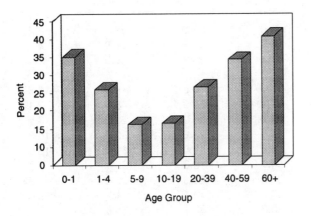

Source: HICE-WMS, PHRD Study Number 2.b, 1996.

reported illness episodes during the two months prior to the survey (Table 4.4). The 1994/95 rural survey by Oxford University and Addis Ababa University indicates that just under 16 percent of individuals surveyed reported illness episodes in the one month prior to the survey, with illnesses lasting an average of nearly 15 days per episode (PHRD Study No. 2.a, 1996). According to the Oxford-AAU survey, 10.2 percent of the sample population reported being disabled or chronically ill.

Figure 4.3 illustrates that, according to the HICE-WMS data, the highest proportion of illness (36 percent) was observed among individuals over the age of 60, followed by infants under the age of 1 (30 percent). Overall, women tend to report a higher incidence of illnesses than men, particularly women over 10 years of age (PHRD Study Number 2.b, 1996). This finding is of particular concern because a high level of female morbidity is likely to have an adverse impact on family welfare given the important role that women play in households. According to the Oxford-AAU survey, among children under 5 years of age, the incidence of illness is highest between the ages of 12 to 23 months, with 19 percent of that age group reporting illnesses over the previous month.

While the incidence of reported illness is somewhat equal across rural and urban areas, there is wide regional variation in the reported incidence of illness in rural areas (Table 4.4). In rural Gambella, for example, nearly 30 percent of the population reported having an illness during the two months prior to the HICE-WMS survey, well above the national average. In contrast, reported illnesses were well below the national average in rural Harari (14.5 percent), rural Addis Ababa (13 percent), and Dire Dawa (5 percent).

Although the Oxford-AAU survey's statistical analysis of the influence of education, income, and other factors on the incidence of illness in Ethiopia proved inconclusive (largely because of likely reporting biases associated with those factors), an analysis of the determinants of the duration of illness suggests that age is positively associated with the duration of a reported illness, while per capita consumption, as a proxy for income, was negatively associated with duration (PHRD Study Number 2.a, 1996). A 1 percent increase in consumption levels is likely to result in a reduction of the length of illness of 1.3 days. Access to primary health facilities, and particularly facilities with adequate medical supplies, also substantially reduced the duration of illness. Although the small sample size of the Oxford-AAU survey suggests caution in conclusions regarding mortality, the analysis also suggests that the level of education of parents, consumption levels, and access to health services are important determinants of the mortality of children under the age of 5.

Utilization Rates

Total outpatient utilization of government health facilities in Ethiopia suggests that, on average, there are about 0.25 visits per person per year, whereas the 1982/83 National Rural Health Survey indicates that Ethiopians are sick on average 7.7 times per year. These data suggest low utilization of health facilities. Only 10 percent of per-

Table 4.4 Illness Episodes and Source of Treatment (percent)

	Percent Reporting Illness	Percent Ill Seeking Treatment	Source of Treatment			
			Government	Private	Individual	Other
National Total	19.4	10.2	43.0	21.8	27.0	8.2
Urban	19.3	13.6	50.0	27.9	17.9	4.2
Rural	19.4	9.5	41.2	20.2	29.5	9.1
Of rural:						
Tigray	22.6	7.4	74.3	10.8	4.1	10.8
Afar	16.2	10.6	27.4	24.9	45.6	2.1
Amhara	21.3	6.6	62.2	11.2	23.5	3.1
Oromia	17.8	10.4	36.5	23.2	30.0	10.3
Somalia	15.5	12.2	6.6	47.6	32.8	13.0
Benishangul	20.7	12.2	64.0	9.8	25.1	1.1
SNNP	20.0	11.4	34.2	20.6	33.4	11.8
Gambella	30.1	21.2	53.3	13.1	4.7	28.9
Hararghe	14.5	12.2	35.3	32.1	25.6	7.0
Addis Ababa	12.6	6.5	20.4	57.7	16.2	5.7
Dire Dawa	4.9	3.1	35.3	33.8	20.7	10.2

Source: PHRD Study Number 2.b, 1996; referred to in Table 4.7.

sons reporting illness actually obtained treatment for their conditions from any health facility, government or private. In contrast, PHRD study Number 2.a (1996) found that of those reporting illness, 55 percent sought treatment in some form. Utilization by the rural population (9.5 percent) is lower than the national average, compared with 14 percent in urban areas. On a regional basis,

the proportion of the rural population who reported an illness and actually sought treatment ranges from 3.4 percent in rural Dire Dawa to 21 percent in Gambella (Table 4.4).

According to the Oxford-AAU data (PHRD Study Number 2.a, 1996), the high cost of treatment was the most-cited reason for not seeking treatment, accounting for 35 percent of all responses. As can be seen in Figure 4.4, the significant relationship between income levels and the utilization of health services is confirmed by the HICE-WMS data (PHRD Study Number 2.b, 1996). Only 7 percent of individuals from rural households with less than Birr 50 per month per capita expenditure levels sought treatment when reporting an illness, compared with 14 percent from rural households with over Birr 201 per capita expenditure levels. A similarly strong pattern is also evident across expenditure levels in urban areas.

Poor quality of facility was the second most common response cited for not seeking treatment in the Oxford-AAU survey (13 percent). This factor was relatively more important among the most wealthy quartile than for the poorer

Figure 4.4 Utilization of Health Facilities by Expenditure Group

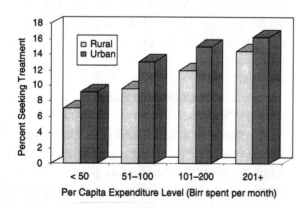

Source: HICE-WMS Survey (PHRD Study 2.b, 1996).

groups in the HICE-WMS data. The HICE-WMS data also suggest that distance to health provider is another important determinant of whether treatment is sought.

A statistical analysis conducted using the Oxford-AAU data set suggests that, along with expenditure levels and distance to health provider, the educational status of mothers is a particularly important determinant of whether treatment is sought. If the mother of an individual has completed her primary education, the probability that treatment is sought increases by approximately 60 percent. The analysis also suggests that older people are less likely to obtain treatment. Finally, for persons older than 6 years, being male and belonging to a large household are both strongly and positively associated with obtaining treatment.

Both access to and utilization of child immunization services are very low in Ethiopia. Service coverage is inadequate relative to need, yet utilization of available, accessible services is also poor. Overall, the proportion of children who have received measles, BCG, and DPT immunizations (combined) is just under 22 percent (Table 4.5). Only 19 percent of children in rural areas have received all three immunizations, compared with 46 percent in urban areas. Both the education level of mothers and per capita expenditure levels have a significant impact on child immunizations. Among children whose mothers have no primary education, just under 20 percent have received their immunizations, compared with just over 30 percent of children whose mothers have a primary education. Only 20 percent of children from households with per capita expenditures of less than Birr 50 per month were immunized, compared with 29 percent of those from households with per capita expenditures of more than Birr 201 per month.

Choice of Provider

Of those reporting an illness in the HICE-WMS survey (PHRD Study Number 2.b, 1996) who ac-

Table 4.5 Proportion of Children Immunized for Measles, BCG, and DPT (All Three)

Total	21.9
Urban	46.4
Rural	18.8
Mother's Education Level	
No Education	19.9
Primary Education	30.1
Postprimary Education	51.4
Per Capita Expenditure Level	
< 50	19.8
51–100	21.1
101–200	25.3
201 +	28.6

Source: PHRD Study Number 2.b, 1996.

tually sought treatment, only 43 percent utilized government facilities. Results from the Oxford-AAU survey (PHRD Study no. 2.a, 1996) support this finding. Populations of urban areas are more likely to use government facilities (approximately 50 percent) than those of rural areas (41 percent). Resorting to private individuals and private institutions, including traditional healers. pharmacies, and drug vendors, is much more common in rural areas than in urban areas. The choice of health provider also varies across regions in Ethiopia. In rural Somali, for example, as few as 7 percent of those seeking treatment choose government facilities. The use of government facilities is also low in rural Addis Ababa (20 percent) and rural Afar (27 percent). Government facilities are much more heavily used in Tigray (74 percent), Benishangul (64 percent), and Amhara (62 percent) regions.

There is a slight relationship between expenditure levels and the use of government services, such that wealthier households are somewhat more likely to use nongovernment facilities (PHRD Study Number 2.a, 1996; PHRD Study Number 2.b, 1996). However, a more detailed breakdown of utilization by type of provider reveals some important differences in the choice of providers by income group, which suggest impor-

Table 4.6   Type of Provider Utilized by Expenditure Group (percent)

	Poorest	Lower Middle	Higher Middle	Richest	Total
Nearest Hospital	7.7	16.1	20.4	19.1	16.0
Nearest Clinic	40.0	35.0	31.2	30.8	34.3
Pharmacy	24.6	15.7	18.0	11.3	17.1
Hospital/Clinic (not nearest)	11.3	11.8	10.4	16.9	12.7
Home of Health Worker	11.3	10.7	10.0	14.9	11.7
Traditional Healer	5.0	10.8	9.7	7.0	8.3

Source: PHRD Study Number 2.a, 1996.

tant differences in the quality of treatment obtained (Table 4.6). Wealthier households are much more likely to utilize hospitals, for example, than poorer households. In contrast, poorer households are more likely to obtain treatment from clinics and, in particular, pharmacies and rural drug vendors.

Distance to provider is also a significant determinant of choice across provider types. PHRD Study Number 2.a also found that, while the education level of the mother is an important determinant of whether to seek treatment, it does not seem to influence the choice of provider. The quality of the clinic (as measured by the reliability of drug supplies) matters significantly in the choice of providers (with the logical exception of pharmacies). Whether a woman is ill or a woman heads the household are both strongly associated with the utilization of pharmacies. Finally, women and female-headed households are much more likely to consult traditional healers than men or male-headed households.

Health Expenditure at the Household Level

Estimates of expenditure on health care per treatment vary widely, from Birr 9 (PHRD Study Number 2.b, 1996 based on HICE-WMS data) to Birr 33 (PHRD Study Number 2.a, 1996 based on Oxford-AAU data). According to the HICE-WMS data, the urban population spends on average more than twice the amount per treatment than that spent by the rural population, suggesting large differences in expenditures per treatment across locations within both rural and urban areas.

While HICE-WMS data show no significant effect of overall expenditure levels on health spending per treatment, data from the Oxford-AAU survey suggest a marked relationship between the two (Table 4.7). The poorest households spend approximately Birr 18 per treatment, compared with Birr 46 spent by the wealthiest households. In addition, the poor on average spend proportionately more on medicines (78 percent) than wealthier households (74 percent), but less on treatment (9 percent versus 13 percent). This finding is consistent with the poor's greater utilization of pharmacies and drug vendors relative to the rich.

Overall, treatment at hospitals is more expensive than that of other providers. This is due, in part, to the fact that hospitals are utilized primarily for more serious illnesses, and therefore treatments are likely to be more expensive. Treatment at the home of a health worker and at pharmacies are the least expensive sources of health care, at Birr 15 and Birr 19 per treatment, respectively. Average expenditure on traditional healers is surprisingly high, at over Birr 50 per treatment,[2] although treatment costs appear to vary significantly across expenditure groups.

---

[2] This finding needs to be treated with caution given that in this survey, the majority of patients are poor rural peasants and therefore the amount spent on traditional healers seems large.

Table 4.7   Expenditure per Treatment by Expenditure Group

	Lowest Expenditure Quartile	Lower Middle	Higher Middle	Highest Expenditure Quartile	Total
Average Expenditure	17.5	18.8	42.2	46.3	32.7
Share of Expenditure to (in percent):					
Medicines	78	72	66	74	72
Treatment	9	14	14	13	13
Transport	7	7	10	8	8
Other	6	5	10	5	6
Average Expenditure by Provider (in Birr):					
Nearest Hospital	47	43	88	69	64
Nearest Clinic	13	11	24	38	21
Pharmacy	12	17	26	22	19
Hospital (not nearest)	33	39	134	122	94
Clinic (not nearest)	7	8	28	59	32
Home of Health Worker	28	7	25	11	15
Traditional Healer	14	32	16	137	50
Type of Facility:					
Government	18	18	58	52	36
Private	18	18	25	34	25
NGO	2	29	71	69	44
Traditional Healer	14	32	16	137	50

Note: Data presented here are derived from only one round of the Oxford-AAU survey on which this analysis is based.
Source: PHRD Study Number 2.a, 1996.

Average spending on each type of provider is lower per treatment for the poorer households than for the richer, although care should be taken with the interpretation of this data, because of its very small sample size. Spending levels on private and public facilities are virtually the same on average for the poorest groups, suggesting that lower expenditures by poorer households are not only related to the subsidies or exemptions that they are provided in the public facilities. Average per treatment expenditures on public health facilities by the wealthier half of the sample are almost double those spent on private facilities. NGO facilities cost much less for the poorer households than for the higher expenditure ones. Overall, these data suggest that the wealthy are able to spend more for better services, regardless of provider type.

Data on total per capita health expenditures suggest important differences in spending patterns between rural and urban populations and socioeconomic groups. Preliminary results from the 1995/96 HICE-WMS survey (PHRD Study Number 2.b, 1996) report that national per capita health expenditures are Birr 8 annually, Birr 7 per capita in rural areas, and Birr 12 per capita in urban areas. The Oxford-AAU data report per capita spending on health at just under Birr 19 annually (Table 4.8). Both the HICE and Oxford-AAU data indicate a strong relationship between spending on health and total expenditure levels. The poorest quartile of the population spends on average just over 6 birr per capita each year, whereas the wealthiest quartile spends approximately 38 birr per capita. The poorest households allocate a somewhat larger share of their budget to health than do the wealthiest, 2.2 percent compared with 1.4 percent. Analysis of this data produced evidence of a very low expenditure elasticity for health, sug-

Table 4.8   Annual Household per Capita Health Expenditures (Birr)

	Poorest	Lower Middle	Higher Middle	Richest	Total
Total Expenditure	286	656	1,326	2,714	1,105
Health Expenditure	6.30	10.50	19.90	38.00	18.80
Share of Total on Health (percent)	2.2	1.6	1.5	1.4	1.7
Iddir Expenditure	2.70	5.00	6.20	7.20	5.30
Share of Total on Iddir (percent)	1.1	0.9	0.7	0.3	0.7

Source: PHRD Study Number 2.a, 1996.

gesting that health care is considered a necessity in Ethiopia, not a luxury.

Households also spent a considerable portion of income on *iddir* (funeral insurance), which in some cases also includes health and disaster coverage. *Iddir* is more than 40 percent of the health expenditures of the poor, and close to one-third of health expenditures for the wealthier households. Overall, *iddir* comprises about 0.7 percent of total household expenditures, while medical expenditure is close to 1.7 percent of total expenditures. Spending behavior toward *iddir* suggests that it, too, is considered a necessity, and local clinics capitalize on this behavior by encouraging increased spending on insurance.

SUPPLY OF HEALTH SERVICES

Health Services and Utilization

Nine programs for the prevention and control of diseases and major public health problems comprise the health care delivery system in Ethiopia:

- malaria and other vector-borne diseases;
- tuberculosis;
- leprosy;
- family planning;
- HIV/AIDS and sexually transmitted diseases (STDs);
- expanded immunization;
- diarrheal diseases;
- acute respiratory diseases; and
- micronutrient deficiency diseases

Coverage and utilization rates for these programs are remarkably low (see Figure 4.5). For example, in 1995, it is estimated that less than 20 percent of pregnant women received antenatal care. That compares with over 60 percent for Sub-Saharan Africa over the 1985–90 period. According to the 1990 National Family and Fertility Survey, institutional deliveries are only 6.1 percent of estimated births. Family planning service utilization was approximately 6.5 percent in 1994/95, compared with 51 percent across all developing countries. While growth monitoring has improved significantly since 1992, the current utilization rate of 23 percent is less than half the rate targeted by the Ministry of Health (MOH) for the year 2000. STD program coverage is also low, at around 12 percent, although the limited data available call for caution in the interpretation of that estimate (PHRD Study Number 11, 1996).

Water and sanitation are also important components of primary health care. Estimates of the proportion of the population in Ethiopia with access to safe drinking water range from 18 to 26 percent. According to data from the Ministry of Water Resources, 80 percent of rural and 20 percent of urban populations did not have access to safe drinking water in 1992. Various studies have indicated that, because of the distance of much of the population from water points, combined with

Figure 4.5   Health Services and Utilization Rates

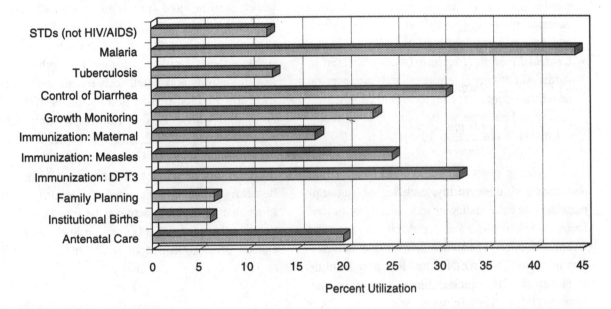

Source: PHRD Study No. 11, 1996.

low incomes and the high price of water in some areas, water consumption is very low. It ranges from 5 to 20 liters per capita per day in rural areas and 30 to 40 liters per capita per day in urban areas. Access to sanitation facilities is also quite low, ranging from 7 to 10 percent of the population.[3]

Availability of Facilities

Service delivery in the health sector was structured according to a six-tiered system (refer to Table 4.10 for regional comparisons of health facilities):[4]

- *Community Health Posts*, typically staffed by a community health agent and traditional birth attendant, provide health education, treatment of common illnesses and minor injuries, attend deliveries, and register births and deaths;

- *Health Stations*, staffed by 1–3 health assistants, provide basic preventive and curative services including antenatal care, family planning services, immunizations, environmental health care, uncomplicated deliveries, and supervision of health posts;

- *Health Centers*, staffed by a medical doctor or nurse and other technical and administrative personnel, provide preventive and curative ambulatory care, laboratory services, beds for labor and delivery and for critical patients awaiting transfer to hospitals, and supervision of health stations and training of community health staff;

- *Rural Hospitals*, with all categories of health personnel excluding specialists, provide preventive and curative ambulatory care, inpatient care, minor and emergency surgery, and radiology services;

---

[3] The dry pit latrine is the most widely used excreta disposal technology in Ethiopia although defecation and urination in the open are more common, especially in rural and semiurban areas (Teka 1993).

[4] Under the government's revised health sector development program, the health care delivery system will be reorganized into a four-tiered system, consisting of primary health care units (incorporating former health centers, health stations, and health posts and providing comprehensive primary care services), district hospitals (incorporating former rural hospitals and acting as referral and training centers), regional hospitals (providing specialist services and training), and specialized hospitals (providing comprehensive specialized services).

- *Regional Hospitals* serve as referral centers for rural hospitals and health centers and provide surgical, medical, obstetric and gynecological, and pediatric services; and
- *Central Referral Hospitals* (mostly located in Addis Ababa) provide specialized care, serving as referral centers for regional and rural hospitals, train health personnel, and conduct medical research (Indevelop 1996).

Health posts and health stations are frontline units and, theoretically, each higher unit supports the one below it. Other specialized institutions focus on specific diseases, research, training, and technical support. These include the Ethiopia Nutrition Institute (ENI), the National Research Institute of Health (NRIH), and the Jimma Health Science Institute (JHSI). The Ethiopian Pharmaceutical and Medical Supplies Corporation (EPHARMECOR) is responsible for the importation of medical supplies, as well as the manufacture of some essential drugs and medical equipment.

The majority of hospitals, health centers, health stations, and health posts are run by either the federal or regional governments (see Table 4.9). The majority of pharmacies, drug shops, rural drug vendors, and private clinics are operated by private and NGO management.

One of the important factors explaining the poor coverage of health services in Ethiopia is the limited physical access of the population to health facilities and staff. This is dramatically illustrated by the low facility-to-population ratio (Table 4.10). Only 89 hospitals serve a population of more than 53 million people. If the numbers of health stations and health centers are combined, the ratio of facilities to population is 1:19,327, compared with a 1:8,046 ratio of a comparable measure for Sub-Saharan Africa as a whole (World Bank 1994a). Given the current population, the number of health centers would have to be nearly tripled and the number of health stations more than doubled to achieve the standard of one health center per 100,000 people and one health station per 10,000 people set by the MOH prior to 1991.

Table 4.10 shows the uneven distribution of health care facilities across regions in Ethiopia. In terms of hospitals and health centers, Gambella, Tigray, Benishagul-Gumuz, Dire Dawa, Afar, and Addis Ababa have higher facility-to-population ratios relative to the national average. In terms of health stations, Gambella, Dire Dawa, and Benishangul-Gumuz also have higher facility-to-population ratios than the national average. Somali, Amhara, and SNNPR consistently emerge as the most disadvantaged regions in terms of health facility-to-population ratios.

Many existing facilities are in an advanced state of disrepair. A recent survey of facilities

Table 4.9   Supply of Health Facilities

	Total Facilities	Facility-to-Population Ratio	Percent Government	Share: Public	Private	NGO
Hospitals	89	1:587,620	91	0	1	8
Health Centers	191	1:273,813	93	0	0	7
Health Stations	2,515	1:20,795	77	0	10	14
Pharmacies	159	1:328,919	5	20	71	4
Drug Shops	152	1:344,067	0	1	99	0
Rural Drug Vendors	1,352	1:38,682	0	2	98	0
Health Posts	1,175	1:44,509	100	0	0	0
Private Clinics	196	1:266,827	0	0	100	0

Source: PHRD Study Number 11, 1996.

Table 4.10 Summary of Health Facilities-to-Population Ratio in All Regions by Type of Facility

Region and Population	Hospitals	Health Center	Health Stations	Pharmacy	Drug Shop	Rural Drug Vendors	Health Post	Private Clinic
Tigray (3,136,267)	1:261,335	1:224,019	1:22,243	1:348,474	1:522,711	1:19,241	1:11,530	1:224,019
Afar (760,000)	1:380,000	1:190,000	1:22,353	1:760,000	1:380,000	1:18,095	—	—
Amhara (13,834,297)	1:1,257,663	1:307,429	1:28,291	1:728,121	1:601,491	1:60,944	1:49,232	1:288,214
Oromia (18,732,525)	1:738,953	1:293,235	1:21,863	1:543,348	1:279,906	1:38,093	1:55,477	
Somali (2,320,000)	1:773,333	1:331,428	1:35,152	1:773,333	1:2,320,000	1:464,000	—	—
Benishangul-Gumuz (460,459)	1230,229	1115,115	1:5,673	—	1:1,460,459	1:11,807	—	—
SNNPR (10,377,028)	1:1,153,000	1:305,207	1:24,474	1:1,297,128	1:1,037,703	1:27,236	1:39,158	—
D/Dawa (251,864)	1:83,955	1:251,864	1:13,992	1:31,483	1:83,955	1:13,256	—	1:251,864
Gambella (181,862)	1:162,397	1:54,132	1:4,776	—	—	1:32,479	—	—
Harari (131,139)	1:26,228	No H.C.	1:26,228	1:26,228	1:131,139	1:26,228	—	1:43,713
Addis Ababa (2,112,737)	1:132046	1:132,046	1:29,343	1:29,343	1:54,172	1:162,518	—	1:77,107
National (52,298,178)	1:584,494	1:272,356	1:20,308	1:327,170	1:342,237	1:38,476	1:44,272	1:121,827

— = Not available.
Source: PHRD Study Number 11, 1996.

found that 47 percent of those hospitals, 33 percent of health centers, and 47 percent of health stations require major repair or complete replacement of the facility (PHRD Study Number 11, 1996).

Given the small number of facilities relative to the population, it is not surprising that the distance to health centers and cost of transportation to reach these facilities, is quite high for much of Ethiopia's population. A review of health facility records indicates that among those who actually utilize health services, the average distance to reach hospitals was 34 kilometers, and 7 kilometers each to the nearest health centers and health stations. Across all facility types, the average distance traveled by patients from rural areas was 27 kilometers compared with 17 kilometers for urban dwellers (PHRD Study Number 11, 1996).

Staffing and Inputs

The Ethiopian health service delivery system is characterized by the shortage, poor distribution, and lack of relevance and necessary skills of its health staff. Indeed, in a recent survey of health personnel, 99 percent of respondents felt that the current health care and management staffing patterns were unsatisfactory in terms of number, mix, and quality to meet the objectives of the health care system (PHRD Study Number 11, 1996).

Ethiopia has very low ratios of health personnel to population. The country has about one-third the number of doctors to population, and one-sixth the number of nurses, as the average for Sub-Saharan Africa (World Bank 1994a). Table 4.11 compares the ratio of personnel to population in 1978 and 1994. Overall, little improvement has been achieved over that period. In 1994, there was only one doctor for every 35,000 people, compared with one for every 38,200 in 1978. In most of the rural areas and small towns, the delivery of health care is primarily dependent upon the availability of health assistants, where only slight gains have been made since 1978. On average there are only 2 nurses to one doctor (compared with the Sub-Saharan Africa average of 5 nurses per doctor), and 3 health assistants to one nurse.

There are extreme biases in the distribution of personnel across regions, with a very large proportion of staff working in Addis Ababa. Although Addis Ababa accounts for a relatively small share of the overall population, nearly 63 percent of all doctors worked in Addis Ababa in 1990, 46 percent of all nurses, and nearly 34 percent of all health assistants. Biases in the distribution of personnel worsened substantially between 1981 and 1990. More recent efforts to relocate centrally-placed staff to the regions have been modestly successful. Similar to the health facility-to-population ratios, Somali, Oromia, and SNNPR are also at a disadvantage relative to other regions, by having the highest population-to-health assistant ratios while Gambella, Addis Ababa, and Harari have the lowest population-to-health assistant ratios.

Staff resources are also poorly distributed with regard to the type of care provided. A government study of time allocation of health staff indicates that a high proportion of time is devoted to curative services rather than preventive services by all categories of health personnel. The proportion of time spent daily on curative care was 48 percent by doctors, 35 percent by nurses, and 34 percent by health assistants. The study also found a high percentage of inactivity during the day for all types of staff, a finding that underscores concerns about the quality of services and the motivation of staff. On average, doctors were inactive for over 34 percent of the day, while nurses and health assistants were inactive for 25 percent and 38 percent of their day, respectively.

The massive loss of trained personnel to the private and NGO sectors, and emigration to other countries, is a particular problem for the health sector in Ethiopia. The main cause of attrition was low salaries, which have remained almost fixed over the past 20 years. Eighty-two percent of health staff surveyed expressed dissatisfaction with remuneration, particularly in light of higher payment levels in the private and NGO sectors. Other reasons for attrition included the lack of educational opportunity, poor career development opportunities, poor quality of equipment

Table 4.11 Health Sector Staffing and Distribution

	Ratio of Personnel to Population		Share of Personnel in Addis Ababa (percent)	
	1978	1994	1981	1990
All Medical Doctors + Health Officers	1:38,200	1:35,054	47	63
Medical Doctor Specialists	1:124,500	1:157,036		
General Medical Practitioner and Health Officers	1:60,000	1:45,078		
Nurses	1:20,400	1:13,973	39	46
Pharmacist	1:280,000	1:109,979	32	65
Sanitarians	1: 92,600	1:90,627	31	50
Other Technicians	1:79,400	1:63,208	40	54
Health Assistants	1:5,400	1:4,624	19	34

Source: PHRD Study Number 11, 1996; Indevelop 1996.

and facilities, and general job dissatisfaction. Teaching staff attrition is particularly high.

Job dissatisfaction is correlated with the level of education of the health worker; that is, the higher the level of education, the higher the proportion of dissatisfied workers. Nearly three out of every four doctors and six out of every ten pharmacists expressed general job dissatisfaction. In contrast, only one out of three health assistants are dissatisfied (PHRD Study Number 11, 1996).

Poor and inappropriate training has led to an underutilization of the limited human resources available to the health sector in Ethiopia. The recent Task Force on Human Resources Development for Health found that the current training curricula are inappropriate to the health needs of Ethiopia, as they emphasize theory rather than practice, and a curative, hospital-based orientation rather than one that focuses on prevention (Social Services and Administration 1994). Training does not provide for career development or advancement. There is no systematic continuing education or in-service training program, and no performance assessment mechanisms.

Other factors have contributed to limited output by health training centers in Ethiopia. As a result of the disruptions caused by the civil war, inadequate financing, and the attrition of training staff in particular, health training centers are currently operating at only 55 percent of their reported capacity. Between 1991 and 1995, only 2 of 11 health assistant training schools and 2 of 11 nursing schools produced graduates every year (PHRD Study Number 11, 1996).

Medical Supplies and Pharmaceuticals

One of the major determinants of the quality and quantity of health care provided to patients is the availability of appropriate supplies and equipment. In the absence of direct information on the quality of services, the condition and availability of supplies, including equipment, can serve as an indicator of quality. The scarcity of equipment in Ethiopia today seriously compromises the quality of health care. For example, there is approximately one hospital bed for every 5,243 people in the country, one functioning x-ray machine per 591,136 people, and one HIV screening center per 867,000 persons. Out of the 89 hospitals in the country, only 46 percent have surgical theaters, an extremely inadequate number in view of the large number of outpatient and inpatient admissions in these hospitals. Even simple equipment, such as baby scales and examination tables, are scarce or nonexistent at all levels of facilities.

The availability of drugs has a significant effect on the level of utilization of services and patient outcomes. Until 1994, EPHARMECOR was the major drug procurement and distribution agency, owning a number of distribution centers and operating the only domestic pharmaceutical production plant (EPHARM). EPHARM produces approximately 20–30 percent of the nation's drug consumption, including 39 essential drug items. In early 1994, EPHARMECOR was restructured into a public enterprise, with its pharmacies and distribution centers to be handed over to the regional health departments (Indevelop 1996). Additional private production and importation mechanisms are currently being contemplated to complete the restructuring of EPHARMECOR. Community-owned pharmacies (along the lines of the Bamako Initiative), as well as NGO-supported revolving drug funds, are also being explored as a means of improving the distribution of essential drugs.

Poor procurement and distribution systems are responsible for the scarcity of basic drugs, a problem that compromises the quality and cost of health care. Throughout the 1980s and early 1990s, the supply of drugs declined owing to the deterioration in the country's foreign exchange, a reduction of the health budget, and the reduction of the share of nonwage expenditures within the health budget. Distributional inefficiencies, in part a result of inadequate storage facilities, exacerbated the drug shortage. Since mid-1992, drug shortages have led to rapidly increasing prices, placing many drugs beyond the reach of most consumers. At the same time, the shortage of supplies has served to erode consumer confidence in the quality of care, particularly at public health institutions. Only 65 percent of surveyed hospitals, 28 percent of surveyed health centers, and 57 percent of health stations had at least 75 percent of the recommended supplies of basic drugs on hand at the time of the survey (Table 4.12). The data indicate that the situation is more serious for health institutions in rural areas, where there are few alternative sources of drug supply.

Consultation with the consumers of health services in Ethiopia underscored many of the issues outlined regarding the quality and availability of services. Forty-eight percent of respondents confirmed that they had faced some type of difficulty while seeking health care, such as inadequate facilities and equipment within the institutions (43 percent of respondents), the lack of finance (34 percent), and the lack of essential drugs (23 percent).

POLICY AND INSTITUTIONAL FRAMEWORK

Ethiopia's National Health Policy was approved by the Council of Ministers in September 1993. According to the policy document:

Table 4.12 Availability of Basic Drugs (percent of recommended supplies)

Level of Availability	Hospitals	Health Centers	Health Stations
75% and above	65	28	57
50%–74%	29	61	32
Less than 50%	6	11	11

Source: PHRD Study Number 17, 1996.

. . . health, constituting physical, mental and social well-being, is a prerequisite for the enjoyment of life and for optimal productivity. The government therefore accords health a prominent place in its order of priorities and is committed to the attainment of these goals utilizing all accessible internal and external resources (TGE, 1993, p. 23).

The 10 principles on which the policy is based include:

- Democratization and decentralization of the health system.
- Development of the preventive and promotive components of health care.
- Development of an equitable and acceptable standard of health service system that will reach all segments of the population within the limits of resources.
- Promotion and strengthening of intersectoral activities.
- Promotion of attitudes and practices conducive to the strengthening of national self-reliance in health development by mobilizing internal and external resources.
- Assurance of accessibility of health care for all segments of the population.
- Collaboration with neighboring countries and regional and international organizations to share information and strengthen all activities contributing to health development, including the control of factors detrimental to health.
- Development of appropriate capacity, based on assessed needs.
- Provision of health care for the population on a scheme of payment according to ability, with special assistance mechanisms for those who cannot afford to pay.
- Promotion of the participation of the private sector and nongovernmental organizations in health care.

To achieve the objectives outlined in this policy, the health care delivery system is being reorganized from the six-tiered system described above into a four-tiered system, consisting of: (a) primary health care units (PHCUs), each with 5 satellite community health clinics (CHCs), providing comprehensive primary care services; (b) district hospitals (DHs), each acting as a referral and training center for 10 PHCUs; (c) zonal hospitals (ZHs) providing specialist services and training; and (d) specialized hospitals (SHs) providing comprehensive specialist services, and in some instances serving as centers for research and post basic training.

To make the health system more democratic and decentralized, the government will strengthen regional, zonal, and district/woreda health departments. Government policy also envisages a greater role for the private sector in health service delivery and financing, within an appropriate regulatory and monitoring framework to ensure coordination of public and private sector activities. The health sector policy will be supported by a range of other sectoral policies related to reducing population growth, improving basic literacy and education levels, particularly for females, and socioeconomic development, focusing on growth in agriculture and related labor-intensive industrial development fostered through a range of economic policies.

To realize these policy objectives, the government has developed the Health Sector Development Program (HSDP), which emphasizes improved access to primary health care services as its highest priority, accompanied by improvements in other components such as IEC, medical supplies, and personnel. A more detailed discussion of this program will be presented in Chapter 8.

DECENTRALIZATION: MANAGERIAL AND INSTITUTIONAL FRAMEWORK

Successful implementation of the government's health policy and investment strategy will require coordinated action across government agencies, the private sector, local communities, NGOs, and donors.

Government Agencies

The management of government health services has historically been centralized at the Ministry of Health in Addis Ababa but also includes regional health bureaus and zonal and woreda/district health departments.

The government system has been fraught with numerous organizational and management inefficiencies and weaknesses that contribute to the low level of health service coverage in the country. To address these concerns, the government has adopted the Health Policy and Health Sector Strategy, which assures the accessibility of health care for all segments of the population, makes provision for a streamlined and decentralized health service delivery system, and reorients the emphasis of care from curative to preventive services.

The new policy stresses decentralization. The Ministry of Health will mainly be responsible for formulating public health policies and strategies, as well as supporting and supervising their implementation. The ministry will therefore focus more on preparing operational guidelines, setting standards for staffing, drugs and supplies, and providing technical support. Government health policy will be implemented primarily through the regional governments, which have been given responsibility for nearly all health facilities and health personnel training centers. Regional governments have also been given considerable financial authority over nearly 90 percent of the total national health budget. Finally, the new policy provides for autonomous and participatory local management at the facility level.

To be successful, the new policy must overcome local shortages of skilled personnel and

implementation capacity, find ways to raise revenue at the regional level, and expand the infrastructure, communications, and logistics resources
available to the regional authorities. This policy
has already led to the reassignment of personnel
and personnel decision-making responsibilities to
the regions, although significant local capacity-
building in the health sector is still required. Regional and zonal facilities are relatively well
staffed and functional, although full levels of staffing have not yet been attained in many regions and
the quality of staff training is still a major concern.
Woreda-level management, however, is practically nonfunctional and is one of the main organizational challenges to be addressed in the near
future.

The policy of decentralization in the
health sector is intended to increase cost recovery.
As local institutions gain a greater stake in the collection and use of resources, they are likely to be
more diligent in the collection of payments from
patients and take greater care in waiving fees to
the poor.

Private Sector

In spite of its relatively small and undeveloped
character, the private sector plays a critical and
rapidly increasing role in the provision of health
services in Ethiopia. While a number of economic
reforms undertaken since 1992 have facilitated
private sector provision of health services, the
government is only just beginning to recognize
the potential of the private sector in this area.
Given the extremely poor availability and coverage of government-run health facilities, a rapidly expanding role for the private sector in the
provision of health services makes a great deal
of sense.

The private sector owns and operates private hospitals, clinics, and drug distribution centers, many of which are run by a growing number
of public sector health employees who work in

private practice outside of normal working hours.
There is currently one private hospital in Addis
Ababa and 182 private clinics nationwide. Nearly
23 percent of all health stations, 75 percent of all
pharmacies, 99 percent of all drug shops, and 99
percent of all rural drug vendor operations are under private sector and NGO management.

The growing importance of the private
sector raises some concerns about the quality of
care that it provides. For example, a recent government study of private clinics in Addis Ababa
found that only a small proportion of private clinics were adhering to established technical standards and government regulations (PHRD Study
Number 13, 1996). The heavy reliance of poor
households on private drug vendors for primary
curative case suggests that, although the poor
gain access to a wide array of drugs, they are less
likely than the nonpoor to be getting the drugs
they need.

With the strengthening of economic
growth in Ethiopia, it is likely that there will be
growing demand for privately provided health
services. A number of recommendations have been
made by donors to ensure that the private sector
can meet that demand, while minimizing the added
burden on scarce government budgetary resources.
These include privatizing at least some government hospitals, revising regulations on the role of
the private sector in drug procurement and distribution, and contracting essential support services
to the private sector. Additionally, support for improved supervision and quality control in the private sector and for the training of private sector
drug vendors and pharmacists has been proposed.

Community Participation

Community participation is a key element in the
provision of social services in Ethiopia. The government recognizes that the delivery of health
services can benefit significantly from local participation, through the fostering of innovative

ideas for problem solving and crisis management, as well as increased participation at various health project levels of management. Local participation can also ensure that services are provided at a lower cost, especially if increased interest is translated into volunteerism. Resources are likely to be more effectively utilized when the community is given greater control over the planning and implementation of their own health and educational services.

In the health sector, the recruitment of community health agents and traditional birth attendants has been an important component of the government's health policy at the community level since the mid-1980s, but the level of financial support given to these staff has often been limited (TGE 1993). In a 1995/96 survey of 30 communities, 43 percent reported their active participation in local health committees (PHRD Study Number 12, 1996). In many areas, community members have made substantial contributions of labor, materials, cash, and communal land in support of health services. In 1990, it is estimated that community labor contributions alone accounted for approximately 26 percent of capital expenditure in the health sector, compared with 24 percent from external donor assistance (Social and Administrative Affairs 1993).

Many of these community-level contributions have been organized through traditional burial, credit, and savings institutions. Interviews of the members of 58 of these community institutions indicate that nearly half actively participate in various types of developmental, social, and community activities. In addition to providing resources, these traditional community self-help mechanisms may also provide models for more effective financing of health services. The *iddirs*, or funeral insurance funds, act also as a type of mutual assistance fund. *Iddirs* have been proposed as a model for rural health insurance schemes, as a means to increase individual access and overall community financial contributions to local health services.

Nongovernmental Organizations

NGO health activities are closely linked to government primary care programs. These activities include the distribution of drugs, family planning, disease prevention, and water and sanitation. NGOs operate just under 200 health clinics and 8 hospitals, with a strong orientation toward the rural areas.

The government's new health policy acknowledges the involvement of NGOs in the Ethiopian health care system and sees its assistance in formulating, implementing, monitoring, and evaluating primary health care activities as complementary to government programs. A recent survey of NGOs indicates that 14 percent of them have significant levels of community involvement in their health programs (PHRD Study Number 13, 1996).

COSTS AND FINANCING

The lack of sufficient funds is the single most important limiting feature of the health care system. Correct estimates of the true costs and financial requirements of the health sector will allow for more accurate and long-range planning for the sector. Only by knowing what quantity of resources are both needed and possible, can rational decisions be made about changes in the operation of the health sector.

Levels and Composition of Financing

The share of health sector expenditures in the total national budget has increased dramatically in recent years. Between 1989 and 1995, health expenditures rose from 2.8 percent to 5.4 percent of the total budget and were planned at 6.2 percent for 1996. During that period, the real value of the health budget increased by 36 percent, in spite of an overall decline in real GDP of about 12 percent. Government health spending rose substantially from 1 percent during the 1980s to 1.8 percent of GDP in 1994. In spite of these dramatic increases in the level of spending, the US$1.50 per capita health expenditures in Ethiopia still compare unfavorably to the Sub-Saharan African average of US$14 (World Bank 1994).

The public sector health budget is composed of about 60 percent recurrent and 40 percent capital expenditures, although the capital budget has been rising rapidly in recent years. Recurrent expenditures have traditionally been paid from the Treasury, while capital expenditures have been financed by loans and foreign assistance in addition to Treasury allocations. This share of Treasury financing of capital expenditures has fluctuated from 78 percent in 1987 to 33 percent in 1992 and back up to 63 percent in 1995. It would appear that Treasury funds fluctuate according to the fluctuations in loans and foreign assistance. In 1994/95, foreign assistance to the health sector totaled Birr 27 million, and the contribution of loans was Birr 58 million.

Historically, a number of inefficiencies have occurred in the allocation of government resources in the health sector. Health sector expenditures in Ethiopia have tended to emphasize urban-based, curative services rather than rural-based care and preventive and public health programs. Until 1991, urban hospitals received around 50 percent of the recurrent budget, compared with only 20 percent for health centers and health stations. Curative services comprised almost 79 percent of total health expenditures in 1994, with only 16 percent spent on preventive services and 6 percent on community services (PHRD Study Number 3, 1996). There is a similar misallocation of resources across diseases. For the ten diseases that constitute 76 percent of DLYs lost in Ethiopia, total spending amounted to only 45 percent of recurrent expenditures.

Health facilities in Addis Ababa received a disproportionately large share of resources

through the 1980s, from 33 percent of the recurrent budget in 1981 to 36 percent in 1991. The share of the recurrent budget going to salaries increased substantially in the 1980s, from approximately 52 percent in 1980 to nearly 65 percent in 1990. This increase came at the expense of spending on drugs and facility maintenance and reflected, in part, a shift in the mix of government health staff toward a greater concentration of highly paid doctors (Indevelop 1996).

Since 1992, however, there has been a gradual but significant restructuring of the budget. A large share of the recent increases in health spending have gone to drugs and other nonsalary items in the recurrent budget. As a result, the proportion of salaries in the recurrent budget declined to 53 percent in 1996. Similarly, there has been a reallocation of resources away from facilities in Addis Ababa, to just over 27 percent of the recurrent budget in 1993. Outside of Addis Ababa, the share of resources directed to primary care facilities has also increased. Spending on hospitals declined somewhat, to 42 percent of the total recurrent budget in 1994, and is expected to fall to just over 38 percent in 1996. There has been a similar reorientation within capital budgets, where spending on health centers and health stations now accounts for 40 percent of the capital budget compared with 17 percent in 1994.

Support for public health services has also increased in recent years. At the regional level, the allocation for programs to address malaria and other vector-borne diseases has increased to between 8 and 15 percent of recurrent health spending in 1994. If the contributions of international assistance for primary care programs such as Expanded Program on Immunization (EPI) and Maternal and Child Health (MCH) are included in the recurrent budget, public health services account for more than 20 percent of the 1994 total budget. This support for public health programs, along with reallocations of resources toward health centers and health stations, suggests that over 52 percent of total regional recurrent expenditures are focused on primary health care-related services, which are likely to yield the greatest health status improvements from available resources (World Bank 1994a).

The transfer of control over resources to regional governments is another important shift in health sector finance since 1992. Of the total national budget, regional governments controlled 85 percent of health expenditure in 1994, 88 percent in 1995, and 86 percent in 1996. The regional governments controlled 83 percent of the recurrent budget and 95 percent of the capital budget for 1996. The share of the regions' recurrent budget that is allocated to hospitals has continued to decline since 1993, yet there has been only a slight change in the proportion of the budget allocated to primary care. The difference appears in the steady increase in the share allocated to the regional bureaus, largely to finance the increasing administrative responsibilities at this level. Per capita budget allocations made by the regions vary substantially (Figure 4.6). The highest per capita health budget is in Gambella (66 percent of which is allocated to capital expenditures), while the lowest levels are in Oromia, Amhara, SNNP, and

Somali (PHRD Study Number 6, 1996). These differences reflect the differing preferences of each region relative to all other competing claims for public resources. Another important reason for the differences in per capita spending is the mix of health care facilities and programs each region inherited when they were formed after 1991 (World Bank, 1997b).

Sources of Financing

Financing for the health sector can be obtained through a number of possible sources, including government revenues, donor aid and foreign loans, user fees, health insurance payments, and community contributions. As indicated in Figure 4.7 and Table 4.13, the sources of health financing in Ethiopia have changed substantially between 1986 and 1996. As might be expected given the increase in the budgetary allocation to the health sector, the government's share of health financing has similarly increased from 23 percent of the total in 1986 to 43 percent in 1996. The role of external grants and loans has also increased over the period, though its share of the capital budget diminished somewhat in 1996 compared with 1986. The contribution of health insurance and

Figure 4.6   Per Capita Health Budget by Region

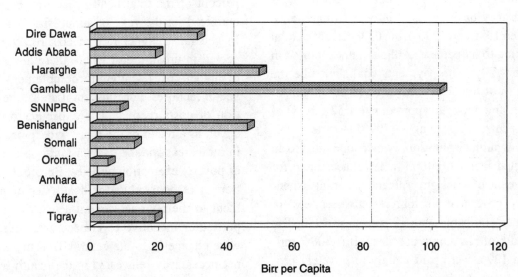

Birr per Capita

Source: PHRD Study Number 6, 1996.

Figure 4.7 Sources of Financing in the Health Sector, 1986 and 1996

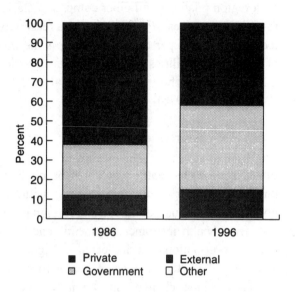

Source: World Bank 1987; PHRD Study Number 6, 1996.

other sources, such as NGOs, remained relatively small throughout the period. Although the contributions of private insurance and NGOs are currently limited, both have the potential to be major contributors to health financing in Ethiopia, as will be discussed.

Estimated payments from private sources—obtained through user fees paid to the government and other care providers—remain substantial, although they have declined in overall importance between 1986 and 1996, from 63.4 percent of total financing to 39 percent. Although not captured in Figure 4.7, private payments continue to be the single most important source of recurrent expenditures, amounting to approximately 52 percent of total recurrent spending in 1996. User fees collected at public institutions, which amounted to an estimated Birr 79 million in 1996, accounted for 22 percent of total government recurrent expenditures (government resources plus user fees) in that year, compared with 19 percent in 1986. The vast bulk of remaining user fees, Birr 308.7 million in 1996, were paid mainly to privately pro-

vided health services and NGO-supported facilities. They accounted for 41 percent of total recurrent expenditure in 1996 compared with 62 percent in 1986. It is important to note that these payments to private sector providers exceeded even the net recurrent expenditures of the government in 1996.

Cost Recovery

At both government and nongovernment facilities, users pay for registration, medical certificates, diagnosis, and dental and ophthalmologic services. In-patients are also charged on a daily basis, and the charge per bed per day varies depending on the class of service. Patients given the first class service pay much more than those given third class. The rates charged by government-owned facilities were first issued almost 50 years ago and have not been substantially revised since, although charges can vary between facilities located in the same town or different towns and by ownership. While fees have remained stagnant, health care costs have increased substantially over that period, creating a wide gap between the expenditures and revenues of health facilities.

In the 1995/96 regional health sector budget, user fees were expected to cover only 5.5 percent of the total health recurrent expenditure budgeted for the year, or about Birr 19.8 million. In general, a higher rate of cost recovery is expected in urban areas, where there are a number of higher-cost hospitals to complement primary health facilities. For most rural areas, the proportion of costs recovered is expected to be quite small, as a result of the more widespread poverty in rural areas and the inconsistent implementation of poverty exemption policies. Before the devolution of responsibility for health sector management to the regional governments, there was no particular incentive to collect user fees, which were channeled to the central Treasury and were not necessarily reinvested in the health sector.

Table 4.13   Financing the Health Sector in Ethiopia

	FY 1986				FY 1996			
	(in million Birr)			Share of Total Expenditure	(in million Birr)			Share of Total Expenditure
	Recurrent	Capital	Total		Recurrent	Capital	Total	
Individual Private Payments	226.5	0.0	226.5	63.4	388.4	0.0	388.4	39.3
Fees Paid to MOH Facilities	19.0	0.0	19.0	5.3	79.7	0.0	79.7	8.10
Fees Paid to Other Facilities	207.5	0.0	207.5	58.1	308.7	0.0	308.7	31.2
Government of Ethiopia	79.0	3.4	82.4	23.1	281.7	142.0	423.7	42.9
External Assistance	20.0	22.0	42.0	11.8	75.2	95.9	171.1	17.3
Health Insurance	0.6	0.0	0.6	0.2	5.0	0.0	5.0	0.5
Other Local Sources	5.7	0.0	5.7	1.6	...	...	...	...
Total	331.8	25.4	357.2	100.0	750.3	237.9	988.2	100.0
Total Health as Share of Government Expenditures			12.6				10.2	
Total Health as Share of GDP			3.2				2.7	

Source: For FY 1986, World Bank 1987; for FY 1996, PHRD Study Number 6, 1996.

The actual capacity of the population to pay for public health services is uncertain. As already mentioned, the most important reason cited for not seeking treatment by respondents in the Oxford-AAU survey was the cost of treatment, suggesting a low capacity to pay for services, especially among the poorest. Actual revenue from fee-paying patients has been estimated to be Birr 79.7 million, or just over 22 percent of total expenditures. However, this level of cost recovery capacity is insignificant when compared with the cost recovery capacity of facilities run by NGOs. According to a recent survey of 31 NGOs currently operating health facilities, 16.1 percent are able to recover between 91 and 100 percent of costs through user fees, while 6.5 percent have a cost recovery capacity of 81 to 90 percent, and the remaining have a 70 percent recovery capacity.

While treatment fees at health care facilities are in principle relatively low, user fees exist even in the government facilities for registration, tests, and medicines. Transport and living expenses while in treatment may also be substantial.

To help alleviate the financial burden on the poorest segments of the population, a system of exemptions allows poor households to obtain health services at no cost. Targeting is administrative, and in some areas letters from local kebele officials are often needed to obtain exemption cards. Free care is available to the indigent, prisoners, refugees, and the military, while civil servants receive a 50 percent reduction in fees at public facilities.

A 1995 WHO study estimates that 30 to 80 percent of patients currently receive exemptions from user fees. In contrast, a small set of provider surveys conducted in Amhara and in Southern Region in 1996 by Oxford University suggest that the percentage of "free" or exempt patients is only about 10 percent, and in clinics often even lower. Clinics in the highly impoverished area of North Shewa reported only 3 to 4 percent of patients receiving exemptions. Exemption rates appear to be somewhat higher in the two hospitals surveyed. This result is surprising in that these urban facilities are likely to serve a higher proportion of wealthy patients, although costs associated with hospitals are also higher. Finally, in all clinics and hospitals, the percentage of exemptions appears to be declining. According to facility records, free outpatients visits constituted about 22 percent of the total in 1993/94, 19 percent in 1994/95, and only 10 percent in 1995/96 (PHRD Study Number 2.a, 1996).

Adequacy and Sustainability of Financing

In 1994, the World Bank estimated that an essential package of primary health care services would cost approximately US$12 per capita in Sub-Saharan Africa (World Bank 1994a). In that same year, even after an unprecedented expansion in its health budget, the government of Ethiopia actually spent only about US$1.50 per capita on the health sector, a level well below the World Bank's minimum target. Even within the context of current budgets, there is evidence that the health sector is underfinanced, given the frequent failure to meet project targets, the lack of operating expenses available even when capital projects have been completed, and the low salary levels for professional staff that have contributed to the loss of skilled personnel in public institutions.

It is difficult to determine the extent to which government revenue and other components of government expenditures will increase over the next 15 to 25 years. The sustainability of even current health expenditure levels will depend on the rate of expansion of the overall economy, the extent to which that expansion in output increases household incomes and the demand for health services, the extent to which any increase in incomes and demand for health services translates into higher levels of recovered costs in the health sector, and the general rate of increase in other sources of government revenues and competing expenditure priorities. Given the Ethiopian economy's heavy dependence on the agricultural sector and the large interannual variability in GDP,

growth in health spending is unlikely to be particularly steady year in and year out.

Under the terms of its Health Sector Development Program, the government's own estimates of spending required for its planned expansion of the health system is approximately Birr 5.0 billion (Birr 4.5 billion with an additional 10 percent contingency allowance) for the period 1997–2002 (FDRE 1997). This assumes that nominal GDP will grow at an annual rate of 10 percent, government revenues will increase annually at 10 percent, and current expenditure will grow annually at 8 percent. Once again, other analysts have raised concerns about the reliability and sustainability of GDP growth, although the government has emphasized that its estimate of GDP growth is conservative. Calculations made by Indevelop (1996) using projected rates of population growth and assuming a somewhat ambitious 8 percent real annual growth in GDP from 1994 to 2020 and no change in government expenditures as a percent of GDP and the health budget share from 1994 levels, indicate that per capita expenditure on health would rise from the current US1.50 to only US$5.53 per capita by 2020. Therefore, it is unlikely that Ethiopia will easily meet the World Bank's minimum standard per capita expenditure level for an essential package of primary health care services of US$12 without either a very rapid and sustainable rate of GDP growth or a significant additional reallocation of budgetary resources to the health sector.

Future Options for Financing

Rather than relying solely on projected increases in GDP, higher overall government revenues and expenditures, another significant reallocation of budgetary resources to the health sector, or long-term dependence on donor contributions, Ethiopia has a number of options for reducing the financing constraint on the health sector. However, while each option must be given due consideration and could yield large returns in the future, it is unlikely that any one of these other sources of financing, or some combination, will substantially ease the health sector's resource constraints in the short term. Difficult decisions regarding the allocation of public funds will remain. Other options for financing include:

Greater efficiency in the public sector. A number of ways to utilize public resources in the health sector more efficiently are possible. In particular, the current efforts of the government to redirect resources from expensive, hospital-based services to less expensive primary care services, as well as an emphasis on preventive rather than curative care, should significantly improve the efficiency of resource use. However, this reallocation of resources across levels of care requires detailed planning, particularly in the case of the reallocation of personnel to regional facilities. Other possible options to gain greater efficiency include the improved management of drugs to streamline procurement and distribution and reduce wastage, consideration of economies of scale in the construction and staffing of new health facilities, revision of current staffing mixes that are currently biased toward high-cost physicians, improvements in health management information systems, and a greater overall emphasis on improved health systems management. To the extent that improved management increases the availability of drugs at government facilities or other factors that contribute to the perceived quality of care provided, for example, the likely resulting increase in utilization of those facilities would raise additional revenues from user fees.

Higher user fees. One potential impact of decentralization in the health sector is an increase in levels of cost recovery, as local institutions have an increasingly greater stake in the collection and use of those resources. A policy of fee retention at the facility level is embodied in the 1993 National Health Policy. However, the actual ability

of the government to collect more revenue through higher user charges is uncertain. Although the fee structure at government facilities has remained relatively unchanged over the past 50 years, the cost of health services remains an important reason for the low level of utilization of health facilities in Ethiopia. Whereas a very low expenditure elasticity suggests that Ethiopians consider health expenditure a necessity, conflicting evidence suggests that a significant increase in user fees would reduce demand significantly or place an additional burden on household budgets. While a restructuring of user fees may be appropriate to more fully reflect differences in the cost structure of health services between primary and tertiary care facilities, for example, the level of poverty in Ethiopia suggests that higher fees are appropriate only if accompanied by other efforts that simultaneously increase the demand for health services and the level of utilization of public health facilities.

Better-targeted exemptions. There is also conflicting evidence on the extent to which exemptions are granted in Ethiopia and the implications of that policy on health sector financing and the demand for health services. As discussed, estimates of the share of patients receiving exemptions range from as low as 10 percent to as high as 80 percent, depending on location and facility type. However, even given lower-end estimates, there is evidence that the targeting of exemptions in Ethiopia is poor (PHRD Study Number 2.a, 1996). Similarly, if the higher estimate of exemptions is actually the case, then it is difficult to explain low levels of health services utilization among poor households. Given the level of poverty and the influence of costs on health service utilization in Ethiopia, there is a clear need to differentiate fees for some segments of the population, based on their demographic characteristics, income levels, geographic location, proximity to services, or other criteria. Improved targeting implies higher administrative costs, but the decentralized management of the health sector by local authorities and the communities themselves should help minimize the information costs of any revised exemptions policy. The use of refined geographic targeting—methods which can differentiate not only levels of poverty across very small geographic areas, but also likely disease prevalence and access to health services—would also reduce the administrative costs of targeting. The number and type of exemptions might be allocated woreda by woreda, for example. Given the constraints on the health budget and the implications of user fees on the utilization of health services by the poor, some additional research is justified to clarify these questions of the targeting of exemptions in the health sector.

Expansion of private health insurance. Improved insurance coverage offers some promise to reduce the burden of health costs on patients. Health insurance can potentially increase the level of payments made into the health system while simultaneously reducing the number of people dependent on government-financed care. Currently in Ethiopia, however, insurance relating to health is provided only to some segments of the formal sector, including those employed by the government and state-owned enterprises. Government employees and family members are allowed 50 percent reduction from the charge they must pay for treatment and other facilities, although they must pay full costs for any necessary drugs. Finally, some private companies also provide such health-related insurance to their employees.

Overall, in 1995, the number of persons covered by medical aid policies represented only 0.03 percent of the total population, although it accounted for a somewhat disproportionate 0.5 percent of total expenditures in the health sector. The only establishment that currently provides private health insurance service is the Ethiopian Insurance Corporation (EIC), which sells policies relating to medical aid insurance, workmen's

compensation, and personal accident. In general, the expansion of coverage in the formal sector, particularly among private sector employees, should be a realistic objective. Compulsory contributions to a social health insurance scheme, based on payroll deductions for formal sector employees, has also been recommended as a means to expand health services coverage and limit the burden of health care on individuals (Indevelop 1996). By expanding levels of facility utilization and cost recovery among formal sector employees, these insurance schemes would allow the government to focus more of its resources on those in the informal and rural sectors.

Other insurance schemes, such as those administered by local cooperatives or public health facilities, might also be developed to enable rural communities to make greater contributions to the financing of health services. One possible option is the use of agricultural cooperatives as a source of rural health insurance. While Ethiopia has some experience with rural cooperatives, some restructuring might be required for the purposes of establishing an insurance component, to ensure a stable organization, full participation of members, and an appropriate mechanism for administration of the program. Traditional insurance schemes, such as *iddir*, which finance funerals and other emergency costs out of small monthly voluntary contributions of community members, already exist in most communities in Ethiopia. The concept of *iddir* could also be expanded as a means to provide health insurance coverage to rural populations, although substantial revision would be required regarding contribution levels, illnesses covered, and payment rates per illness type, among other issues. Considerable government input would be required to promote the use of *iddir* for this purpose and to assist communities in the management of this local insurance scheme. The government itself would have to develop its own policies and guidelines on the management and oversight of these community insurance schemes and the extent to which government financial support is required to facilitate these efforts.

Other community financing schemes. A number of NGOs have been active in encouraging the establishment of revolving community drug funds, to improve the access of the rural populations to essential drugs. There is evidence in Ethiopia that these revolving funds can be financially successful and can be applied in both rural and urban settings. UNICEF has been promoting the establishment of community-owned pharmacies, along the lines of the *Bamako initiative*, as another means to improve access to essential drugs. Since 1990/91, seven community-owned pharmacies have been opened in Bichena (Amhara region), Sululta and Mana Kersa (Oromia region), Yirga Chefe and Dammot (SNNPR), and Kechene and Yeka (Addis Ababa). The funds necessary to establish these pharmacies were obtained from UNICEF, while WHO provided the technical support. Supervisory services have been provided by the Ministry of Health, which has prepared a procedures manual regarding the management of the pharmacies. The funds provided by UNICEF are repaid after three years of operation, at which time most pharmacies have accumulated enough capital to continue operation independently. Significant expansion of these activities will require continued technical guidance and supportive policies on the part of the government.

Private sector initiatives. Since 1992, there has been a rapid increase in the number of private health care providers in Ethiopia. As previously mentioned, practically all drug vendors and drug stores are privately owned, as are more than 70 percent of pharmacies, facilities that represent an important dimension of Ethiopia's health care delivery system, particularly for the rural poor. Visits to the homes of health workers or to private health clinics and health centers are also important components of the system and are utilized more by wealthier individuals. Currently, ex-

cluding pharmacies, there are 183 private health facilities (1 hospital and 182 clinics) throughout the country (PHRD Study Number 13, 1996).

With continued economic growth in Ethiopia, there is a strong likelihood of growing demand for privately provided health services. Greater private sector participation would then allow the existing government budget to be reallocated to promote expansion of services to more vulnerable populations. However, private sector participation in the health sector will not be an immediate panacea, since private sector capacity is currently small and relatively undeveloped. In addition, particularly given the private sector's already important role in distributing essential drugs in rural areas, expanding the role of the private sector in health services is likely to bring benefits primarily to better-off urban populations. In rural areas, further private sector participation is likely to bring additional improvements in the availability and use of essential drugs rather than large investments in private diagnostic or preventive services.

A number of recommendations have been made to ensure that the private sector can meet the likely increasing demand for health services, while minimizing the pressure on already limited government budgetary resources. These include the continued expansion of privately funded primary care facilities and the privatization of some or all aspects of (a) hospital management; (b) drug procurement and distribution; (c) laboratory and other technical services; (d) public health programs, such as malaria control and family planning services, and (e) nontechnical "hotel" services at health facilities. To accomplish this, the government will be required to improve access to land for facilities construction, provide a tax holiday and an exemption from duties on health equipment, ensure a well-trained labor pool and reasonably low-cost financing options, and provide a streamlined administrative framework for doing business within the Ministry of Health, among other things. Finally, the government must support strong supervision and quality control in the private sector and the training of private sector drug vendors and pharmacists to improve the quality of care they provide to their customers.

PROGRAM IMPLICATIONS FOR THE HEALTH SECTOR

Since 1992, the government has taken important steps to improve the quantity and quality of health services for the population of Ethiopia. In addition to increasing the overall share of health in the budget, the government has begun to reallocate resources away from urban hospital-based curative services toward more preventive care that is increasingly focused on the population in rural areas. Through the HSDP, the government will embark on a program of needed investments in health infrastructure and staffing, while revising its health training programs to improve staffing mixes and ensure a more appropriate set of skills. The restructuring of EPHARMECOR, the reorganization of the structure of health facilities, and the devolution of responsibility to local authorities, among other steps, will likely lead to increased efficiency of operations and improved quality of care by ensuring greater responsiveness of health institutions to local needs.

If the objectives of the health sector reforms are to be fully realized, however, a number of key issues need to be addressed. First, to increase the utilization of services, interventions to increase supply need to take into account issues of demand. Second, key stakeholders must be effectively mobilized to make the decentralization process work. Third, financial constraints must be addressed through alternative sources of funding, more efficient allocation of scarce resources, and strategic planning to effectively sequence or phase interventions.

The future demand for health facilities and services in Ethiopia will depend not only on changes in the size and demographic composition of its population, its increasing urbanization, and the rise of HIV/AIDS as a health concern, but also on:

- increased access to good quality primary health care services such as improved immunization coverage, which should change the pattern of disease among vulnerable women and children, especially since children and maternal conditions combined account for 50 percent of all deaths and 56 percent of DLYs lost in Ethiopia.

- growth in incomes, because cost was one of the major reasons cited (aside from distance and quality) for not seeking treatment by households surveyed by HICE-WMS and Oxford-AAU.

- Improvements in the educational status of the population, accompanied by increased coverage of effective Information, Education, and Communication (IEC) programs, better dissemination, and coordination of information. These factors should help increase health and nutritional awareness and therefore positively influence the demand for health services.

- The increased availability of facilities must be accompanied by essential drugs, medical supplies, and equipment and staffed with trained, well-qualified personnel. Increasing access by constructing new health facilities is a necessary but insufficient condition to increase utilization because quality of facilities was also cited as an important determinant of demand for health care services.

The government's policy of decentralization must overcome local shortages of skilled personnel and inadequate implementation capacity (through training and setting of proper incentives to prevent further staff attrition), some inherent difficulties in raising revenue at the regional level, and the limited infrastructure, communications, and logistics resources at the disposal of regional authorities.

. Even with the development of alternative financing sources, the health sector will continue to face serious financing constraints as it seeks to meet expanding needs for facilities, drugs and other supplies, and well-qualified staff. Limited and conflicting information regarding the level of private sector capacity, the degree of cost recovery actually achieved, and the degree to which exemptions are provided to patients creates uncertainty about the extent to which the current constraints to health sector financing can be alleviated in the short to medium term. If the HSDP objectives are overoptimistic under available finances and implementation capacity, greater care must be taken in the selection of capital investments and assurances made that resources will be available within the recurrent budget to actually finance operations and equip new and renovated facilities with needed supplies and personnel.

The financing constraint also underscores the importance of better targeting of exemptions and actively exploring alternative sources of funding. The approval of the proposed health financing strategy cannot be overemphasized.

- Given the constraints on the health budget (improved targeting might entail increased administrative costs) and the implications of user fees on the utilization of health services by the poor, some additional research is needed to address targeting/exemption issues. On the other hand, the decentralized management of the health sector by local authorities could help minimize the information costs of any revised exemptions policy since they themselves are better informed (relative to the central government) about who would be eligible for exemptions within their own communities.
- The use of indigenous systems such as the *iddir* could be expanded to provide health insurance to rural populations (according to PHRD Study 2.a, rural households spend a portion of their income on *iddir* or funeral insurance, which in some cases also includes health and disaster coverage). Government input would be re-

quired to promote the wider use of *iddir* for this purpose. Some policies and guidelines would also need to be developed regarding the management of these community insurance schemes and the extent to which government financial support is required to facilitate these efforts.

- Other insurance schemes such as those administered by local cooperatives or public health facilities might also be developed to enable greater financial contribution from rural communities in the financing of health services. One possible option is the use of *agricultural cooperatives* as a source of rural health finance. However, while Ethiopia has some experience with rural cooperatives, some restructuring might be needed to establish an insurance component that is well organized, is supported by its members, and has an appropriate mechanism for program administration.

Financing constraints point to the importance of better management and more efficient allocation of resources. Thus, the government must not provide all services but must focus on interventions with the largest public impact, such as essential health services that address the major disease burden and enhance health and nutrition status.

- Improved antenatal and maternal care can minimize the incidence of infant deaths, maternal mortality, and low birth weight. Integrated management of childhood illness, school health/deworming, measles case management, and immunization is likely to be highly cost-effective in minimizing the heavy disease burden borne by children under five years of age. Moreover because there is considerable overlap in the symptoms of a number of childhood diseases such as ARI, malnutrition, diarrhea, and measles, a single diagnosis for a sick child may be inappropriate. The integrated initiative will focus not only on the management of the child's illness but also on promoting preventive measures. Clustering health services for women and children can reduce service delivery costs, as well as women's time and travel costs.

- It is essential to exploit the synergy between interventions such as IEC, safe water, and proper sanitation facilities and preventive health and nutritional interventions to minimize the onslaught of infectious and preventable diseases. Coordination must be strengthened among the different ministries such as Health, Agriculture, Education, and Water Resources/Sewerage. Although local communities will implement programs, the central government has a vital role in ensuring coordinated, intersectoral activities.
- It is crucial to address health and nutritional needs at every stage of the human life cycle, from birth to old age, because each stage builds upon the previous one. It may be more costly and even too late to intervene only at later stages.

Experience in some African countries suggests that cost-effective packages of basic services can be delivered at the community level. A number of decentralized health programs have demonstrated that it is possible to improve health service delivery by improving the tools for community-level supervision, monitoring, and evaluation. This approach enhances the participation of local community groups, providing an additional source of resources and manpower. This will also help forge a partnership between communities and health service providers that is essential for the continuous improvement of services. Ethiopia has started a pilot project that gives management and financial responsibilities to local communities. In particular, the Ethiopia Social Rehabilitation and Development Fund (ESRDF) supports community activities that relate to basic social services such as health, rural water supply/sanitation, and education.

The ability to develop and exploit the capacity of the private sector in the provision of health services will also require substantial changes in government policies, not only to support private sector efforts through investment incentives and by eliciting private sector feedback and participation in health sector planning activities, but also to coordinate activities and ensure quality of services through an appropriate regulatory framework.

Strategic planning also entails considering the different burden of disease patterns across regions. Priorities may vary significantly across regions, and the central government will need to be flexible in providing support to local authorities. Strategic planning also involves exploring different modes of health service delivery. For example, in cases where nearby health facilities are not available, local health center staff could conduct outreach activities, visiting these areas on a regular basis. Different approaches to reaching pastoralist populations could also be tried. One option is mobile clinics, although these may not be cost-effective and may be difficult to manage given the poor roads in rural Ethiopia. Water troughs could be constructed in key locations, enabling nomadic populations to settle longer together with their animals and in turn making them easier to locate and reach. Clearly, options to reach the pastoralist populations exist, but these options need to be studied carefully and their advantages and disadvantages weighed. In this regard, the FDRE plans to conduct a study on mechanisms to deliver health services to pastoralist/nomadic populations. Finally, strategic planning entails prioritizing, given resource and capacity constraints. Careful phasing of expansion activities will entail deciding what needs to be done when, where, by whom, and how.

5

NUTRITION

The high levels of malnutrition in Ethiopia are among the most serious detriments to the well-being of the nation's population. Poor nutrition undermines child development, the cognitive abilities of schoolchildren, and the productivity of the workforce. However, nutritional deficiency cannot be viewed as an isolated condition. Nutritional deficiency is a risk factor in a number of other diseases. It exacerbates their negative consequences and may itself be a consequence of other health problems. Although the complexity of the problem makes it difficult to isolate the specific contribution of nutritional deficiencies to the well-being of the population of Ethiopia, it also suggests that the benefits of nutrition interventions are likely to support efforts to address other health problems, such as acute respiratory infection and diarrheal diseases.

This chapter addresses the level of malnutrition in Ethiopia in comparison with other low-income countries in the region, the extent to which expected improvements in per capita food or total consumption (income) might lead to nutritional gains, especially for the children of Ethiopia, and the nature of the interface among income (consumption) growth, nutrition, education, and health. This synthesis of issues will shed light on the roles of income-augmenting and/or food security interventions, policies aimed at enhancing private consumption rather than expanding public goods, such as health, education, nutrition, and family planning.

MALNUTRITION IN ETHIOPIA

Child Malnutrition

Table 5.1 presents a summary picture of rural malnutrition in Ethiopia for 1983, 1992, 1994/95 (three survey rounds), and 1995/96 (rural and urban), disaggregated by gender. In rural areas, the proportion of both male and female children under age six who were stunted increased between 1983 and 1992, from 60 percent to 64 percent. While the 1994/95 survey indicates a slight reduction in the level of stunting, albeit at still very high levels, the rate seems to have increased again to an unprecedented 68 percent in 1995/96. The proportion of children wasted seems to have increased rather steadily over the reported periods, particularly through the early 1990s. There appears to be no significant difference between male and female children. Data for 1995/96 suggest that malnutrition is significantly worse in rural areas than in urban areas.

Table 5.2 provides data on stunting, wasting, and underweight of children by age groups for rural areas in 1992 and for the country as a whole in 1995. For both years, the data show a general increase in the proportions from 6 months of age, peaking at 24 months of age, and a slight decline in the older age groups. Between 1992 and 1995, except for the age group 12–23 for male children, which registered a slight decline, the

Table 5.1   Prevalence of Stunting and Wasting for Children under 6 Years, 1983–96

	Gender	Rural		Rural 1994/95			1995/96		
		1983	1992	Round 1	Round 2	Round 3	Urban	Rural	Total
Stunting	Female	58.6	65.7	53.7	55.3	55.2	...	...	63.8
	Male	60.9	62.7	53.4	58.4	56.5	...	...	65.2
	Both	59.8	64.2	53.5	56.9	55.9	56.3	68.7	64.9
Wasting	Female	7.6	7.2	9.2	12.5	13.3	...	...	11.1
	Male	8.6	8.7	11.5	9.0	14.2	...	...	10.5
	Both	8.1	8.0	10.4	10.7	13.7	9.3	10.4	10.8

... no data.

Note: Stunting: z-score less than -2 for height-for-age; wasting: z-score less than -2 for weight-for height.

Sources: PHRD Study Number 2.b, 1996; PHRD Study Number 2.a, 1996; and Central Statistical Authority 1992.

proportion of children stunted, wasted, or underweight worsened or remained about the same. The general pattern of increase in the proportion of malnourished children after 6 months of age observed in Ethiopia is similar to the pattern observed in other low-income countries, although, again, the proportions in Ethiopia are alarmingly high.

No clear pattern emerges regarding the relationship between household expenditures per capita and malnutrition. Table 5.3, which provides data on average weight increases by consumption quartiles, suggests that children in the lower consumption groups have a higher degree of fluctuation in body weight. Between rounds 1 and 2 of the 1994/95 survey, the poorer groups experienced slightly higher weight increases than those better-off groups, and between rounds 2 and 3 they experienced larger weight declines. For 1995–96, data in Table 5.4 suggest that prevalences of stunt-

Table 5.2   Prevalence of Malnutrition by Age and Sex, 1992 and 1995

Age in Months	Stunting		Wasting		Underweight	
	Rural 1992	National 1995	Rural 1992	National 1995	Rural 1992	National 1995
Males						
<6	...	38.4	...	6.6	...	12.0
6–11	59.0	70.1	6.5	7.8	42.5	42.9
12–23	74.5	68.5	13.0	10.2	59.7	53.7
24–35	65.5	64.6	6.9	13.1	50.4	55.7
36–47	63.1*	66.1	7.9*	9.1	45.3*	41.7
48–59		65.4		11.4		42.9
All Ages	65.7	65.2	8.7	10.5	49.3	46.2
Females						
<6	...	42.3	...	6.3	...	29.1
6–11	53.8	65.5	6.1	7.2	36.2	32.9
12–23	70.8	71.4	10.2	9.4	50.0	48.9
24–35	63.1	63.0	7.0	12.9	50.4	48.2
36–47	61.0*	65.7	6.2*	12.9	44.5*	46.8
48–59	...	59.9	...	12.6	...	46.5
All Ages	62.7	63.8	7.2	11.1	45.9	44.9

... no data.

Note: Stunting: z-score less than -2 for height-for-age; wasting: z-score less than -2 for weight-for-height; underweight: z-score less than -2 for weight-for-age.

* For ages 36–59 months.

Sources: PHRD Study Number 2.b, 1996; Central Statistical Authority 1992.

Table 5.3 Average Weight Increase between Rounds for Children under 6, by Consumption Group, 1994/95

Increase between	Consumption Group			
	Poorest	Lower	Higher	Richest
Round 1 and 2	1.11	1.06	1.01	0.97
Round 2 and 3	-0.12	-0.12	0.14	0.11

Source: PHRD Study Number 2.a, 1996.

ing and underweight decline as per capita expenditures rise, while the reverse seems to hold for wasting.

Data on the levels of wasting and stunting by mother's education are presented in Table 5.5. The table indicates that the proportion of children malnourished is much lower among children of educated mothers than for the children of mothers who did not complete primary school- ing; the drop in the proportion is truly remarkable for both wasting and stunting in all rounds. Two caveats are in order, however. First, very few mothers have completed primary schooling in general. Second, the impact of mother's schooling may still be high, but not as dramatic, controlling for other influences, such as income, mother's own health, and others.

Data on regional variations in stunting and wasting are presented in Table 5.6. A com-

parison of changes in the proportions of malnourished children between 1983 and 1992 (positive change indicating a worsening, and a negative change indicating an improvement) shows significant regional variations in the experience of malnutrition over the past decade. The data suggest a universal worsening of conditions according to the underweight measure, while the situation is more mixed in terms of the stunting and wasting measures. In the regions of Arsi, Gojam, Sidamo, and Welega (according to previous administrative boundaries), the change in nutritional status was negative for all measures.

Finally, nutritional deficiencies of children under the age of 5 account for a significant share of the burden of disease in Ethiopia. It is the fourth most important cause of both mortality and life-years lost, ranking behind perinatal and maternal conditions, respiratory infections, and measles. Nutritional deficiencies in Ethiopia directly account for 7.8 percent of all deaths and 9.3 percent of DLYs lost. For the Eastern Africa region as a whole, nutritional deficiency was found to be a direct determinant of 5 percent of the region's mortality. However, taking into account the interaction of nutritional deficiency and other diseases, the total direct and indirect contribution to mortality was 29 percent (World Bank 1996b). Although a detailed analysis of the indirect effects of nutritional deficiency is available for Ethiopia, the regional analysis suggests that the combined

Table 5.4 Prevalence of Malnutrition by Household Per Capita Expenditure Group, 1995/96

Expenditure Group	Stunting			Wasting			Underweight		
	Severe	Moderate	Total	Severe	Moderate	Total	Severe	Moderate	Total
<50	49.9	20.2	70.1	4.5	4.8	9.3	24.0	29.0	53.0
50–100	45.3	19.6	64.9	5.3	6.4	11.7	18.2	28.2	46.4
101–200	42.3	19.4	61.7	5.2	5.4	10.6	16.1	23.8	39.9
>200	38.0	18.3	56.3	6.9	4.5	11.4	12.9	21.9	34.8
Total	45.3	19.6	64.9	5.2	5.6	10.8	18.9	27.0	45.9

Note: Severe is less than -3 z-score; moderate is less than -2 z-score.
Source: PHRD Study Number 2.b, 1996.

Table 5.5   Prevalence of Malnutrition in Rural Areas by Mother's Education, 1994/95

	Stunting			Wasting		
Primary School?	Round 1	Round 2	Round 3	Round 1	Round 2	Round 3
No	54.6	57.6	57.2	10.6	11.0	14.4
Yes	46.3	52.4	48.6	4.9	4.8	10.8

Note: z-scores less than -2.
Source: PHRD Study Number 2.a, 1996.

direct and indirect effects of nutritional deficiency are likely to explain a substantial share of the total burden of disease.

Other Nutrition Problems

Apart from protein-energy malnutrition, Ethiopia's children also suffer from other serious nutrition problems. For example, estimates of low birthweight range from 13 to 17 percent, based on available hospital information (compared with about 7 percent among developed countries). This could be attributed to maternal malnutrition. The mean weight gained by pregnant women in Ethiopia is only 5 to 6 kilograms, compared with 12.5 kilograms in developed countries.

Micronutrient deficiencies, including iodine deficiency, vitamin A deficiency, and nutritional anemia are also prevalent. Prevalences of iodine deficiency disorder are as high as 71 percent in certain populations, while the national level among schoolchildren is nearly 31 percent and almost 19 percent among all household members. The deleterious effects of iodine deficiency on pregnancy outcomes have been found to be high: about 13,600 neonatal deaths, 14,800 stillbirths, and 20,000 miscarriages in 1990. As for vitamin A deficiency, the average prevalence of Bitot's spots was 1 percent, compared with the 0.5 percent maximum level set by WHO. The number of children affected is staggering: about 5 million children under 6 years of age show manifestations of subclinical vitamin A deficiency. Vitamin A deficiency causes blindness and, in association with diarrhea and measles, can increase the mortality rate of children under 5 years of age. In general, micronutrient deficiencies are much higher among children of pastoralists than among children living in foodgrain and cash crop areas.

The nutritional status of adults is also a concern in Ethiopia. Body-mass indices (BMIs), calculated from 1994/95 nutrition survey data, are shown in Table 5.7 for three rounds and by consumption groups. It shows the percentage of

Table 5.6   Regional Changes in Malnutrition, 1983–92

	Change from 1983 to 1992		
Region	Stunting	Wasting	Underweight
Arsi	6.0	1.1	15.6
Bale	4.3	-0.1	6.2
Gamo-Gofa	-11.3	1.7	7.9
Gojam	6.0	0.7	6.0
Gonder	-3.3	1.6	7.3
Ilubabor	10.3	-1.1	13.1
Kefa	5.8	-0.9	8.0
Shewa	1.9	-2.0	5.5
Sidamo	2.8	4.0	17.0
Welega	6.6	0.1	8.1
Welo	-3.5	-3.9	3.6
All Ethiopia	4.2	-0.5	9.6

Note: Malnutrition is defined as z-scores less than -2; negative change implies improvement in nutritional status.
Sources: Central Statistical Authority 1992; Webb et al. 1992.

Table 5.7   Malnutrition of Adults by Consumption Group in Rural Areas, 1994/95

	Consumption Group			
Round	Poorest	Lower	Higher	Richest
1	32.7	28.3	28.0	21.5
2	23.7	22.0	21.9	19.7
3	28.3	26.3	24.3	22.0

Note: Undernutrition is defined as adults with BMI less than 18.5.
Source: PHRD Study Number 2.a, 1996.

adults with BMI below 18.5 for each consumption group and for each round. Unlike the case of child malnutrition, there appears to be a close association between consumer expenditure group and adult malnutrition: poorer households clearly have a larger proportion of malnourished adults than the richer households. The data also suggest a significant seasonal pattern, particularly among the lower consumption groups.

POVERTY AND MALNUTRITION

The major direct causes of malnutrition in Ethiopia are the inadequacy of food intake, both in terms of the quantity and quality of foods consumed, the extremely high burden of disease in the country, and inappropriate feeding practices. As indicated in Figure 5.1, Ethiopia has been plagued by chronically low and variable levels of food production. An estimated 52 percent of the country is food insecure with average consumption of approximately 1,770 kilocalories per capita, 16 percent below the minimum level ac-

Figure 5.1   Foodgrain Production and Population Affected by Drought, 1985–96

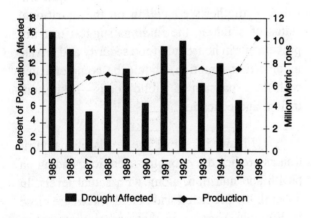

Source: FDRE 1996c.

cepted by the government. To achieve the FAO/WHO recommended per capita calorie intake of 2,000 kilocalories per person per day, total food production has to increase by 6.5 percent per year. Over the past decade, a period that does not include the full extent of the drought and famine in the early 1980s, the population affected by drought has ranged from as low as almost 5 percent to just over 16 percent. Until the bumper harvest of 1996, Ethiopia experienced huge production deficits of approximately 1 million tons annually.

Overall, the burden of disease in Ethiopia is nearly double that of neighboring Kenya, for example, as discussed in detail in Section 4.2 and is particularly focused on the under 5 population. The extent of morbidity in Ethiopia is a major contributing factor to the levels of malnutrition in the country. While breastfeeding is widely practiced, particularly in rural areas, it is often initiated somewhat later than typically recommended. Supplemental foods are often introduced late and may be inappropriate. In some cases, fresh butter or water is given instead of breastmilk immediately after birth, depriving the infant of colostrum. Although the data presented touch on only some aspects, underlying these determinants are parental factors such as mother's age and education level; household factors such as farm productivity, income, and asset holdings; and community factors such as access to health care services including immunization, sanitation, and protected water. Individual factors such as the child's age and gender are also of some importance as determinants of malnutrition rates.

In spite of Ethiopia's history of drought and chronically low levels of food production and household access, some studies have shown that child nutrition may be more responsive at the margin to health inputs than to food availability at the household level. This is not to argue that a decrease in food availability would not have consequences on children and communities, but that nutritional gains from the expansion of public goods may outweigh the gains from expansion of private production and consumption.

The current state of malnutrition in Ethiopia deviates substantially from the values predicted by the relationships between malnutrition and per capita incomes and consumption of low-income countries in Africa. These relationships, as measured between monthly per capita consumption expenditure corrected for purchasing power parity (PPP), dietary energy supply, and the prevalence of underweight children, are illustrated for a small sample of African countries in Figures 5.2a and 5.2b. In fact, whatever measure of malnutrition is used, the actual values for Ethiopia are much worse than the values predicted by the relationships for low-income countries of Africa. In Figures 5.3a and 5.3b, the same relationship is shown but with PPP-corrected GNP per capita, and the findings are the same. These findings suggest that Ethiopia has a lot of catching up to do and that low incomes and consumption levels are not necessarily the most binding constraints to improved nutritional status. The evidence suggests that direct interventions and provision of public goods will be necessary to close the gap. It is likely that a part of that catching up must come from enhanced public spending not just on nutrition per se, but more generally on health and nutrition.

Although local-level data on poverty and consumption are hard to come by and there are the usual problems of comparability between the data sets, Table 5.8 presents an analysis of the direction of change in consumption-based poverty incidence and the severity of poverty for three regions of Ethiopia. That information is contrasted with the actual change in two indicators of malnutrition for the same regions over roughly the same time period. The table suggests that while the incidence and severity of poverty fell in all three regions, the incidence of malnutrition in

creased in all but one case. In Goma-Gofa region, there has been a dramatic decline in poverty incidence and severity; in this region, the stunting of children has also declined. The conclusion that emerges again is that in Ethiopia, moderate improvements in consumption or reductions in poverty are unlikely to register corresponding decreases in malnutrition.

To better understand the role of investments in public goods to address malnutrition, relative to the role of private consumption, a simple regression equation was estimated for the few countries for which data are available on overall health and nutrition spending, PPP-corrected consumer expenditure per capita per month, and the nutritional status of children. These estimates show that the elasticities of children underweight with respect to both public expenditure on health and nutrition, and with respect to private expenditure per capita, are statistically significant. These elasticities imply that an annual US$1 increase per capita on health and nutrition would reduce malnutrition by 2.75 percentage points, whereas an average US$1 increase in private consumer expenditure per capita per year would reduce malnutrition only by 0.03 percent. These results illustrate the possibly dramatic returns to investments in health and nutrition in Ethiopia. Coupled with the previously noted substantial impacts of mother's education on the nutritional status of children, the findings suggest that improvements in household food security and private income (consumption) should be complemented with the expansion of public goods—health, nutrition, and education.

Figure 5.4 shows the levels of malnutrition as predicted by country-specific spending on health and nutrition, along with actual levels. In general, the predicted and actual values are close in Ethiopia, suggesting that underinvestment in health and nutrition is a major factor in high levels of malnutrition. Moreover, the levels of malnutrition drop with increases in per capita public

Figure 5.2a   Actual and Predicted Dietary Supply by PPP-Corrected Mean Consumption per Month

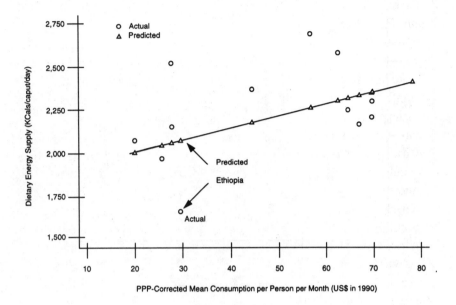

Source: Subbarao and Mehra 1996, based on data from Chen, Datt, and Ravallion (statistical addendum), 1994.

Figure 5.2b   Actual and Predicted Prevalence of Undernutrition by PPP-Corrected Mean Consumption per Month

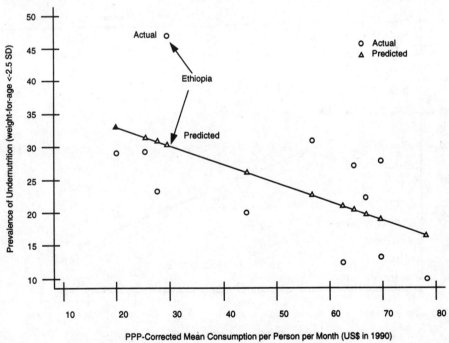

Source: Subbarao and Mehra 1996, based on data from Chen, Datt, and Ravallion (statistical addendum), 1994.

Figure 5.3a   Actual and Predicted Dietary Supply by PPP-Corrected Mean Consumption per Month

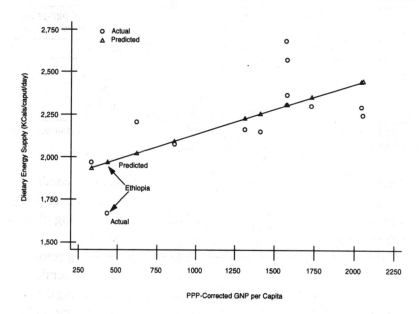

Source: Subbarao and Mehra 1996, based on data from Chen, Datt, and Ravallion (statistical addendum), 1994.

Figure 5.3b   Actual and Predicted Prevalence of Undernutrition by PPP-Corrected Mean Consumption per Month

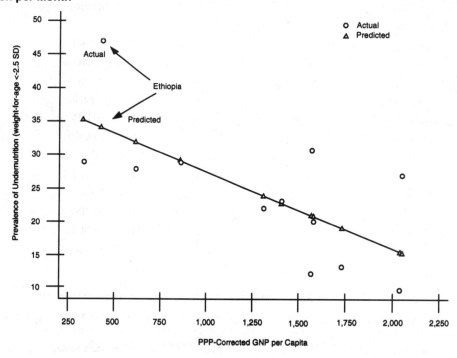

Source: Subbarao and Mehra 1996, based on data from Chen, Datt, and Ravallion (statistical addendum), 1994.

Table 5.8   Changes in the Incidence and Severity of Poverty and Malnutrition in Selected Regions

Region	Change in Poverty, 1989–94		Change in Malnutrition, 1983–92	
	Incidence	Severity	Stunting	Wasting
Doma, Gamo-Gofa	—	—	— (55%)	+ (7%)
Debre Berhan, Shewa	–	–	+ (62%)	– (6%)
Gara Godd, Sidamo	–	–	+ (65%)	+ (10%)

+ moderate increase; – moderate decrease; — substantial decrease. Numbers in parentheses are percent malnutrition for 1992.
Source: Central Statistical Authority 1992.

spending on health and nutrition. Simulations suggest that if Ethiopia were to spend the same amount per capita as other countries in the sample, the percentage of children malnourished would have been less than half of the present level.[1]

PROGRAMS AND POLICIES

From the foregoing situational analysis and socioeconomic determinants of malnutrition, it is clear that:

- children in the age group 6 months to 24 months are most in need of intervention;
- interventions should be targeted to pregnant women and mothers of young children to bring about changes in behavioral patterns with respect to self-care,[2] feeding practices, and child care;
- food supplementation should be directed not merely to overcome PEM, but also to address micronutrient deficiencies;
- such interventions should be nationwide covering food deficit as well as food surplus areas and cut across all income (consumption) groups; and
- such early-childhood development initiatives should be combined with efforts to improve mothers' education.

Interventions to combat malnutrition in Ethiopia fall into three major groups:

- those aimed at reducing chronic household-level food insecurity,
- those aimed at reducing temporary food insecurity from drought and conflict, and
- those aimed at improving the biological utilization of food by focusing on improved health, water, sanitation, and nutrition.

In all three groups of interventions in Ethiopia, the government's efforts are heavily complemented by donor contributions and NGO participation. Indeed, most donor programs are operated through government ministries.

The government's strategy for addressing chronic food insecurity includes efforts to: (a) ensure widespread economic growth, particularly in the smallholder rural sector; (b) address national food availability of food supplies through both greater investment in agricultural productivity and the exploitation of comparative advantage in trade; and (c) promotion of food entitlements for specific household groups through employment and income-generating programs, as well as through targeted transfers of food and other resources to particularly vulnerable groups.

---

[1] These and other simulations assume that public spending automatically results in "access" of services to the poor. In reality, access problems are acute in Ethiopia, and interventions have to be carefully designed to overcome the problem of access of the poor to publicly provided areas.

[2] The Ethiopian woman's diet is also usually unbalanced and insufficient to enable her to perform her activities such as fetching water and collecting fuel wood, as well as taking care of the young and sick. Although she is usually the caretaker of the household, she is usually uneducated about proper nutrition.

Figure 5.4   Actual and Predicted Underweight and Health Expenditures (including nutrition) by Selected Low-Income African Countries

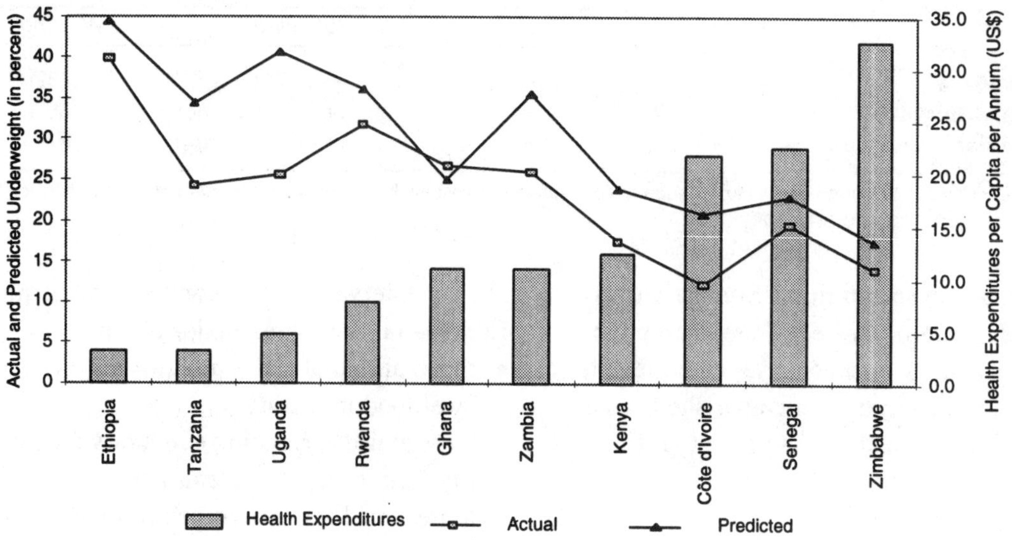

Source: United Nations (ACC/SCN), 1994.

In addition to general relief feeding programs, public works and other temporary employment programs are also essential components of the government's efforts to address transitory food insecurity as well. According to available estimates, about 10 percent of food aid has been through food-for-work in recent years, with the remainder distributed as free food relief. Within the next five years, in order to address perceived food aid dependency among some segments of the population, the government has determined that 80 percent of food aid will be channeled through employment generation schemes in various sectors (social, infrastructure, environmental assets, etc.). The remaining 20 percent will be distributed as free food to disabled people, refugees, and other particularly vulnerable groups.

Public works programs have been in operation in Ethiopia for many years. However, the economic relevance, technical quality, and net incomes generated from public works have not been rigorously examined. The few studies that have reviewed the food security aspects of public works

point out that payment in-kind may have forced the program to operate only in areas where food can be transported. One study compared the amount of employment offered by food- and cash-for-work programs across the country during 1990 with the population in need of assistance for that year (Webb, Richardson, Seyoum, and Yohannes, 1994). The employment offered was sufficient to cover the minimum requirements of only 24 percent of people in need. The bulk of even these obviously small efforts are being met by NGO activities.

Cross-country experience suggests that properly designed public works programs can strongly complement developmental efforts. Public works program need not be exclusively oriented toward relief. Government policy has begun to shift food aid and public works to development activities. In Ethiopia, public works activities have been linked with priorities for development in rural areas, in the construction of roads, small-scale irrigation, improvements in water supply and sanitation, and schools and clinics.

It is particularly important to evaluate the experience with public works program in terms of its impact in combating household food insecurity, providing net income support, and indirectly leading to improved nutritional status. The issues that need an analysis include: (a) how to render access to the program to those in need, (b) how to avoid spreading scarce food aid resources too thinly across the country, (c) what is the trade-off between auctioning food aid and using the cash for supporting a cash-for-work program versus a food-for-work program, and (d) how to maximize transfer benefits to the poor without necessarily reducing the stabilization benefits of the program.

Finally, a third set of programs directly addresses the nutritional status of Ethiopia's most vulnerable population groups. Given the evidence presented earlier, the highest priority for nutrition programs should be given to high-risk groups, especially children under the age of 5 and pregnant and lactating mothers. Current efforts underway include food supplementation programs such as school feeding, an accelerated child health development program implemented with UNICEF support, a range of maternal and child health services, including growth monitoring, provided through various government and NGO facilities, and a number of programs to control micronutrient deficiencies. The government has proposed a National Food and Nutrition Program of Action for 1995–2000. In addition to antipoverty measures, disaster prevention and mitigation measures, investments in market stabilization, and agricultural research, the action program includes nutrition research and training, nutrition education, and micronutrient interventions as major components.

However, many of these programs have not had the desired effect on malnutrition among schoolchildren. Supplementary rations through school-feeding and other programs are rarely suf-ficient to address severe malnutrition. The coverage and performance of immunization, water and sanitation, and disease-control programs has had limited impact on the population at large. Coverage of growth monitoring efforts, for example, is estimated to be only 23 percent of the under 5 population (PHRD Study Number 11, 1996). Poor quality of services, shortage of resources and extreme poverty of patients have contributed to a worsening of primary care services. Inefficient and ineffective utilization of even the limited resources available and their inequitable distribution across the country have aggravated the problem of underfunding. Results from recently initiated micronutrient programs have yet to be thoroughly evaluated.

Looking at the analysis of the burden of disease in Section 4.2, the diseases that affect children under the age of 5 years (ARI, diarrhea, nutritional deficiencies, and measles) account for 33 percent of deaths in Ethiopia and 39 percent of DLYs lost. Since children under 5 represent less than 20 percent of the population, the evidence is clear that they share a disproportionate burden of ill health. When perinatal and maternal conditions are added, the health problems of mothers and children combined account for 50 percent of deaths and 55 percent of DLYs lost. However, unlike in some other countries, such as Zimbabwe and India, Ethiopia has no program that delivers a combination of services (food supplementation, health inputs, immunization, etc.) to preschoolers and/or pregnant women.

Little information is available regarding actual expenditures on nutrition-related programs by the government and donors. In 1994/95, actual expenditure on MCH programs, which include growth monitoring and breastfeeding components, constituted approximately 0.6 percent of the total spent on eight selected health programs, including EPI, family planning, malaria control, tuberculosis and leprosy control, HIV/AIDS, potable water, and health education (PHRD Study Number 6, 1996). The budget of the National Food and Nutrition Program of Action for 1995–2000, which includes food security, research and training, and nutrition interventions, is ambitious, at approximately US$560 million over the period. Most of this is to be generated by domestic resources (FDRE 1995).

PROGRAM IMPLICATIONS FOR NUTRITION

The proportions of wasting, stunting, and underweight children in Ethiopia are staggering not only in drought-prone regions but nationwide. Nor is the phenomenon necessarily confined to specific consumption groups, since evidence to that effect is somewhat contradictory. There is some relationship between certain measures of malnutrition and income/consumption status, but evidence suggests that regions with a moderate decline in the incidence of poverty did not experience a corresponding decline in the incidence of malnutrition. The problem with respect to micronutrient deficiencies is almost as serious as protein-energy malnutrition. Although not analyzed in detail, adult malnutrition is just as worrisome: nearly one-third of adults among the poorest, and one-fifth among the richest, have BMIs lower than 18.5.

Of the many causal factors that lead to malnutrition, mother's primary schooling seems to make a significant difference to children's nutritional status. The most binding constraint for children's nutrition in Ethiopia seems to be not so much a failure of household-level food security and private consumption, however, but the failure to prevent infections and morbidity and to target food supplementation programs to the weakest among the population, especially preschoolers and mothers.

In spite of this evidence, as with much of the Sub-Saharan Africa region, public policy in Ethiopia has focused primarily on energy availability and consumption at the household level as a means to improve nutritional outcomes, thereby equating the problem of hunger with that of malnutrition. While an emphasis on household food security is important and should continue, the analysis given here underscores the importance of policies other than food security—particularly investments that enhance the availability and impact of public goods, including: (a) health care interventions that reduce infections and provide preventive care; (b) investments in education, particularly of women, and incorporation of nutrition in school curricula; (c) strengthening of community-based programs such as growth monitoring and promotion; (d) targeted food supplementation for preschoolers and mothers; and (e) improved investments in health, water, and sanitation infrastructure.

6

POPULATION

Ethiopia has the second largest population in Sub-Saharan Africa. The government has recognized the large and rapidly growing population as a critical obstacle to rapid and widespread economic and social development. Through its impact on access to resources and the quality of the environment, extreme population pressure can dampen per capita income growth and undermine the ability of the economy to absorb an expanding labor force. On the one hand, through its effects on incomes, rapid population growth may minimize potential growth in the demand for social services at the household level. On the other hand, an expanding population base will require more and more resources simply to maintain the quality of, and access to, social services. Other changes in the population structure, particularly those threatened by the continued high rates of infant and maternal mortality and the rapid spread of HIV/AIDS in Ethiopia, also present significant challenges to development and the delivery of social services.

Therefore, developing effective population and reproductive health programs is crucial to the success of the government's overall development strategy. Toward that end, this chapter will explore the structure of population growth in Ethiopia, as well as the issues related to changing levels of fertility, mortality, and the prevalence of HIV/AIDS and other sexually transmitted diseases (STDs). Women's behavior is a major determinant of the demand for family planning and reproductive health services, so the many influences on women's behavior, particularly the role of women's education, will be a special focus.

Thus, knowledge, attitudes, and practices (KAP) will be addressed. The chapter will also assess the constraints to the improved supply of family planning and reproductive health services, as well as options to alleviate those constraints.

OUTCOMES

Population Growth and Structure

Ethiopia's population was approximately 54 million people by mid-1994. Annual population growth estimates vary from 3.1 percent between 1980 and 1990, to as low as 1.7 percent during the 1990–94 period. By comparison, annual population growth in Sub-Saharan Africa was 3.0 percent through the 1980s (Figure 6.1), declining only somewhat to 2.7 percent more recently (World Bank 1996a). As indicated in Chapter 2, even the most optimistic scenarios for declining fertility in Ethiopia imply a substantial increase in its population base over the next 25 years, from current levels to approximately 92 million in 2020. At the other extreme, assuming no decline in fertility over the next 25 years, Ethiopia's population would more than double to just over 113 million. The scenario considered most plausible in terms of likely changes in fertility levels places the population at 97.9 million by 2020.

Again, the population of Ethiopia's urban centers has grown relatively more rapidly than that of the rural areas. According to pre-liminary census reports, Addis Ababa recorded 3.8 percent

Figure 6.1   Population Growth (1980–90) and Total Fertility (1994) Rates

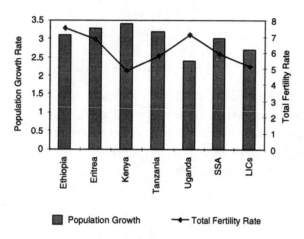

Source: PHRD Study Number 4, 1996.

annual growth in the inter-censal period, while other urban centers recorded 4.1 percent annual growth. In rural areas, the population is estimated to have grown at an annual rate of 2.23 percent. Currently, urban areas constitute approximately 13.7 percent of the population, with that share expected to rise to just under 20 percent by the year 2020. From a base of approximately 7.3 million in 1995, the urban population is expected to increase to between 18.2 million under the low growth scenario detailed in Chapter 2 and nearly 22 million in the high-growth scenario. Again, the most likely scenario places the urban population at 19 million by the year 2020.

Table 6.1   Age and Sex Distribution of the Population, 1995 and 2020 (percent)

	1995			2020		
	Male	Female	Total	Male	Female	Total
0–19	28.5	27.8	56.3	24.6	24.3	48.8
20–39	12.3	13.9	26.2	15.8	15.5	31.2
40–59	6.2	6.0	12.1	7.1	7.8	14.9
60+	2.9	2.5	5.4	2.3	2.7	5.0
Total	49.9	50.1	100.0	49.7	50.3	100.0

Source: PHRD Study Number 4, 1996.

In 1995, according to Table 6.1, there was no large difference in the proportion of males to females in the population of Ethiopia across any age group. The population under the age of 20 accounts for over 56 percent of the population currently, although, as discussed in Chapter 2, by the year 2020 the population will likely have aged significantly. While the population between 20 and 60 years of age currently makes up just over 38 percent of the total population, that share is expected to rise to approximately 46 percent over the next 25 years.

Fertility

As also discussed in Chapter 2, the total fertility rate (TFR) estimates for women between the ages of 15 and 49 years range from 5.8, according to a preliminary analysis of the 1994 national census, to 7.5 percent in 1994 and 7.0 percent in 1995 based on World Bank estimates. These rates compare with fertility of approximately 4.9 in neighboring Kenya, 5.8 in Tanzania, and 5.9 for the Sub-Saharan Africa region as a whole (Figure 6.1).

The determinants of fertility in Ethiopia include direct influences, such as marital status, contraceptive use, postpartum infecundability, and abortion, as well as indirect influences, such as women's socioeconomic status, education, urbanization, religion, ethnicity, and health, among others. According to National Family Fertility Survey (NFFS) data, 34 percent of women in the sample married before the age of 15, 41 percent between the ages 15 and 17, and 12 percent between the ages 20 and 21. Although still quite low, age at first marriage has increased over time. NFFS data suggest that the mean age of women who married before 1966 was 14.9 years, compared with 15.5 for those who married between 1966 and 1970, and 15.8 and 17.1 for those who married between 1971 and 1975 and after 1976, respectively. Similarly, time series information suggests that the mean age at marriage for women in Addis Ababa also increased from 17.2 years in 1967 to 24.6 years in 1990. Urban women in Ethiopia tend to marry slightly later than those in rural areas, as do those with some education. Mean ages at first marriage also varied based on religion and ethnicity.

However, age at first marriage by itself may not always be an important factor influencing fertility. Other factors such as effective marriage date, the age at which first births occur, duration of marital unions, and marital status are also important. In some rural parts of Ethiopia, the day marriages take place and the day cohabitation begins differ. Available data indicate that a significant proportion of women in Ethiopia have their first births at a very early age; 39 percent of rural women became mothers before they reached age 18, compared with 35 percent in urban areas (Central Statistical Authority 1993).

Exclusive breastfeeding is another factor that has a suppressing effect on fertility in Ethiopia. According to the 1990 NFFS, about 97 percent of ever-married women had breastfed their last child. Although some differences in breastfeeding practice can be observed between urban and rural women and across education levels, those differences are small. Nearly 86 percent of ultimate births were breastfed until about 20 months after delivery.

Finally, a multivariate analysis in 14 African countries indicates a consistently strong relationship between female education, fertility, and contraceptive practice (Ainsworth, Beegle, and Nyamete 1995). According to that analysis, the impact of completed primary school for both urban and rural women reduces the number of children ever born by 0.3 to 0.6 children. The impact of secondary school experience is to reduce children ever born by 0.9 to 1.4 children. The mean number of children ever born to illiterate women was 3.9, while it was 2.7 for those who had non-formal education. The mean number of children born to women who had primary education went down to 1.8 and to those who had junior secondary education and senior secondary education to only 0.9. Rates standardized for age also showed that mean parity declined as education increased.

Mortality

Since 1980, Ethiopia has made important reductions in its infant mortality rate, although it is still among the highest in Sub-Saharan Africa and other low-income developing countries. Recent estimates of infant mortality range between 112 and 120 deaths per 1,000 live births, while child mortality estimates vary between 168 and 204 deaths per 1,000. The high level of infant mortality is partly attributable to a high rate of perinatal and neonatal deaths, which are often the result of the poor health of the mother and the low birth weight of infants. In contrast, the deaths of children older than one month are mainly the result of disease and malnutrition in the children themselves (WHO 1986). The neonatal mortality rate in Ethiopia during 1980–84 has been estimated at around 57 per 1,000 live births, suggesting that over 50 percent of infant deaths were among infants under one month of age. The percentage of live births with low birth weight in Ethiopia is estimated to be between 13 and 17 percent, a major factor contributing to neonatal mortality. Spacing births is an important way that mothers can help prevent infant deaths. Reduction of infant mortality rates is striking for babies born more than two years after a-preceding birth. For instance in Kenya a child born within a less than two-year interval is 1.6 times more likely to die.

National and regional levels of maternal mortality are not well known in Ethiopia. Estimates range between 452 and 1,528 deaths per 100,000 live births. The lower end of that range is comparable to neighboring countries, while the upper limit represents a level of mortality more than double the high-end estimates of other countries in Eastern Africa. Lack of good antenatal, delivery, and postpartum care, maternal malnutrition and anemia, high parity, and septic abortions all contribute to the high rate of maternal mortality. Coverage for antenatal care in Ethiopia is approximately 19.8 percent (compared with nearly 60 percent in Sub-Saharan Africa), while only 6.1 percent of all births are institutional deliveries.

STDs and HIV/AIDS

Sexually transmitted diseases (STDs) are among the major health concerns in Ethiopia. Although there are a few recent studies of STD prevalence nationwide, a study of sex workers in Addis Ababa found a prevalence of gonorrhea of 30 percent, nearly 24 percent for trichomoniasis, 20 percent for vaginal candidiasis, and 37 percent for syphilis. The 1982/83 rural health study found that STD prevalence was 4.8 per 1,000 (based on reported illnesses), ranging from 11.3 percent to 0.9 percent across various regions of the country. With approximately 155,000 cases treated out of an expected 1.3 million, the national coverage rate for STD programs is currently estimated to be approximately 12.1 percent (PHRD Study Number 11, 1996).

The number of AIDS cases reported to the Ministry of Health from January 1986 through the first quarter of 1995 was about 18,042, (Table 6.2). However, according to the Epidemiology and AIDS Department of the Ministry of Health, in cooperation with the Futures Group, the actual number of AIDS cases has been estimated at approximately 1.45 million for 1995, which implies a prevalence of 4.7 percent (Table 6.3). Table 6.3 suggests that new AIDS cases in 1995 amounted to 171,000, while the number of AIDS-related deaths totaled approximately 315,000. Seventy-six thousand children were estimated to be born HIV-positive in 1995 as well.

Out of the total reported cases, about 54 percent were from Addis Ababa hospitals and 42 percent of AIDS patients were residents of Addis Ababa city. The reported number of AIDS cases in 1994 was more than 6 times higher than that reported in 1991. Data reported during January 1986 to April 1994 show that the prevalence of AIDS was significantly higher among the 15–49 age groups, which account for approximately 93 percent of all cases. The ratio of men to women reporting AIDS is 1.58:1 over the entire 1986–1995 period (Table 6.2). Thirty-four percent of AIDS patients were identified to be married people.

According to projections developed for this report, the estimated number of people infected with HIV will rise from 1.45 million in 1995 to about 2.2 million by the year 2000 and 3.9 million by 2020. While the gross numbers are expected to continue to increase, the adult prevalence is assumed to level off at 6 percent in the year 2005. Total deaths from AIDS are estimated to increase to nearly 500,000 annually by 2015. Another study used three different scenarios to

Table 6.2   Reported AIDS Cases, 1991–95

	Male	Female	Total	M/F Ratio	Annual Share of Total
1991	586	300	886	1.95	4.91
1992	1,984	1,272	3,256	1.56	18.04
1993	3,187	1,937	5,124	1.65	28.39
1994	3,309	2,249	5,558	1.47	30.88
1995 (1st quarter)	1,476	1,000	2,476	1.48	13.63
Total (1986–95)	11,042	7,000	18,042	1.58	100.00

Source: PHRD Study Number 11, 1996.

Table 6.3 HIV/AIDS Projections, 1995–2020 (thousands)

	1995	2000	2005	2010	2015	2020
HIV Population						
Total	1,450	2,163	2,511	2,807	3,300	3,865
Males	725	1,082	1,256	1,404	1,651	1,934
Females	724	1,080	1,255	1,402	1,649	1,931
Adult Prevalence	4.7	5.9	6.0	6.0	6.0	6.0
New AIDS Cases						
Total	171	281	393	427	475	551
Males	86	141	197	214	238	276
Females	85	140	196	213	237	275
Annual HIV+Births						
Total	76	94	109	116	122	
Percent	2.7	3.0	3.2	3.3	3.4	
Annual AIDS Deaths						
Total	315	321	393	435	498	
Per 1,000	5.5	4.8	5.0	4.9	4.9	

Source: PHRD Study Number 4, 1996.

project HIV/AIDS cases in Ethiopia. Under the medium variant scenario, HIV cases were projected to be about 2.7 million by the year 2000 and 8.6 million by the year 2010. Under the same scenario, the number of deaths due to AIDS was projected to be 895,000 and 5,822,000 for the years 2000 and 2010, respectively (Asmerom 1994).

Even under the most optimistic scenarios, the health, social, and economic consequences of the debilitation and ultimate loss of human lives will place a severe strain on the weak economy of Ethiopia. The impact of AIDS includes the direct loss of labor, land, and remittance income, for example, as well as losses associated with the cost of caring for the sick. The treatment of AIDS patients will significantly increase the demand on the existing health care system. Currently, the costs of treating AIDS patients are estimated to range from a low of US$85 to a high of US$628 per patient. About 16 percent of hospital beds nationwide are occupied by AIDS patients. The situation is worse in Addis Ababa, where 30 to 40 percent of hospitals beds could be occupied by

HIV/AIDS patients. It has also been estimated that by 2009, expenditure for AIDS care would amount to one-third of the MOH's entire budget (Abdulhamid 1994). Thus, AIDS has strong budgetary implications apart from the physical strain on health care delivery system. There is further risk that, to combat AIDS, resources are likely to be diverted from the treatment and control of other important diseases. AIDS treatment will likely also increase the demand for foreign exchange for pharmaceuticals.

DEMAND FOR SERVICES

Preference for Children

According to the 1990 NFFS, only 6 percent of women expressed an interest in having fewer than 4 children. Just under 18 percent were interested in between 6 and 9 children and 4 percent expressed a willingness to have 10 or more children. The overwhelming proportion, approximately 60 percent, stated no preference, indicating that the matter was in the hands of God. The percentage of women who stated that they wanted no more children, according to the 1990 NFFS, was 23.7 percent of all women: 22 percent of the rural and 44.5 percent of the urban women.

As indicated in Figure 6.2, the NFFS data indicate that those women who want no more children have to a large extent already achieved large family sizes. Ninety-three percent of those without children desired a child, while, of those with eight and nine children, only 40 percent and 32 percent, respectively, desired more children. Women's level of education also seems to influence slightly the number of desired children. Of those with no education, 77 percent reported desiring more children, compared with 67 percent of those with primary education, 71 percent of those with junior secondary education, and 65 percent of those with senior secondary and higher education.

Knowledge and Use of Contraceptives

The use of contraceptives in Ethiopia is very marginal, although increasing somewhat in recent years. Contraceptive prevalence is about 7 percent of married women currently (World Bank 1996a),

Figure 6.2   Percent of Women Desiring More Children, by Number of Surviving Children

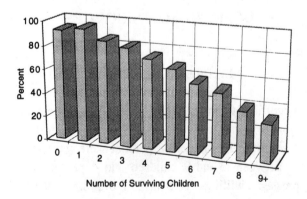

Source: PHRD Study Number 4, 1996.

up from as low as 4.8 percent based on 1990 NFFS data. By contrast, contraceptive prevalence is 20 and 33 percent respectively in Tanzania and Kenya. At such low levels of use, the current contribution of contraception to fertility decline is very small. However, although the fertility-inhibiting effect of contraception is low at the moment, raising the contraceptive prevalence rate is the single most important direct intervention in reducing fertility in Ethiopia.

As indicated in Table 6.4, approximately 69 percent of family planning acceptors use the pill, 17 percent use condom, 7.3 percent use IUD, 5.2 percent use injections, and 0.1 and 0.5 percent respectively are sterilization and Norplant users. It is important to note that this method mix may represent the availability of supplies rather than client preference. By the year 2020, the government anticipates contraceptive prevalence to expand to 44 percent, with a significant shift in the method mix away from the pill and toward increased use of sterilization, injection, IUD, and Norplant.

Although total prevalence is low, the 1990 NFFS data indicate that 63 percent of women knew about family planning methods, including over half of all rural women and nearly all urban women. Out of all women aged 15–49 years, 7.5 percent use at least one method of family planning. For rural women, the proportion was 4.2 percent, while for the urban, it was 26 percent. In contrast, among currently married and nonpregnant women, 4.8 percent reported current use, 2.6 percent for the rural areas, and 24 percent for the urban population. For the currently married, nonpregnant women of Addis Ababa, 32 percent reported current use of contraceptives in the 1990 study.

The 1990 NFFS study indicates that among the total population, 25.8 percent of women who have knowledge of at least one method of family planning but who never used a

Table 6.4   Current and Projected Use of Family Planning, 1995–2020

	1995	2000	2005	2010	2015	2020
Total Users (000s)	617	1,170	1,940	3,122	4,906	7,216
Share (percent)						
Condom	17.0	16.5	16.0	15.5	15.0	14.5
Sterilization	0.1	1.3	2.5	3.8	5.0	6.2
Injection	5.2	7.7	10.1	12.5	15.0	17.5
IUD	7.3	10.5	13.6	16.8	20.0	23.1
Norplant	0.5	4.1	7.8	11.4	15.0	18.6
Pills	69.0	58.0	47.0	36.0	25.0	14.0
Other	0.9	1.9	2.9	4.0	5.0	6.0
Total	100.0	100.0	100.0	100.0	100.0	100.0
Prevalence Rate	7.0	11.4	16.5	24.0	33.6	44.0

Source: PHRD Study Number 4, 1996.

method reported their intention to use one in the future. The corresponding percentages for rural and urban areas was 22 and 38 percent, respectively. Among women with knowledge of family planning but who have never used family planning and have no intention of future use, 35 percent were fatalistic and believed that destiny determined the number of children, while 15 percent claimed lack of deep knowledge about family planning prevented use. Fear of side effects and the disapproval of husband were other reasons given for no intention of future use.

The use of family planning is associated with several factors, including the age of a woman, number of living children, the educational level of a woman and her husband, religion and ethni- city, place of residence, and work status or occupation. In Ethiopia, the use of family planning was observed in the NFFS study to increase with the age of a woman until the ages of 25–29 years, after which it starts to decline slowly.

According to NFFS data, the relationship between family planning use and degree of urbanization was found to be significant, with the percentage of women using contraceptives increasing from 2.6 percent in rural areas to 19 per-

cent in regional urban centers. In Addis Ababa, family planning use was 32.8 percent. The use of family planning also increased with the educational level of a woman. The proportion of women who use family planning methods was only 2.7 percent for those with no education, 4.9 percent for those with non-formal education, 19 percent for those with primary education, 37 percent for

Figure 6.3   Use of Family Planning Methods by Educational Experience of Women

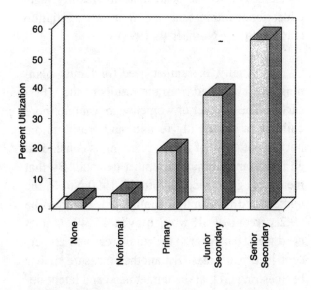

Source: PHRD Study Number 4, 1996.

those with junior secondary education, and 56 percent for those with senior secondary education. For the country as a whole, 4.2 percent of those who were working and 5.7 percent of those who were not working reported being current users of family planning. In contrast, in Addis Ababa, current use of contraception is higher among currently working women (45 percent) than nonworking women (27 percent). The NFFS data also provides evidence that the use of family planning is also influenced by the educational level and occupation of the husband.

Other Determinants of Demand

In Ethiopia, family planning services have largely been available without any fee. Although little data is available regarding actual household expenditures on family planning and other reproductive health services, a study was conducted to assess willingness of clients and potential clients to pay for services. A survey in two periurban areas and in the main commercial center of Addis Ababa among potential clients of family planning services found that the majority (71 percent) were willing to pay for services. That willingness, however, was very much related to certain factors such as support of family planning, contraceptive use, distance to the nearest health facility, age, educational attainment and religious affiliation (PHRD Study Number 4, 1996).

Finally, the unmet need for family planning was estimated from the results of the NFFS survey. The number of women who want no more children, are currently fecund, and are in union, but are not users of family planning is considered an important measure of unmet demand. By that measure, again, according to the 1990 NFFS, the unmet need for family planning was found to be 19.2 percent of all women aged 15–49. Unmet need was 18 percent in the rural areas and 26 percent in urban areas. By another measure, it has been estimated that the unmet need and latent demand for family planning services equals 55 per-

cent of currently married couples, including 32 percent of couples who wanted to space their next child and 23 percent who wanted to stop childbearing (UNFPA 1995).

PROGRAMS AND POLICIES

Program Coverage and Finance

In Ethiopia, most family planning services are delivered through, or integrated with, the public health care system as part of the maternal and child health (MCH) care program. However, the distribution of public health facilities in the country appears very weak and limited in coverage.

A review of health statistics data indicates that about 95 percent of hospitals, 95 percent of health centers, and 70 percent of health stations in the country were providing family planning services in 1995 (MOH 1995). While the share of facilities that provide family planning and reproductive health services is fairly large, actual coverage is limited, given the low levels of overall coverage in the health system. Nationwide, as indicated in Table 6.5, coverage for antenatal care is 19.8 percent, maternal immunizations (TT2) 17 percent, institutional births 6.1 percent, and family planning services 6.5 percent. Coverage for STD treatments is estimated to be approximately 12 percent, and there is currently only one HIV screening center per 867,000 persons in the country (PHRD Study Number 11, 1996). The data in Table 6.5 also indicate significant differences in program coverage across regions.

In addition to the generally poor state of health service delivery in Ethiopia, one of the most critical obstacles to greater coverage of family planning and reproductive health programs is the poor coordination of service delivery with information, education, and communication (IEC). However, a recent attempt to improve mechanisms

Table 6.5 Coverage of Selected Reproductive Health Programs by Region (percent)

Region	Antenatal Care	TT2	Deliveries	Family Planning	STDs
Tigray	18.8	7.6	13.1	6.8	1.4
Afar	4.9	6.3	0.5	1.5	4.2
Amhara	13.8	11.1	4.2	4.7	34.9
Oromia	22.7	23.4	5.3	3.1	3.0
Somalia	2.4	...	1.2	0.6	...
Beneshangul	16.8	24.3	8.8	4.7	2.0
SEPAR	22.8	21.2	4.8	2.6	0.9
Gambella	28.8	45.4	10.5	7.5	89.3
Hararghe	29.5	28.5	16.6	12.1	...
Dire Dawa	9.3	21.1	9.7	7.4	12.5
Addis Ababa	37.2	11.3	19.7	56.1	1.4
National	19.8	17.1	6.1	6.5	12.1

Source: PHRD Study Number 4, 1996.

to provide services through community-based distribution (CBD), which uses local people as distributors, either on a paid or volunteer basis, has been promising.

Population Policy

In Ethiopia, family planning services began with the establishment of the Family Guidance Association of Ethiopia (FGAE) in 1966. The FGAE was the sole provider of family planning services until about 1980, when the Ministry of Health also began participating. However, it was only after the results of the 1984 census that concerted efforts were made to limit the high population growth rate, as well as address directly the health problems of mothers and children. Since then, a number of projects supporting family planning were formulated with the assistance of the United Nations Fund for Population Activities (UNFPA) and a number of NGOs began to participate in promoting family planning services.

Several improvements were made in family planning services over the years. However, problems remained and were evident in the poor coordination of service delivery; inadequate delivery of information, education, and communication; and low levels of implementation capacity (Abdulhamid 1994). In addition, various institutions had different objectives and were not adequately coordinated.

Ethiopia's 1993 population policy starts with the understanding that, together, the rapid population growth, its young age structure, and the uneven spatial distribution of the population seriously undermine the development prospects of the country. The general objectives of the government's policy are to:

- close the gap between high population growth and low economic productivity;
- expedite economic and social development through holistic, integrated development programs;
- reduce the rate of rural-to-urban migration;
- maintain and improve the carrying capacity of the environment;
- raise the economic and social status of women; and
- improve the social and economic status of other vulnerable groups—youth, children, and the elderly.

To achieve those objectives, the policy explicitly targets improvements in fertility, contraceptive use, maternal child and infant mortality, female participation in education, and women's economic and social rights, among other specific outcomes.

With the formulation of the population policy, a more comprehensive strategy began to be elaborated. The National Office of Population, which is a focal point in promoting family planning, was established to coordinate the activities of both governmental organizations and NGOs. Similar offices under the NOP were also established in some regions. A plan of action, which elaborates objectives and activities for the period 1994–1999, was also prepared for the implementation of the policy. Major activities in information, education, and communication; family planning service delivery; career counseling; women's microenterprises; and population and environment are planned or already underway, as are efforts in research and counseling in reproductive health.

At present, there are several governmental and nongovernmental institutions participating in promoting family planning. In several ministries, focal points were formulated, including in the Ministry of Health, Ministry of Education, Ministry of Labor and Social Affairs, Ministry of Agriculture, and Ministry of Information and Culture. Although many continue to require technical assistance from the center, a number of regional governments have also established population offices and developed their own regional plans of action, based on the national plan. Furthermore, a number of other NGOs are also involved in the area. The FGAE still plays a major role in the provision of contraceptives. FGAE served a total of 351,808 acceptors between 1991 and 1994, including 73,258 new acceptors. The FGAE also provides family planning counseling services and has IEC programs. To date, the private sector plays only a limited role in the provision of family planning services.

The types of family planning services given or areas of concentration of the different institutions differ, depending on their objectives. For instance, some NGOs are mainly concerned with the increasing prevalence of HIV/AIDS. Others are concerned more about promoting the health of mothers and children. For some institutions, the concern emanates both from the health aspect and from the socioeconomic consequences of rapid population growth.

Finally, little information is available regarding actual levels of expenditures on family planning and reproductive health-related programs by the government and donors. In 1994/95, actual public expenditure on family planning programs was reported to constitute approximately

1.2 million Birr, or 1.5 percent of the total spent on eight selected health programs, including the expanded program on immunization, maternal and child health, malaria control, tuberculosis and leprosy control, HIV/AIDS, potable water, and health education. Spending on HIV/AIDS was reported at only 418,000 Birr, or 0.6 percent of the selected programs mentioned (PHRD Study Number 6, 1996).

PROGRAM IMPLICATIONS OF PROJECTED POPULATION CHANGES

Projected Population Changes

The analysis here points to the likelihood of a large increase in the size of Ethiopia's population over the next 25 years, as well as the continued rapid pace of urbanization and a sizable aging in the structure of the population. These factors, combined, will have an important impact on the resources required for the provision of family planning and reproductive health services over that period.

For example, given the population projections described in Chapter 2, the population of women aged 15–49 years is projected to increase from approximately 12.4 million in 1995 to 25.2 million in 2020. Under the scenario where contraceptive prevalence rates are projected to increase from 7 percent in 1995 to the government's targeted level of 44 percent in 2020, a substantial increase in family planning commodity costs might also be expected, from US$64 million to US$457 million in constant 1995 dollar terms, an annual increase of just under 8 percent.

That change in the structure of the population will also have important implications for the provision of antenatal care and coverage of tetanus toxoid immunizations. Simply maintaining current coverage for maternal immunizations (estimated to be nearly 17 percent in 1995) would require a more than 26 percent increase in resources over the next 25 years. A doubling of coverage would greatly expand resource requirements in the future, by as much as 152 percent between 1995 and 2020, an annual increase of 3.7 percent. Achieving total coverage would raise costs by as much as 8.3 percent annually.

Finally, the number of actual HIV infections is estimated to rise from a current 1.45 million to anywhere between 2.8 and 8.6 million by 2010, and AIDS-related mortality is estimated to expand to between 500,000 and 5 million annually in the same period. The economic and health care impacts of AIDS in Ethiopia were assessed using a range of different scenarios. Under the low-cost scenario, for the period 1995–2005, the costs of outpatient and inpatient treatments were estimated at US$34 million and US$79 million, respectively, while the high-cost scenario gave cost of US$258 million and US$369 million, respectively. The loss of income due to the disease was estimated at US$54 billion for estimated lives lost that period (US$2,087 per life lost). Unless some policy changes are made, by the year 2005 about 28 percent of hospital beds will be occupied by AIDS patients.

Integrating Services

Best practice in integrating family planning, maternal and child health care, and prevention and treatment of STDs into a comprehensive reproductive health care package are now providing good results in several African countries. Ethiopia could benefit from such experiences (Box 6.1).[1]

- Reproductive health policies and strategies need to be integrated with social policies that address poverty reduction and human development. Such policies would ideally include the education and empowerment of women, as well

---

Box 6.1   Experience in Raising Contraceptive Prevalence Rates in Three Countries

Botswana, Kenya, and Zimbabwe raised contraceptive prevalence rates to about 30 percent in Botswana and Kenya and up to 43 percent in Zimbabwe. The family planning programs in these countries attempted to address existing demand for contraception by emphasizing the benefits of child spacing and providing temporary methods, often the pill. The three countries have used different delivery systems: Botswana relied on its extensive system of health posts and health centers to provide contraceptives. Kenya emphasized outreach activities but also relied more on private voluntary organizations to complement services. Zimbabwe placed primary emphasis on community-based distribution (CBD) in rural areas. In addition, in these countries, most users choose effective modern methods of contraception.

Successful programs offer a wide range of methods and provide the information needed to teach clients to use those methods correctly. The more choices there are, the more likely it is that clients will find the method that suits their particular needs.

Source: Africa DHS 1992.

---

as the sensitization of men who are traditionally the decision makers in households and communities.

- Coordination and collaboration need to be strengthened between the family planning programs, the expanded program on immunization, the Department of AIDS Control, and the Department of Health Education. Health auxiliaries such as community health workers and traditional healers need to be effectively integrated into the family health program.

---

[1] Some efforts in Ethiopia to use community-based distribution (which uses local people as distributors, on a paid or voluntary basis) have improved provision of services to isolated rural areas.

Adolescent Health

The reproductive health needs of adolescents must be better met because of the changing conditions in which young people live. In Ethiopia, where early marriage is common, pregnancy during adolescence is a threat to the health of the young mother and baby. Providing training in counseling techniques and sensitization and information on family planning and reproductive health issues to youth leaders and organizers is important. Young people can be trained to counsel and assist their peers in making the right decisions regarding their reproductive health.

Family life education in schools and other venues can also help teenagers make informed choices about sexual behavior and the prevention of STDs. Programs that also help teenagers cope with pregnancies can be valuable.

Elimination of Harmful Practices

It is critically important to educate communities and help them understand the harmful effects of some prevailing practices. In particular, elderly women, husbands, village chiefs, and other influential community leaders need to be informed about the adverse health impact of female genial mutilation. They need to be made aware of its physical consequences, which can be sometimes life threatening. Aside from pain, females who undergo female genital mutilation are likely to experience hemorrhaging, shock, urinary tract and pelvic infections, painful menstruation, fistulas, cysts, obstructed labor, and increased risk of stillbirth and maternal mortality. Female genital mu-

tilation is also a cultural issue, however, and needs to be approached with sensitivity and caution.

Quality improvement through trained personnel and availability of drugs and contraceptives is vital. Sound logistics and a warehouse system are important in this regard. Alternative service delivery systems are needed to accommodate regional differences, especially in reaching the nomadic populations in Somali and Afar regions.

Improvement in the Socioeconomic Status of the Population, Especially of Women

In many developing countries, factors contributing to high rates of STDs and HIV/AIDS include increasing urbanization and the disruption of traditional social structures, increased mobility for economic reasons, poor medical facilities, and high unemployment rates. Women's occupation and their husband's occupation were found to be the major determinants of AIDS infection. Among the different occupational groups of husbands, those working in bars and merchants were among the high-risk groups for AIDS. Women who are bar ladies were also found to be among the high-risk groups. The rate of HIV infection is highly correlated with prostitution. An associated factor is the relatively low level of female education, for where there are fewer alternative economic opportunities for women, prostitution is more frequent. Reducing the risk of HIV in these circumstances will require strong public action to effect significant social changes in the role and status of women (including increasing female education) as well as promoting the use of condoms and treating coexisting STDs.

7

EDUCATION

Overall participation rates are extremely low at all levels of education in Ethiopia. Ethiopia's primary gross enrollment rate (GER) is less than 30 percent, one of the lowest in the world, while the average GER for Sub-Saharan Africa is 72 percent.

Of the small percentage of children who attend school:
- female participation rates are lower than those of males, especially in rural areas;
- the majority are over-aged, as indicated by the fact that the average age of entry to Grade 1 is 11 years old; and
- repetition rates and drop out rates are both relatively high.

Four additional problems characterize the education sector:
- severe urban-rural and regional differences in participation and access;
- poor quality;
- low efficiency; and
- massive resource deficit.

Against this background, the FDRE has proposed a comprehensive Education Sector Development Program (ESDP) for the period 1997–2002 as part of a longer-term program of 20 years. To meet the program objectives, the FDRE will need to consider the underlying causes of rural Ethiopia's poor rates of school attendance and decide which programs and activities need to be

Figure 7.1 Gross Primary Enrollment Rates in the World

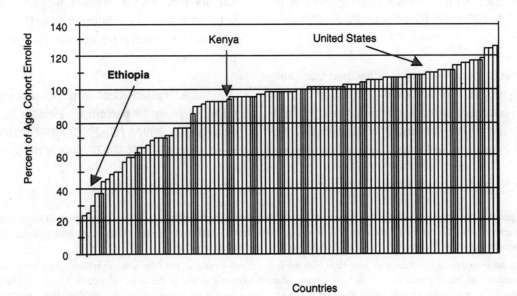

Source: World Bank 1995b.

given immediate priority. Aside from having one of the lowest primary school participation rates in Africa, Ethiopia is also one of the world's poorest countries. Thus, the choices that will be made will be largely driven by need and efficiency considerations given the gap between available resources and resources required to meet the stated objectives.

This chapter will present an overview of the structure and performance of the education sector in Ethiopia, followed by an analysis of the determinants of household demand for education and an assessment of supply-side conditions based on empirical and qualitative evidence obtained from the household, community, and provider/institutional surveys. School enrollment in Ethiopia is affected by both demand and supply considerations, and the distinction between these two is not always straightforward. Given that previous analyses undertaken in the education sector have focused on the supply side, our discussion focuses on the constraints that Ethiopian households face and means by which they can be encouraged and assisted to invest more in their own human capital.

GENERAL STRUCTURE AND PERFORMANCE OF THE EDUCATION SECTOR

Ethiopia's educational system has two main subsectors that are institutionally separate: (1) the formal education subsector, which consists of academic and technical training at the primary, secondary, and tertiary levels; and (2) nonformal education, which includes technical and vocational skills training for youth and adults.

Between 1962 and 1994, general education was divided into three levels: primary school (Grades 1 through 6); junior secondary school (Grades 7–8); and senior secondary school (Grades 9–12). Education reforms in 1994 revised the structure so that it now consists of: primary education (Grades 1–8), where Grades 1–4 aim at achieving functional literacy and Grades 5–8 prepare students for further education; general secondary education (Grades 9–10), which enables students to identify areas of interest for further training; and a second tier of secondary education (Grades 11–12) that prepares students for higher education.

Primary School

Poor participation rates characterize Ethiopian primary school attendance. The highest recorded primary GER[1] for Ethiopia was 38 percent in 1986, only slightly more than half that of Sub-Saharan Africa overall (World Bank 1994b). This is due to very low enrollment rates in rural areas. Nearly universal primary education has been achieved in urban centers. Low enrollment in the rural areas is therefore mainly responsible for the low national average.

A dramatic decline in primary school enrollment from 38 percent in 1986 to 22 percent occurred in 1992[2] (UNESCO 1993, 1994). The most recent HICE-WMS (1995/1996) indicates

---

[1] The gross enrollment ratio is calculated as the ratio of currently enrolled students (regardless of their age) to the total eligible population in the relevant age group. The net enrollment ratio is the ratio of currently enrolled students of the relevant age group to the total eligible population in the relevant age group. This measures the extent of over-aging of the student population.

[2] It is possible that the social dislocation associated with the civil war prevented children from going to school during this period. If this is the explanation, we would expect the decline to be temporary and enrollments to rise gradually as infrastructure is rebuilt and people gain confidence in the new government. However, there are also reports that parents were forced to send their children during the Derg period. If so, weak demand for schooling may reflect lingering resentment of the previous regime's imposition of formal education. This, combined with the possibility that enrollment figures were artificially inflated under the previous regime, suggests that we cannot expect demand to increase simply as a result of supply-side reforms.

Table 7.1   Major Education Statistics, 1995

| Education Level | Enrollment | Teachers | Schools | Enrollment | | Student/ Teacher Ratio |
				MOE	PHRD	
Primary	3,098,422	94,657	10,503	26	29[a]	33
Secondary	370,916	11,235	32	77.4	12[a]	33
Tertiary	15,820	1,937	b	0.5	<1[a]	8.2
Tech/Vocational	2,364	454	17			
Total	3,487,792	108,561	10,847			

a. PHRD Study Number 1.a, 1996.
b. 2 universities, 13 colleges, and 3 institutes.
Source: Ministry of Education (MOE).

that enrollments have increased to 29 percent. On the other hand, 1995 estimates by MOE indicate that primary GER has increased to 34.6 percent for grades 1–6 and 30.1 percent for grades 1–8, but both are still below the levels attained during the late 1980s.

Net enrollment ratios (NERs) measure the extent of over-aging in the student population and, at 16 percent, are lower in Ethiopia than GERs. The average age of entry into Grade 1 in Ethiopia is 11 years. Only 12 percent of those currently in school entered Grade 1 at 7 years of age, 14 percent at the age of 8. The great majority (62 percent) en-

Figure 7.2   Primary Gross Enrollment Trends for Ethiopia and Sub-Saharan Africa

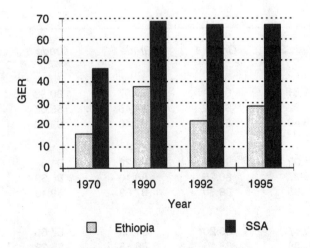

Sources: World Bank 1993c, 1995b; PHRD Study No. 1.b, 1995/96.

tered primary school at the age of 10 years or more.

Promotion rates in 1995 ranged from 66 percent to 88 percent across Grades 1–6. Not surprisingly, the highest dropout-rate was also from Grade 1. In 1995, dropout rates for Grades 1–3 and Grades 4–6 were 22 percent and 13 percent, respectively (PHRD Study Number 1.b, 1996).

The repetition rate for all primary grade levels in 1994 was 11 percent. Students tend to repeat the higher grade levels of primary education (nearly 20 percent in Grade 6) in order to improve their chances of proceeding to secondary school. The high dropout rates and low promotion rates in Grade 1 likely reflects children's difficulty adjusting to school, especially since they enter school at a relatively late age.

Urban-Rural Differences

Enrollment ratios indicate wide disparities between urban and rural areas. The total primary GER was 91 percent in urban areas and only 18 percent in rural areas. NERs in rural areas were also lower (16 percent) than those in urban areas (60 percent). On average, children in rural areas enter Grade 1 at a later age (at least 11 years) compared with children in urban areas (9 years).

Promotion rates in rural areas were 11 to 22 percent lower than those in urban areas, but

Table 7.2   Net Enrollment Ratios by Schooling Level, Urban/Rural, and Gender

Urban/Rural and Gender	Primary	Junior Secondary	Senior Secondary	Tertiary	Total
Net Enrollment Ratios					
Urban					
Male	0.62	0.28	0.26	0.02	0.36
Female	0.58	0.20	0.21	0.01	0.29
Total	0.60	0.24	0.23	0.01	0.32
Rural					
Male	0.10	0.01	—	—	0.05
Female	0.05	0.01	0.01	—	0.03
Total	0.08	0.01	—	—	0.04
Urban + Rural					
Male	0.18	0.06	0.04	—	0.10
Female	0.13	0.05	0.06	—	0.08
Total	0.16	0.05	0.05	—	0.09

Source: HICE-WMS, PHRD Study Number 1.b, 1995/96.

Grade 1 promotion rates were the lowest in both the cities and countryside. Moreover more students in rural areas dropped out of school than those in urban areas (30 percent relative to 10 percent for Grades 1–3 and 16 percent relative to 10 percent for Grades 4–6). Repeater rates in both urban and rural areas were, however, similar, at roughly 4 percent for Grades 1–3, and 2 percent versus 3 percent in rural and urban areas, respectively, for Grades 4–6.

Regional Differences

The wide gap in student enrollment across the regions is a function of a number of factors, the most important of which is accessibility. Primary GERs vary across regions, with Afar and Somali regions having the lowest GERs (below 15 percent) and Addis Ababa and Gambella having the highest (over 60 percent).

Table 7.3   Promotion Rates by Grade

Region of Residence	Grade 1	Grade 2	Grade 3	Grade 4	Grade 5	Grade 6
Rural						
Male	60.81	79.99	71.61	80.54	79.67	80.93
Female	54.11	93.70	91.32	87.82	88.45	85.65
Total	58.26	83.36	76.40	82.25	82.40	82.42
Urban						
Male	83.56	94.36	91.02	90.97	90.26	91.86
Female	76.31	92.13	96.37	80.25	86.10	86.39
Total	76.94	93.27	93.95	86.30	87.63	89.13
Urban + Rural						
Male	66.94	86.00	79.57	86.20	84.56	87.66
Female	64.51	92.63	94.98	82.15	86.65	86.22
Total	66.01	88.47	85.86	84.75	85.62	87.03

Source: HICE-WMS, PHRD Study Number No. 1.b, 1996.

Table 7.4   Enrollment by Gender, 1995

Education Level	Male	Female	Total		Percent Female
Primary	1,923,775	1,174,647	3,098,422	37	40
Secondary	209,568	161,348	370,916	43	47
Tertiary	13,915	2,060	15,975	12	34
Technical/Vocational	2,210	424	2,634	16	—
Total	2,149,468	1,338,479	3,487,947	38	

Source: Ministry of Education; PHRD Study Number 1.A, 1996.

Gender Differences

There is a bias against girls in the Ethiopian educational system, particularly in rural areas (although the disparity is admittedly less stark relative to what has been observed in other countries). In 1995, girls made up only 40 percent of all primary school students. The GER for boys was 33 percent compared with 24 percent for girls. The GER for girls in rural areas was only 11 percent, less than half that of boys. On the other hand, the primary GER of girls in urban areas exceeded that of boys (94 percent versus 88 percent). Among regions, female primary participation rates are highest (greater than 45 percent) in Addis Ababa, Amhara, Harari, and Dire Dawa and lowest in Somali, Benishangul-Gumuz, and SNNPR (less than 30 percent).

Girls generally start school later in life than boys. The national average NER for girls was 13 percent, while it was 18 percent for boys. Primary education NERs were 62 percent for males and 58 percent for females in urban areas, and 10 percent for males and 5 percent for females in rural areas. Only 38 percent of urban boys and girls joined Grade 1 at the age of 10 years and above, compared with the 73 percent of boys and 68 percent of girls in rural areas that entered Grade 1 at the age of 10 years and above.

The percentage of males dropping out of school in Grades 1–3 was higher than that of girls (23 percent versus 18 percent). In rural areas, this pattern persists through Grade 6. With the exception of Grade 1, more girls than boys are promoted in rural areas. Fewer girls in rural areas repeat Grades 1–3, while the opposite is true in urban areas.

Secondary School

The 1995 GER for secondary school was very low (19 percent for junior secondary and 9 percent for senior secondary). The net enrollment rate was only 5 percent in 1995. Countrywide, the Ministry of Education estimate of repetition rates averaged 16 percent. According to the ministry, only 1 out of 10 children who enter primary school complete the 12th year of secondary school.

Urban and rural differences are greater at higher education levels, with GERs of 6 percent in junior secondary and 2 percent in senior secondary schools in rural areas, compared with 73 percent and 38 percent, respectively, in urban areas.

Regional disparities also become greater at the secondary level, as the highest participation rates in senior secondary school are in the cities (40 percent in Addis Ababa, 31 percent in Harari, and 19 percent in Dire Dawa), while all the other regions have participation rates of 5 percent or lower.

The bias in favor of boys still holds in junior secondary school, where 46 percent of the students are girls, but GERs are 22 percent for boys and 17 percent for girls). This bias virtually disappears in senior secondary school, where 49 percent of the students are girls, and the GERs for both boys and girls are 9 percent. Repetition rates for females were also higher (20 percent) than for boys (11 percent) in 1994 (FDRE 1995). More females repeated Grades 7 to 10, while the percentage of males repeating Grades 11 and 12 was three times that of girls repeating (PHRD Study Number 1.a, 1996).

The percentage of males discontinuing schooling until Grade 8 was higher than that of girls in rural areas. However, beyond Grade 8, female dropout rates were higher than male dropout rates because females get married and drop out of school. In urban areas, on the other hand, female dropout rates were higher than male dropout rates for all grades except for Grades 7–8.

Tertiary Schooling

Less than one-half of 1 percent of the school age population in Ethiopia is able to gain access to tertiary education. On average, 30 percent of the students who take the Ethiopian School Leaving Certificate Examination each year pass the exam, and only 10 percent of those who pass are accepted by tertiary education institutions. According to the Ministry of Education's records, total enrollments in 1995 numbered 15,820 registered at two universities, twelve colleges (including teacher training colleges), and three technical institutes (specializing in polytechnic education, health sciences, and water technology). While this is an improvement over the 1975 enrollment of 7,000 students, it is still low compared with other African countries.

Based on the results of the HICE-WMS survey, the GER at the tertiary level is less than 1 percent. In fact it is not significantly greater than 0, and about 2 percent in urban areas. The per-

centage of female participation is 34 percent in tertiary schools, according to the HICE/WMS survey, although this is much higher than the 13 percent participation rate given by the Ministry of Education for 1995.

From 1992 to 1994, commercial and science majors accounted for 25 percent of total enrollments, agriculture 17 percent, engineering 16 percent, pedagogy and the natural sciences 14 percent, and medicine, 11 percent. Women tend to be concentrated in colleges of social science, business and economics, education, and health.

Technical and Vocational Education

School leavers who choose not to continue into the second "cycle" of secondary education face limited opportunities for formal pre-employment training. At present, the maximum enrollment capacity of technical and vocational schools is 6,000 students. However, the total actual enrollment in these schools in 1995 was less than 2,700 (Ministry of Education 1995).

HOUSEHOLD DEMAND FOR EDUCATION

Why are enrollment rates in Ethiopia so low? Is the low enrollment due to a lack of household demand for schooling? If demand is constrained, is it because the perceived benefits of education are few or because of the high cost of schooling? How much are households spending for education and how much are they willing to pay to educate their children? To answer these questions, the following section (1) summarizes household heads' attitudes toward schooling; (2) examines other factors that might influence household demand for education, such as direct and indirect costs of schooling, as well as the returns from schooling in Ethiopia; and (3) discusses the results of the empirical analysis of the household surveys.

Table 7.5   Household Heads' Attitudes toward Schooling

	Agree	Disagree		Agree	Disagree
It is useless to send girls to secondary school since they will eventually get married.	30	69	I want my son to have more education than myself.	99	1
Girls who have been to school are less polite and obedient than other girls.	26	70	I want my daughter to have more education than myself.	99	1
Girls who go to school do not learn how to be good wives and mothers.	32	68			
It is important for girls to learn how to read and write.	95	5			
				Quit	Finish
Children who go to school are better able to look after their parents in their old age than others.	79	19	Imagine that someone in the village has a young son who does not enjoy school and wants to quit. What should he/she do?	29	50
Children who finish school usually want to leave the village and go to a town or city to find work.	87	10	Imagine that someone in the village has a young daughter who does not enjoy school and wants to quit. What should he/she do?	34	41
				Quit	Move
Children who go to school are better farmers than boys who do not go to school.	47	51			
Children who go to school are less interested in following religious teachings than other children.	48	48	Imagine that someone in the village has a child who wishes to go to secondary school but there is not one nearby. What should he/she do?	9	90

Note: Figures may not add to 100 because of exclusion of "no opinion" category.
Source: PHRD Study Number 1.a, 1996. Based on subsample Oxford University-AAU Survey.

Attitudes toward Schooling

In general, in spite of observed low schooling participation rates, attitudes toward education in Ethiopia are very positive and indicate a strong demand for education (Table 7.5). People perceive education as a means of acquiring greater knowledge and becoming a "better person" (PHRD Study Number 12, 1996). In rural Ethiopia (PHRD Study Number 1.a, 1996), most respondents expressed the desire for their children to have more education than they themselves had attained. The same households have very positive attitudes toward girls attending school. An overwhelming majority of respondents agreed that it is important for girls to learn how to read and write[3] (PHRD Study Number 1.a, 1996).

---

[3] In the community assessment survey, 30 percent of household heads said that girl students face problems at the community level, such as cultural beliefs (for example, girls should stay at home; girls should marry early, girls should do domestic work; and girls may be threatened by crime because of the long distance of schools from their locality).

When asked how households decide which of their children to send to school, the majority (52 percent) said that the head of household, together with his spouse, makes the decision, while 26 percent indicated that the household head alone decides who should go to school. A small percentage (5 percent) reported that children themselves decide (PHRD Study Number 13, 1996). It is also reasonable to assume that decisions about schooling are made with the ability and ambition of the child in mind. This was confirmed by asking parents (in rural households) how they would choose to keep a particular child in school if they could afford to send only one child to school. The two most widely cited criteria were that the child is good at school work and the child enjoys going to school (PHRD Study Number 1.a, 1996).

The students' ambitions with respect to schooling and future employment are generally high, although girls have slightly lower ambitions regarding schooling than boys.[4] There are also gender differences in job plans. Girls are more likely to want to be teachers, whereas boys want to be doctors. Boys are also more willing to move to go to school or find employment. Secondary school students understandably have higher career aspirations than those in primary school. Secondary school students are less likely to want manual work and more likely to want to become doctors than teachers. Secondary school students are more likely to move to obtain more education or a job than primary school students.

Given that attitudes toward schooling are in general positive, why are enrollment rates so low in Ethiopia? One answer might be found in the direct costs to households of schooling. How much are households spending and how willing are they to pay for their children's education?

Household Education Expenditures

Total household education expenditures[5] in Ethiopia amount to Birr 9.5 per month or Birr 114 per year. On a per student basis, households spend Birr 4.9 per month on average or close to Birr 60 annually. Per capita education expenditures account for about 4.5 percent of per capita total expenditures for households. The mean household expenditure increases by school level: Birr 2.2 per student for primary (Grades 1–8), Birr 2.88 per student for secondary (Grades 9–12) and Birr 25.8 per student for tertiary education. Urban households spend almost 40 percent more than rural households on education. The average monthly education per student expenditure for ur-

Figure 7.3   Average Monthly Household Education Expenditures by Monthly Household Total Expenditure Quartile (in Birr)

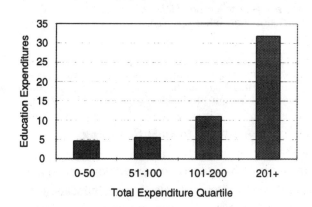

Source: HICE-WMS, PHRD Study Number 1.b, 1996.

---

[4] The rural subsample survey sites were chosen on the basis of their having relatively high enrollment rates relative to other sites. Hence these results should be considered upper-bound relative to a nationally representative survey.

[5] Note that these figures are derived from the first round of the HICE-WMS 1995/96 survey, which was undertaken when school term was ending and educational expenditures are at a minimum. At the time of the survey, enumerators also mentioned that household experienced some difficulty recalling the exact amounts they paid to educate their children. Because of these reasons, the survey is believed to have captured only part of the total household education expenditures.

ban households is Birr 5.50 while it is only about Birr 4 for rural households.

A greater percentage of higher-income households send their children to school (8 percent for the highest income quartile and 5.8 percent for the lowest). Moreover, households with higher incomes spend substantially more on education than households with lower incomes (Birr 31.65 per month by the highest income quartile and only Birr 4.58 by the lowest income quartile). Per capita education expenditures for households in Ethiopia are positively affected by household income, as well as the educational attainment and age of the household head.

PHRD Study Number 1.b (1996) found that half of the total household expenditures of the mainly urban respondents for education were on school fees, about Birr 31 per year on average. Annual per pupil expenditures on school fees increased by school level; from Birr 27 for Grades 1–8, Birr 34 for Grades 9–12, to Birr 310 for tertiary education. A more detailed breakdown of rural household education expenditures (PHRD Study Number 1.a, 1996) indicates that households spent Birr 81 per child in school, of which Birr 50 was allocated to clothing (school uniforms or clothing and shoes bought specifically for school), Birr 18 for school supplies, and Birr 11 for school registration fees. Expenditures on primary schooling (Birr 58 with clothing expense included, and Birr 24 without clothing expense) were substantially lower than expenditures at the secondary level (Birr 141 with clothing expense, and Birr 50 without clothing expenditures)

The PHRD Community Assessment Survey (PHRD Study Number 12, 1996) found that one-third of household heads were willing to allocate approximately 10 percent of their household incomes to education, while another third said that they were willing to spend 25–33 percent of their incomes on education. The remaining one-third of household heads were not willing to al-

locate any of their income to education because of poverty and the general belief that the government should be responsible for the schooling of children. In the Rural Household Survey (PHRD Study Number 1.a, 1996), approximately 61 percent of households were willing to pay up to Birr 40 per student. When asked how much they would be willing to pay to keep their male and female children in school, slightly more households were willing to pay over Birr 40 per year for their sons (39 percent) than for their daughters (35 percent).

Opportunity Costs of Schooling

Given the time demands of schooling, the earnings forgone, or opportunity cost of education, is a major cost component of education in Ethiopia. In agricultural households, the most important cost of schooling may be the opportunity cost of a student's time.

Students in the Rural Household Survey (PHRD Study Number 1.a, 1996) indicate that they spend 6.5 hours per day on school-related activities. On average, travel time to school is about 45 minutes, 4.2 hours are spent in classes, and 1.5 hours are spent studying outside school per day. Secondary school students spend 82 percent more time traveling to and from school, and 52 percent more time studying outside of school than do primary school students.

In the rural areas of Ethiopia, the number of students attending school significantly declines during harvesting season and increases during the lean season (PHRD Study Number 9.b, 1996). A study on labor force utilization in traditional agriculture in Ethiopia (Aredo 1989) indicates that children spend long hours working, especially on herding of animals. The opportunity cost of schooling was the single most important reason cited by rural household members for not attending school in the AAU-Oxford household survey (PHRD Study 1.a, 1996). In particular, boys are required for farm activity and girls are needed for

Figure 7.4a   Why Children Never Attend School in Ethiopia: First Reason

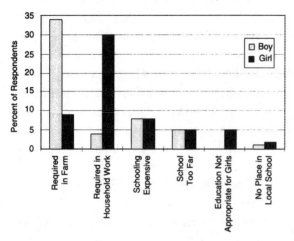

First Main Reason for Not Attending School

Figure 7.4b   Why Children Never Attend School in Ethiopia: Second Reason

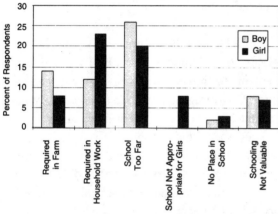

Second Main Reason for Not Attending School

Source: Oxford-AAU Survey, PHRD Study Number 1-A, 1996.

other household activities. School-related expenses and the distance from school are also important but less so, as reasons for not attending school (Figures 7.4a and 7.4b).

When the data set was disaggregated into two age groups, younger children (6–12 years) are considered "too young" to attend school, while older children (13–18 years) cited farm work and household duties as their primary reason for not attending school. Distance and expense were important secondary reasons.

Most rural students who dropped out of school did so because of conflicts between work and school (PHRD Study Number 1.b, 1996). In rural areas, 31 percent of all students quit due to agricultural work. Twice as many boys than girls in rural areas left school because of farm work. In urban areas, 32 percent withdrew from school due to poor scholastic performance, while 17 percent stated that they could no longer afford to go to school. These opportunity costs may, however, be partly or wholly offset to the extent that households perceive high real returns to their investments in education.

Perceived Returns to Schooling

Since education is a long-term investment, returns are generally not realized until many years after the cost has been incurred, thus the decision to invest today will depend upon expected future returns. The individual household's rate of return to schooling depends on the costs incurred, as well as the expected benefits of education.

There is some evidence from the literature of a positive effect of education on farmer productivity, though this is more likely to be the case in an innovative environment where farmers are modernizing than in traditional agriculture.[6] While farmers in rural Ethiopia do have the option of using new, higher-yield crop varieties and some modern inputs, such as fertilizer, farming methods are still quite traditional. It is therefore unlikely in general that households would *perceive* there

---

[6] See Lockheed, Jamison, and Lau (1980) for a discussion of a number of such studies. Cotlear (1989) used a natural experiment to illustrate the effect of education on farm productivity in Peru at different stages of modernization.

to be positive returns to schooling in traditional agriculture. However, an empirical analysis (PHRD Study Number 9.b, 1996) using data from households in North Showa, has shown that aside from farm size and family size, education significantly influenced household income in agriculture. In particular, the income (output) of a literate household head is 16 percent higher than that of an uneducated/illiterate household head.

Households may also recognize that there are higher returns to schooling from formal sector employment, particularly by those educated household members migrating to urban areas. Remittances from people who were educated at the expense of the household but who are no longer household members is also legitimately viewed as a return to education. In any case, the average earnings of educated individuals in Ethiopia are higher than the average earnings of the illiterate population (see Figure 7.5).

Results of surveys of civil servants, workers in a state-owned factory, and private enterprise employees (PHRD Study Number 9.b, 1996) sug-

gest that education and experience are significant determinants of formal sector wages. In contrast, in the informal sector the only significant determinant of wages is entrepreneur's level of capital. In the informal sector, skills are acquired though informal means (observing, assisting others, and through apprenticeship). Evidence in other countries suggests that those with basic numeracy and literacy skills fare better in the informal sector than those who lack these skills (PHRD Study Number 9.b, 1996).

A different type of return to education is that derived from continuing on to the next level of schooling. Rural school administrators who were interviewed suggest that disillusionment with the prospects of finding employment or admission to a postsecondary institution after graduation has caused parents to refrain from sending their children to school in recent years. The fact that girls are less likely to go to school than boys may also provide evidence of the importance of anticipated returns to the decision to send children to school. Since girls normally get married early and leave the household, most benefits from their education will accrue to the family into which they are married, so there is less incentive to invest in girls' schooling (PHRD Study Number 1.a, 1996). Moreover a study that compared the earnings of males and females that have the same educational attainments indicate that the former have higher average earnings than the latter (PHRD Study Number 9.b, 1996).

In summary, households do expect positive returns from schooling, although these gains are perceived to be more likely to accrue to those individuals who are employed in the formal sector in Ethiopia. Rural households that use traditional methods of farming do not perceive that they will benefit much from sending their children to school. This is compounded by their perception of limited prospects for further schooling (completing postsecondary education) and finding formal sector employment.

Figure 7.5 Comparison of Earnings by Educational Attainment in Ethiopia (in Birr)

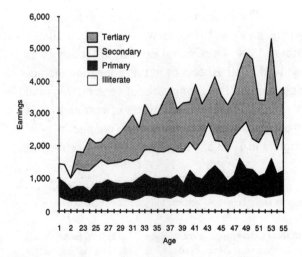

Source: PHRD Study No. 9b (Returns to Schooling), 1996.

Table 7.6   Regression Results: Socioeconomic Determinants of Enrollment, School Performance, and Education Expenditures

	Probability of Being Enrolled	Probability of Not Dropping Out	Probability of Being Promoted	Probability of Late Entry	Household Education Expenditures
Total Expenditures as a Proxy for Household Income	+	+	+	+	+
Education Level of Household Head	+	+	+	-	+
Female Head of Household	+	+	ns	ns	ns
Urban Area	+	+	+	-	+
Male Child	+	+	+	ns	ns
Distance to School	-	-	ns	ns	ns
Number of School-Age Children	+	+	+	ns	+
Both Parents of Child Residing in Same House as Child	+	ns	ns	+	ns

Source: HICE/WMS, PHRD Study Number 1.b, 1996.
ns = not significant.

Other Factors That Affect Household Demand for Schooling

Empirical results (Table 7.6) based on descriptive and regression analysis indicate that household per capita expenditures (as a proxy for household income) and the educational level of the household head are the two key factors that significantly affect the likelihood that children will be enrolled, enter primary school at the age of 7, stay in school, and be promoted.

The results also suggest that children are more likely to attend school and stay in school if: (1) they are males rather than females; (2) they live in urban areas rather than rural areas; and (3) they reside in households that: (a) have more school-aged siblings,[7] (b) are headed by females rather than males,[8] and (c) are located near primary and secondary schools. Distance significantly affects enrollment and dropout rates in rural areas.

SUPPLY-SIDE ASSESSMENT

This section reviews the current situation in the management, provision, and financing of education in Ethiopia and discusses the options for improving the education sector in line with the strategies outlined in the Education Sector Development Program (ESDP).

Management and Administration of the Education System

The Role of the Public Sector. Education management in Ethiopia was highly centralized prior to 1994. The Central Education Ministry was involved in all aspects of public education including planning, budgeting, school construction, and the production and distribution of textbooks and other educational materials. The change in government in 1993 and the shift to a federal structure

---

[7] One explanation for this is that an only child would not have any siblings to share household responsibilities with, thus decreasing her chances of going to school.

[8] This result is consistent with the general observation that mothers care more about the education of their children than fathers. Female heads may also view the education of their children as a means of escaping poverty (there are more female-headed households in the poorest quartile of the rural household sample). However, children whose parents both reside with them are also more likely to be enrolled and to enter primary school at the age of 7.

of administration resulted in the delegation of decisionmaking power to the regions. Mechanisms are in place that will devolve more responsibility and authority to lower administrative levels such as zones and woredas.

Five main managerial and administrative organs constitute the education sector: central, regional, zonal, woreda, and institutional. The powers and duties of the central and regional administrations are clearly defined by law (Table 7.7). The functions of the central Ministry of Education have been reduced to setting fundamental educational policy, broad educational planning and programming, maintaining standards and setting procedures for program implementation, and providing technical assistance where needed (PHRD Study Number 13, 1996; FDRE 1996). The responsibility for planning and executing primary and secondary educational development programs and projects falls on the regions. Regions are also responsible for the allocation and management of resources for primary and secondary schools, and for primary school teacher training. At the regional level, there is a high level of discretion over what resources are allocated to education, but at the subregional level there is less discretion. The zonal education department is directly accountable to the regional education bureau, and the woreda education office is accountable to the zonal education department. The woreda education office manages and controls resources allocated to schools in the woreda, and schools in the woreda are accountable to the woreda education office (EU, Public Expenditure Review 1996).

The Role of NGOs and the Private Sector.
A series of government regulations has been is-

sued at different times to govern NGOs and private educational institutions in Ethiopia.[9] A proclamation issued by the military government in 1975 outlawed the establishment of private schools and nationalized the existing ones. This and the policies of the succeeding government effectively reduced NGO and private school provision from about 30 percent of total institutional capacity in 1975 to only 6 percent in 1995. Given the recent reforms that the new government has introduced through ESDP, the participation of different stakeholders in the country has become even more welcome and important. Thus, it is likely that NGOs and the private sector will play an influential role in the future development of the educational sector in Ethiopia. The government recently issued regulation No. 206/1995 permitting the establishment of private schools.

There were about 286 primary schools with Grades 1–6, 185 junior secondary schools, and 32 senior secondary nongovernment schools in Ethiopia in 1996. In contrast, there were 1,502 private and NGO schools in 1975 (PHRD Study Number 13 1996).[10] Ten percent of the total number of primary students and 8.5 percent of the junior and secondary level students are enrolled in nongovernmental schools. Most of the kindergarten schools are run by communities or by missions. The government does not run kindergarten schools except for a few orphanages administered by the Ministry of Labor and Social Affairs. Only 1 percent or 70,255 of the estimated 5.3 million children of kindergarten age (4–6 years) have access to kindergarten schools.

More than 50 percent of the enrollment in privately operated primary schools is concentrated in Addis Ababa, and 60 percent of the junior

[9] In Ethiopia, the term NGO refers to the usual nonprofit organizations such as the Ethiopian Orthodox church and various missionary organizations, but also to private organizations established for profit.

[10] Estimates of NGO and private sector involvement might be understated since only officially registered institutions were considered for the survey study.

Table 7.7   Responsibilities for Education Management

Area of Responsibility	Ministry of Education	Regional Education Bureau	Zonal Education Department	Woreda Education Office
Policy	Proposed and contributes to national policy	Contributes to national policy and makes plans for region on basis of national policy		
Standard Setting	Sets standards	Implements standards	Implements standards	
Examinations	Prepares national examinations	Implements and supervises national exams		
Curriculum	Sets curriculum for secondary and higher education; assists in preparation of other school curricula	Prepares primary and junior secondary curriculum	Provides feedback and complements curriculum	Ensures implementation of curriculum in schools and provides feedback
Inspection		Inspects schools		
Teachers	Set standards and required qualifications; posts secondary teachers to regions	Pays teachers; recruits teachers and trains primary teachers	Pays primary teachers; offers in-service training	
Teaching and Learning Materials	Bulk procurement	Provides text books and materials	Distributes materials	
School Establishment	Establishes higher education institutions; licenses private higher institutions; sets standards for higher ed. institutions	Establishes schools and junior colleges; licenses private schools	Establishes schools and vocational training centers	
Data	Collate national school census data and assists in system development	Collates regional data	Compiles zonal data	Compiles woreda data

Source: EU PER 1996; Ministry of Education; and Region Education Bureau.
Note: The responsibilities of the different levels vary according to capacity and are evolving continually.

secondary enrollment in private schools is concentrated in Addis Ababa and Oromiya. Three-quarters of the remaining 40 percent enrolled in junior secondary schools are in Amhara and SNNP. Only five regions reported having NGO-operated senior secondary schools. Addis Ababa accounts for 45 percent of the enrollment while Oromiya and SNNP account for 48 percent of student enrollment at this level.

The Role of Communities. The proclamation on the strengthening of the management and administration of schools (Proclamation No. 260, 1991/92) stipulates that communities be involved in school affairs through the establishment of

Government and Community School Committees. Among the duties the proclamation vests on the committees are to ensure the observance of educational guidelines and directives issued by the Ministry of Education, and supervise the proper use of the school's and physical resources. The five-year ESDP also stipulates that local communities should be involved in the management of schools to ensure that schools provide appropriate education to children (FDRE 1996).[11]

The facility level survey (PHRD Study Number 16, 1996) confirmed that parent committees exist in most of the government schools. Across the regions, approximately 97 percent of the government schools surveyed have school committees. School committees are less common in nongovernmental schools at the primary level (69 percent) and nonexistent at the senior secondary level. There were no observable trends in the regional distribution of school committees.

Provision of Educational Facilities and Services

Facilities. The number of educational facilities significantly decreased during the long civil war in Ethiopia. Some were destroyed during the war and others, established in settlement villages, were destroyed as the population returned to their place of origin. Since the end of the war, the number of schools has increased. Between 1992 and 1995, the number of facilities increased by 14 percent, 12 percent, and 18 percent at primary, junior secondary, and senior secondary levels, respectively. By 1994, there were 678 kindergarten schools, 9,276 primary schools, 1,230 junior secondary schools, 330 senior secondary schools, 13 primary school teacher-training institutes, 17 colleges, and 2 universities operating in Ethiopia. Of these schools, 95 percent of the kindergarten schools, 5 percent of primary, 15 percent of junior secondary, and 9 percent of senior secondary were nongovernmental.

A typical rural or peri-urban primary school in Ethiopia consists of four to six classrooms in one or two blocks. These schools may vary in their quality of construction and condition. Most schools are constructed of either mud, wattle, or cement blocks and suffer from inadequate maintenance both inside and in the immediate environment outside.

Because of the relatively high increase in the enrollment of students and the insignificant in-

crease in facilities, particularly in urban areas, the number of students per classroom has been growing. The national norm set by the Ministry of Education for class size is 50 students for primary (1–8) and 40 for secondary (9–12) levels, while the actual class size in the 1994/95 academic year averaged 47 students in primary and 63 students in senior secondary classes (Ministry of Education 1996).

Textbooks. Most children have notebooks, but only a few have textbooks. Across Ethiopia, the current pattern of textbook distribution is 1 textbook to 2 students in primary schools, 1 textbook to 4 students in junior secondary schools, and 1 textbook to 6 students in senior secondary schools (PHRD Study Number 8, 1996). Considerable regional disparities exist in the number of textbooks available. Primary schools in Region 13 and 5 seem oversupplied, while there is shortage in Dire Dawa and Region 6. In junior secondary schools, textbooks are in short supply in Dire Dawa, the Southern Ethiopian People Region, Gambella, and Tigray. In senior secondary schools, the situation is alarming. While Region 5 is oversupplied (with 2 book copies per subject per student), some schools in Region 2 and Dire Dawa have only one book copy per subject for up to 121 pupils.

A facility-level survey (PHRD Study Number 16, 1996) found that of 295 schools surveyed, only 24 percent have adequate laboratories, 17 percent have auditoriums, and only 52 percent have a school library. More than 30 percent of the schools do not have water and electricity, and around 20 percent do not have toilets. Only 35 percent of the schools have a staff lounge, and 75 percent have a sports field.

The equipment and furniture in most schools in Ethiopia have been damaged by exces-

---

[11] In community schools, the parents' committees are mandated with additional duties and responsibilities, which include determining school fees, supervising the administration of the school, and administering aid and donations.

sive use without adequate maintenance. Many schools were not equipped with either furniture or other equipment right from the start. Maintenance capacity is either very limited or nonexistent. In a number of urban schools, 80 children or more are squeezed into poorly lit rooms designed for half that number, and many children do not have chairs or desks. The teachers provide instruction with only a chalk board as an aid. Over 60 percent of the schools surveyed did not have the equipment necessary for teaching social science, mathematics, handicrafts, and home economics. Thirty-three percent did not have sports equipment, while 27 percent did not have any agricultural equipment for instruction (Table 7.8).

Curriculum. Experts agree that the curricula at all levels in the Ethiopian school system before 1994 were either too impractical or too academic. Following the introduction of the new education and training policy, the Ministry of Education has embarked on a program of curricular reform. In preparation, guidelines have been created, staff who will either prepare the new curricula or use them (teachers) have been trained, and evaluation instruments have been developed.

The new curricula will emphasize the development of basic skills in literacy, numeracy, and communications, reduce emphasis on rote

Table 7.8 Unavailability of Teaching Materials in Schools

Teaching Materials	Not Available (Percent of Schools)
Science Equipment	42
Social Science Materials	62
Mathematical Equipment	61
Library Materials	71
Sport Materials	33
Agricultural Equipment	27
Handicraft Materials	73
Home Economics Materials	77

Source: PHRD Study Number 16, 1996.

learning, promote learning in the mother tongue in the first four grades of primary education, provide alternative methods for preparation for tertiary education, and develop a gender-sensitive learning environment.

The introduction of the new curricula is being accomplished step by step. New curricula for Grades 1, 2, 5, and 6 have been put into practice throughout the country. The curricula for Grades 3 and 7 are being tried out and put into practice in 1996/97. Complete revision of all curricula should be completed by the year 2000. The change in the curricula has been accompanied by the preparation of companion textbooks. Textbooks and teachers' guides for Grades 1 and 5 have been distributed to all primary schools. Textbooks and teachers' guides for Grades 2 and 6 have also been prepared and are being distributed. Those for Grades 3 and 7 are currently under preparation. All textbooks have been and will continue to be tried out before general distribution.

Teaching and Administrative Staff

The teachers at primary, junior secondary, and senior secondary levels are recruited from teacher training institutes (TTIs) as well as higher education institutions. Currently there are 13 primary school TTIs that could supply up to 7,350 new teachers every year if used to full capacity. Enrollment in the TTIs in 1994/95 was higher than in previous years, utilizing 88 percent of the total capacity. The average student-teacher ratio in the TTIs from 1992 to 1995 was 17:1, though the variation in this ratio is high. The TTIs are spread over 6 national administrative regions. The current policy of teaching in local languages at the primary level requires that at least one TTI be established in every region. The mismatch in both number and qualifications between the supply and demand for teachers in Ethiopia indicates the lack of an appropriate education manpower development strategy.

Teacher training is carried out in two forms, preservice and in-service training. Preservice training is a combination of academic schooling and specialized training provided before assignment as a teacher, whereas in-service training is provided to upgrade the knowledge and pedagogical skills of poorly qualified teachers and to enhance career development.

The Ministry of Education plans to establish new teacher training institutes and to upgrade some existing ones. In 1996/97, new teacher training programs were initiated at Addis Ababa University, Alemaya University, and Bahir Dar Teachers Institute for senior secondary schools. The Awassa, Gondar, and Jimma TTIs will be upgraded to college level for training teachers for upper primary schools (Grades 5–8).

The widely established qualifications of teachers in Ethiopia are graduation from teacher training institutes for primary school teachers and diploma- and degree-level training for junior and senior secondary school teachers. Nevertheless, a significant number of unqualified teachers are currently teaching in all three levels.

In 1993, only 85 percent of primary school teachers met the required qualifications. The rest were either untrained (10 percent) or had received only abbreviated training (5 percent). The situation at the junior and senior secondary levels was worse. The proportion of professionally trained teachers at the junior secondary level was only 52 percent. The remaining 48 percent had a certificate for lower grades or had no professional training. At the senior secondary level, only 37 percent of the teachers were qualified at the proper level of training. The remainder (63 percent) had no professional training.

Table 7.9 shows that 19,678 (20 percent) teachers out of 96,546 now teaching need professional training. In addition, the 3,375 primary school teachers have only short-term training and need further training. Training for unqualified teachers at all three levels is the obvious priority in designing further training programs for teachers.

The teaching force in primary and secondary education is relatively inexperienced and young. Fifty-four percent of the teachers in primary, 36 percent in junior secondary, and 42 percent in senior secondary schools had fewer than 10 years' experience in 1993/94. Those with 20 years' experience and above constituted only 6.5 percent at primary, 22 percent at junior secondary, and 19 percent at senior secondary levels.

Student-Teacher Ratios. The steady increase in the number of teachers at all levels of education has resulted in low average student-teacher ratios. In 1994/95 there were 83,113 teachers in primary, 11,544 in junior secondary, and 11,235 in senior secondary schools. Female teachers constituted 27 percent of the primary, 12 percent of junior secondary, and 9 percent of the senior secondary teaching force. Out of those teaching at the three levels, 6.3 percent of primary,

Table 7.9   Training Levels of Primary and Secondary School Teachers, 1993/94

Level of Education at Which Teaching	Required Level of Teacher Training	Professionally Trained at Required Level		Short-Term Training		Untrained or Lower Level than Required		Total	
		No.	Percent	No.	Percent	No.	Percent	No.	Percent
Primary	Certificate (T.T.I)	63,744	85.4	3,375	4.5	7,524	10.1	74,643	100
Jr. Secondary	Diploma	5,567	52.4	—	—	5,058	47.6	10,625	100
Sr. Secondary	B.A./B.Sc.	4,182	37.1	—	—	7,096	62.9	11,278	100

Source: PHRD Study Number 15, 1996.

12 percent of junior secondary, and 18 percent of senior secondary school teachers were teaching in nongovernment schools.

Teachers' salaries are the single greatest line item expenditure in education (in 1994/95 the salary bill made up 92 percent of primary school, 84 percent of secondary school and 58 percent of postsecondary education recurrent budget). Thus, the efficient use of teachers is critical. As noted, the Ministry of Education standard for student-teacher ratios in Ethiopia is 50:1 for primary and 40:1 for secondary levels. The average student teacher ratio in 1994/95 was 33:1 over all levels. There were also wide variations between the regions. The student-teacher ratio at primary school ranged between 21:1 in Somali to 51:1 in Addis Ababa. At the junior secondary level, Gambella had the highest ratio (62:1), followed by Addis Ababa (45:1). Afar has the lowest student-teacher ratio (13:1).

Administrative Staff. PHRD Study Number 15 (1996) analyzed data on administrative and general service staff, taking into account factors such as qualification, experience, age, and salary. Data were not available for two regions (Regions 2 and 12).

Most of the 10,933 staff in the sample (Regions 2 and 12 not included) had low qualifications. Staff with an education of Grade 8 and below and those with Grade 9–12 qualification comprised 39 percent and 26 percent of the total administrative staff, respectively. Thus, the majority (65 percent) have attained educational levels of less than or equal to Grade 12. The staff with diploma or degree qualifications make up a small percentage (11 percent) of the total. Twenty-one percent are graduates from teacher training institutions, and the remaining 3 percent are dropouts from higher education institutions.

Thirty-seven percent of the administrative staff have fewer than 10 years of experience, and

39 percent have between 10 to 19 years of service. The majority (64 percent) of the staff are below the age of 40. Approximately 56 percent receive a monthly salary of 299 Birr or less, 42 percent receive salaries of Birr 300–699, and only 2 percent get a monthly salary of Birr 700 or above.

COSTS AND FINANCING OF EDUCATION

This section will discuss the three most important issues of education cost and financing: (1) sources and uses of funds, (2) alternative sources for financing education, and (3) efficiency in the use of those funds.

Sources and Uses of Funds

The major sources of funds for education in Ethiopia are the government, households, and external loans and assistance. The relative importance of these sources depends on whether the expenditures are recurrent or capital expenditures.

Resource flows to education in 1994/95 were estimated to be about Birr 1.4 billion. Of this, 64 percent was obtained from the central and regional governments' treasury, 22 percent from households, and 14 percent from external sources (see Figure 7.6). As shown in Table 7.10, share

Figure 7.6   Sources of Funds for the Education Sector, 1994/95

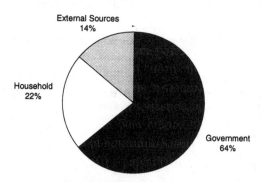

Source: PHRD Study Number 6, 1996.

Table 7.10   Sources of Financing for Education in Government Schools, 1995/96 (in 000 Birr)

Source	Recurrent Costs	Percent	Capital Costs	Percent	Total	Percent
Government	790,051	81	187,600	48	977,651	71
Households	186,692	19	—	0	186,692	14
External Loans	—	0	189,289	48	189,289	14
External Assistance	—	0	16,994	4	16,994	1
Subtotal	976,743	100	393,883	100	1,370,626	100
Percent of Total		71		29		100

Source: PHRD Study Number 5, 1996.

estimates of funding sources for education are roughly same for 1995/96, although the government's share increased to 71 percent and households appeared to contribute less at 14 percent.[12] The sources of funding for the recurrent budget were the government (81 percent) and households (19 percent), in the form of education fees. Capital costs were almost equally divided between government (48 percent) and external loans (48 percent), with the balance provided by external assistance. Overall, 71 percent of education expenditures are on recurrent costs, with the remaining 29 percent designated to capital costs.

Public Spending on Education

Total spending on education varied between 2.5 percent and 3.8 percent of GDP from 1990/91 to 1995/96, increasing in real value over that period. The increases reflect the end of the war and subsequent reallocation away from military expenditures (Table 7.11).

During the same five-year period, total public spending on education increased in real terms, from 5.5 percent of the public budget in 1990 to 11.4 percent in 1994. It increased to 13.8

Table 7.11   Total Education Budget as a Share of GDP and Total Public Budget, 1990/91–1995/96 (in Birr million)

Year	GDP		Total Public Budget		Total Education Budget		Total Education Budget Percentage of		
	Nominal	Real	Nominal	Real	Nominal	Real	GDP	Public Budget	Index[a]
1990/91	19,852	12,031	9,202	5,577	490	297	2.5	5.3	165
1991/92	20,394	11,205	5,673	3,117	528	290	2.6	9.3	182
1992/93	26,394	13,965	5,932	3,138	694	367	2.6	11.7	189
1993/94	27,397	13,978	8,447	4,310	1,034	527	3.8	12.2	196
1994/95	32,065	—	9,966	—	1,145	—	3.6	11.4	—
1995/96	—	—	9,667	—	1,337	—	—	13.8	—

Source: PHRD Study Number 5, 1996.

---

[12] Financing by households is based on household survey results. The survey was done when the school term was ending and educational budgets at a minimum. Households had difficulty recalling the actual amount they paid to educate their children. Because of this, the survey is believed to have captured only part of the household expenditures on education.

percent in 1995. To put these figures in an inter-national context, successful stories of educational reform show that a commitment of 5 percent or higher of GDP and 15 to 20 percent of the national budget are recommended.

Recurrent Budget. The public sector edu-cation budget consists of roughly 70 percent re-current and 30 percent capital costs. Personnel salaries and allowances, constituting 80 percent of total recurrent costs, are by far the largest single expenditure, followed by nonpersonnel services, grants, and materials. The higher share of person-nel salaries and allowances in the primary level recurrent budget suggests that increasing effi-ciency in the use of resources must be a high pri-ority (Figure 7.7).

About 55 percent of the 1994/95 recurrent budget was allocated to primary, 13 percent to jun-ior secondary, 12 percent to senior secondary, and 10 percent to higher education.[13] The remaining 10 percent was allocated to administration and

Figure 7.7 Allocation of Primary School Recurrent Expenditures

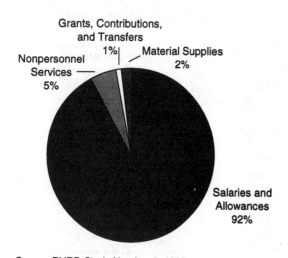

Source: PHRD Study Number 5, 1996.

Figure 7.8 Allocation of Recurrent Budget by Education Level

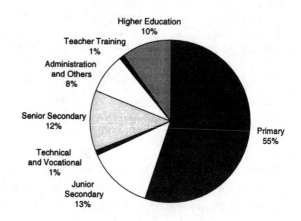

Source: PHRD Study Number 5, 1996.

common services, primary school teacher train-ing, and technical and vocational training (see Figure 7.8).

Regional Recurrent Budget. Since 1991/92, institutions of higher learning have been managed by the Ministry of Education, while institutions of primary and secondary education are admin-istered by the regional governments. The central government provides a lump sum subsidy to the regions, and the regions in turn decide on the dis-tribution of the budget among the various levels of education.

Nearly 14 percent of total public expen-ditures were allocated to education in 1995/96. The central Ministry of Education allocated 4.3 percent of its total budget to the mainly higher educational institutions that it manages. The per-centage shares allocated to the various regions ranged from 15 percent to Addis Ababa to 32 percent to Oromiya.

---

[13] It is difficult to assign every expenditure to a level of education, since some costs are common to all levels. There is no accurate method of apportioning the indirect costs incurred in administration, curriculum development and supervision, or repair and maintenance to the levels of schooling.

Per capita allocations vary widely among regions. For example, Oromiya and Amhara allocated 31 percent and 28 percent, respectively, of their total budgets to education, but Gambella, which allocated less than 20 percent of its total budget to education, had a per capita allocation that was more than five times greater than those of Oromiya and Amhara. This would suggest that population size or better still, school-age population size should be accounted for in budget allocations. On average, regions allocated 27 percent of their 1995/96 total budget to education, but there are striking regional variations in the recurrent budget allocation to different educational levels. The Amhara region spent about 69 percent on primary education while Addis Ababa spent 40 percent. Regions that spent above average—that is, over 55 percent—on primary education were Amhara, Benishangul, Oromia, SNNPR, Afar, Harari, Tigray, and Gambella. Regions that spent

less than the national average on primary education spend more on junior and senior secondary schools. Addis Ababa spent about 49 percent on junior and senior secondary education while Dire Dawa spent 36 percent. Regions spent about 6 percent of their total education budget on administration and other common services. However, regions like Harari, Tigray, Benishangul, and SNNPR spent much more than the average. Approximately 86 percent of regional recurrent expenditures were allocated to personnel expenses (teacher and administrative salaries). With the exception of Dire Dawa, the rest of the regions spent at least 80 percent of their recurrent budget on personnel. Addis Ababa spent at least 95 percent of its regional recurrent budget on this particular line item (Table 7.12).

Total budget allocated by regions per enrolled student varied from Birr 2,080 in Afar to

Table 7.12   Allocation of Government Recurrent and Capital Budget for Education by Region, 1994/95 (percent)

| | | Purpose of Expenditure (Line Items) | | | | | | | | | | | |
| | | Recurrent | | | | | | Capital | | | | | |
No.	Region	Personnel Services	Non-personnel Services	Material Supplies	Grants, Contrib., Transfers	Purch. of Motor Vehicle & Equipment	Total	Bldg., Other Const.	Equipment	Furniture	Taxes	Financial Costs[a]	Other	Total
1	National	82.2	8.0	6.2	1.9	1.7	100.0	66.0	11.9	6.2	7.9	4.4	3.6	100.0
2	Central	52.0	21.0	20.6	4.2	2.2	100.0	38.4	14.6	3.5	23.2	12.3	8.0	100.0
3	Regional	86.5	6.2	4.1	1.6	1.6	100.0	77.5	10.8	7.4	1.5	1.1	1.7	100.0
3.1	Tigray	80.1	8.3	6.3	3.7	1.6	100.0	72.7	21.7	3.8	0.5	0.3	1.0	100.0
3.2	Affar	94.6	1.8	1.6	1.4	0.6	100.0	76.6	9.0	10.6	2.3	1.5	0.0	100.0
3.3	Amhara	85.2	7.1	4.0	1.6	2.1	100.0	76.7	6.1	9.9	1.4	0.7	5.2	100.0
3.4	Oromiya	86.3	6.7	3.9	1.5	1.6	100.0	83.6	7.9	6.8	0.7	0.6	0.4	100.0
3.5	Somalia	90.6	2.2	5.2	1.7	0.3	100.0	80.5	13.0	5.3	0.9	1.1	(0.8)	100.0
3.6	B. Shangul/ Gumuz	81.4	5.3	9.5	2.1	1.7	100.0	71.7	12.5	5.2	3.2	2.8	4.6	100.0
3.7	SNNPR	84.8	6.6	4.6	2.1	1.9	100.0	76.6	10.6	8.1	2.5	2.0	0.2	100.0
3.8	Gambella	84.1	5.3	6.2	3.3	1.1	100.0	74.0	6.7	10.8	2.0	1.3	5.2	100.0
3.9	Harari	89.3	4.7	3.8	0.2	2.0	100.0	83.8	10.8	4.1	0.8	0.5	0.0	100.0
3.10	Addis Ababa	95.4	2.3	2.0	0.1	0.2	100.0	86.1	1.6	10.1	1.6	0.5	0.0	100.0
3.11	Dire Dawa	78.9	9.3	7.0	2.8	2.0	100.0	83.6	2.8	9.2	1.5	0.3	2.6	100.0

a. Interest, commission, insurance, etc.
Source: PHRD Study Number 5, 1996, using data from Ministry of Economic Development and Cooperation and Ministry of Finance.

Birr 243 in SNNPR. The average allocation per student for all regions is Birr 337. Regions that have the highest percentage of enrollment spent more of their total budget on recurrent costs while those with fewer students spent more on capital infrastructure. One explanation for this pattern of spending is that regions that have smaller student populations are trying to increase enrollments by building more schools.

Capital Expenditures. The proportion of capital expenditures in total educational expenditures has increased in real terms at all levels of education over the last 10 years. For example, amounts spent on primary education increased from an average of 26 percent to 37 percent, and on secondary education increased from 18 percent to 29 percent.

The total national capital budget allocation for education in 1995/96 was 63 percent for buildings and other construction, 20 percent for equipment, and 8 percent for furniture. Institutions reporting to the Ministry of Education allocated slightly over 38 percent for buildings and other construction. The regions, on average, allocated 60 percent of their capital budgets for this purpose. In contrast, the regions' 1994/95 capital budget for education was apportioned 77.5 percent for building and other construction; 10 percent for equipment, and 7 percent for furniture. Both Tigray and Benshangul-Gumuz spent less than average on buildings and more on equipment. Among those who spent well above 80 percent of their capital budget on buildings and other construction are Addis Ababa, Harari, Dire Dawa, and Oromiya (Table 7.12). These percentages, however, do not reflect the sometimes considerable nongovernmental institutions' capital expenditures.

Household Contributions (Tuition). Although educational costs have always been largely covered by the government, parents have until recently been required to pay registration fees for their children in Grades 1 to 10. In addition, they purchase

or rent the necessary learning materials. Households spend an average of Birr 4.93 per month on education (PHRD Study Number 1.b, 1996).

As shown in Table 7.13, household contributions make up a larger source of funding for nongovernment schools (25 percent) than for government schools (7 percent). In nongovernmental schools, incomes come mainly from tuition and registration fees. Survey results (PHRD Study Number 16, 1996) indicate that 80 percent of nongovernmental schools collect registration fees, 58 percent collect textbook fees, and 50 percent collect sports fees (see Table 7.14). The tuition fees charged by the nongovernment schools range from 80 Birr to 489 Birr, according to the educational level.

Household contributions are also an important source of funds for government schools. Among the government schools surveyed (PHRD Study Number 16, 1996), 93 percent collect registration fees, 81 percent collect textbook fees, and 84 percent collect sports fees. Other fees are also charged when specific needs arise and are strictly school administered. Outside of textbook fees, none of these other fees are approved by the central authorities.

Fees charged by nongovernment schools are higher than those charged by government schools. Foreign communities and other organizations run schools that charge much higher fees than those reported. Both government and nongovernment schools also grant fee exemptions based on means tests.

Stability of Funding Sources

Education is largely financed by the government. Households also contribute to education, although most of their contributions are not officially reflected in government revenues, except revenues generated from textbooks sales and rentals. Proceeds from research work undertaken by a limited

Table 7.13   Source of Finances as Reported by Schools

Source of Finance	Type of School	
	Government	Nongovernment
Government Budget Allocation	90.0	71.1[a]
Students Fees and Contributions	7.1	25.6
School Internal Revenue	1.6	2.3
Community Contributions	0.7	0.1
Other Income	0.6	1.0
Total	100.0	100.0

a. Not all government schools receive subsidies from the government; only nationalized (community schools) schools get subsidies.
Source: Computed from data in PHRD Study Number 16, 1996.

Table 7.14   Breakdown of Fees Collected from Households by Government and Nongovernment Schools

Does your school collect the following fees from students?	Government Schools		Nongovernment Schools	
	No. of Schools Interviewed	% of Yes Responses	No. of Schools Interviewed	% of Yes Responses
Tuition Fees	228	6	40	68
Registration Fee	249	93	40	80
Construction Fee	226	5	40	30
Maintenance Fee	224	5	40	3
Instructional Material Fee	223	12	40	13
Textbook Fee	241	81	40	58
Uniform Fee	225	7	40	8
Sports Fee	242	84	40	58
Other Fee	243	16	40	10

Source: PHRD Study Number 16, 1996.

number of higher education institutions are reported as revenue.

Unlike recurrent expenditures on education, capital expenditures on education are partly covered by loans and grant assistance. The share coming from the central treasury was over 47 percent for 1995/96. Loans and assistance accounted for 48 percent and 4 percent, respectively, of recurrent expenditures.

The main funding source for recurrent expenditures is the central treasury, while capital expenditures are from the central treasury, loans, and assistance.

Figure 7.9 shows that the share of capital expenditures financed from combining foreign loans

and assistance (43 percent and 42 percent, respectively) in 1990/91 and 1991/92 exceeded 80 percent while by 1994/95 this combined share declined to about 46 percent, increasing slightly in 1995/96 to 52 percent. These fluctuations reflect the highly unstable nature of external loans and assistance.

Alternative Domestic Sources of Financing

For 1997–2001, the ESDP has proposed reforms that will cost Birr 12,252 million (US$1.96 billion), nearly twice the current spending for education. Of this amount, Birr 8,877 million will be financed by domestic sources, leaving a deficit of Birr 3,375 million. Most of this financial burden will fall on the government. If foreign grants or loans are not forthcoming, alternative domestic sources of

Figure 7.9 Trends in Sources of Government Capital Expenditures on Education

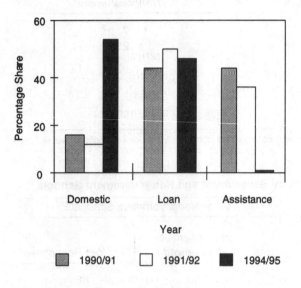

Source: PHRD Study Number 5, 1996.

Table 7.15 Percentage of Different Income Groups Benefiting from Education

Total Monthly Household Expenditure (in Birr)	Percentage of Households Sending Their Children to School	Average Monthly Household Expenditures on Education (in Birr)
0–50	5.8	4.50
51–100	7.4	5.46
101–200	7.9	11.12
201+	8.1	31.65

Source: PHRD Study Number 5, 1996.

financing will have to be devised. Two such alternatives are (1) cost recovery or cost sharing and (2) increasing the nongovernmental flow of resources to education.

Cost Recovery/Cost Sharing. The government's new policy eliminating fees of any kind in Grades 1–10 is intended to address the problem of equitable access to education, but it will deprive schools of one of their current sources of funding. Until 1996, government schools obtained approximately 10 percent of their revenues from student fees, contributions from parents and the community, and other private sources (PHRD Study Number 5, 1996).

Although public spending on primary education generally favors the poor, public spending on secondary and tertiary education appears to favor the affluent. As shown in Table 7.15, higher-income households (8.1 percent) have more children in school than the lowest-income level households (5.8 percent).

Total public spending seems biased against the poor because public spending per student on tertiary education is much higher than public spending per student in primary and secondary education. About 50 percent of total public recurrent expenditure on education is for primary education and 25 percent is for secondary education. While these proportions have remained stable since 1975, the recurrent budget for tertiary education has risen fivefold since 1975 (Birr 17 million to Birr 84 million in 1994). About 64 percent of the recurrent budget for tertiary education is allocated to the Addis Ababa University, which has 59 percent of the total tertiary education enrollment (FDRE 1996).

The high cost of tertiary education and the disproportionate spending on this sector in relation to enrollment rates raises some fundamental questions about further public investment in tertiary education and the possible stimulation of private investment through the introduction of cost-recovery policies.

PHRD studies have shown that the ability and willingness to pay for education exists at all levels but especially at the tertiary level. Thus while there is an opportunity for modest cost recovery at the primary and secondary levels, there is a strong case for cost recovery at the tertiary level. However, the fact that there are insufficient tertiary level facilities to accommodate the potential number of students is a barrier to increased enrollments and consequent cost recovery.[14] The government must also continue to guarantee that qualified but poor students have access to basic education through scholarships or loans.

Increase Nongovernment Share of Resource Flows to Education. The new education policy commits the government to creating the necessary conditions for increased private sector investments in education. The objective of this policy is to "provide choice for education service seekers who have the ability to pay." Households who can afford to pay are expected to send their children to private schools.

Private investors who have already expressed an interest in investing in education have encountered some difficulties (PHRD Study Number 13, 1996). For instance, the amount of land required to build schools is relatively large compared with that needed to create other businesses with similar amounts of capital. The required sizes for classrooms, playgrounds, and parking make private investments in education unprofitable. In addition, private investors are hoping for incentives from the government such as exemptions on duties imposed on imported school materials, favorable lending terms, and tax exemptions on profits earned.

Cost Efficiency

Better management and efficiency of existing resources could significantly reduce the amount of new funding that needs to be generated for the education sector.

Public Spending and Outcomes. Public spending on education in Africa, which has the lowest enrollment ratios of any region in the world, is higher as a percentage of GNP (4.2 per-

cent) than either East Asia (3.4 percent) or Latin America (3.7 percent), regions that have achieved largely universal primary education (World Bank 1996a).

There is no theoretically correct proportion of GNP or public spending that should be devoted to education. Some countries (such as those in East Asia) have been able to improve education with the same or even reduced public spending, by focusing public spending on the lower levels of education and increasing its internal efficiency. Other countries have shown that results dramatically improve simply by increasing the level of public spending.

A cross-country comparison in Figure 7.10 shows that there is a positive relationship between GERs and total expenditure in education as a percentage of GDP (a proxy for the level of effort that a country gives in order to have a good education system). Ethiopia, with a near average

Figure 7.10   International Comparison of Education Expenditures and Primary School Enrollments

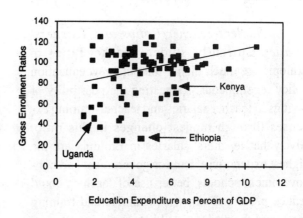

Source: Gargiulo 1996, based on data from World Bank, World Development Report.

[14] Only 10 percent of the 30 percent of students who pass the Ethiopian School Leaving Certificate Exam are accepted in tertiary level schools.

budgetary effort, has one of the lowest primary GERs in the world (29 percent in 1995/96), well below the trend line that would predict a primary level GER closer to 90 percent. Thus, although Ethiopia can increase the budget share of education, its more important task is to improve efficiency. Improved efficiency implies being able to enroll more students with the same budget without sacrificing the quality of education.

What are some areas where efficient management of resources can make a difference? There are currently inefficient mixes of educational inputs, such as staff and instructional materials. This results in slow learning, high repetition rates, and high dropout rates. While input combinations may vary slightly according to local conditions, broad guidelines can be developed on the basis of international, interregional, and interschool comparisons. Modest increases in student-teacher ratios can also improve education if the resources saved are reallocated to other critical inputs such as textbooks. School buildings can serve their purpose more effectively if adequate maintenance funding is assured. Double-shifting can make better use of existing capital resources and, in the short term, will minimize the need for constructing more classrooms.

Student-Teacher Ratios and Teachers' Salaries. Currently, student-teacher ratios in Ethiopia are much higher than the new education policy recommends, suggesting the possibility of savings in teacher salaries and teacher-training expenses through modest changes in this ratio. Given that teachers' salaries in Ethiopia are the highest expenditure item for government and nongovernment schools, better use of teachers could reduce personnel expenses (salaries and training cost), and the savings could be reallocated to improve the education sector.

Nongovernment schools spend more than government schools on other running costs, such as instructional materials, and less on teacher salaries.

Table 7.16 Comparison of Reported School Running Costs, Government and Nongovernment (percent)

Line Items	Government Schools	Non-government Schools	Both
Salaries	91.3	62.5	85.9
Running Costs	2.3	14.6	4.6
Fixed Costs	1.1	7.6	2.3
Instructional Materials	2.2	2.0	2.0
Other Expenses	3.3	13.3	5.2
Total	100.0	100.0	100.0

Source: PHRD Study Number 13, 1996.

When the allocations of recurrent costs of government and nongovernment schools are compared, teachers' salaries are costly for both (Table 7.16). However, nongovernment schools allocate only 62 percent of their total annual recurrent expenditures to teachers' salaries while government schools allocate 91 percent of theirs. Running costs and other expenses for nongovernmental schools are about 6 and 4 times as much, respectively, relative to those incurred by government schools. NGO schools also have higher student-teacher ratios. In 1992/93, student-teacher ratios in nongovernment schools were 47:1 in primary, 48:1 in junior secondary, and 20:1 in senior secondary schools. In government schools, the ratios were 25:1, 30:1, and 33:1, respectively (Ministry of Education 1994).

In spite of the large share of the education budget that is spent on teacher salaries, teacher morale is low because of an inappropriate salary and merit structure that lacks incentives. Ethiopia employs a uniform salary scale for primary school teachers and a different one for secondary school teachers. In this system, a teacher's pay depends on educational credentials and years of experience, not on the quality of teacher's performance, the subject being taught, the working conditions in the school, or the living conditions in the area.

Thus all teachers earn the same salary for a given level of training, irrespective of performance. While a new salary scale has recently been introduced that is expected to improve teacher morale, this fundamental flaw has yet to be corrected.

Double-Shifting. Double-shifting entails compressing a school "day" into half of a day, using six 40-minute periods. Two separate sessions are held, one in the morning and one in the afternoon, in order to share school facilities. In 1994/95, in seven regions of the country, about 25 percent of primary, 40 percent of junior secondary, and 42 percent of senior secondary schools were operating in double shifts. As one might expect, schools in more urbanized regions were more likely to resort to double shifts. For example, 83 percent and 73 percent of primary schools in Harari and Addis Ababa regions operated on a double shift system, while only 15 percent of primary schools in Oromiya did.

Some educators argue that the double-shift system has a negative influence on the quality of education since teaching time is likely to be reduced. However, there is evidence to suggest the contrary. For example, early studies in Malaysia, Chile, and Senegal (Beebout, 1972; Farrell and Schiefelbern, 1974; and Colclough and Lewin 1993) showed that the move to double-shift teaching was not associated with a decline in educational quality.

Language of Instruction. The new education and training policy also allows for diversity in language of instruction in Grades 1–4. It has been found that a child can adapt better to school life and to academics if the language that is spoken at home is also used in school. To date, about 19 ethnic groups have begun using their language in school instruction. Others are expected to follow suit.

English is and will continue to be used as the medium of instruction at the secondary and tertiary levels. The shift from local language instruction toward English as a medium of instruction has created difficulties for both teachers and students and underscores the need for better preparation of primary students in the English language.

The language policy also has cost implications in terms of textbook production. Primary school textbooks will be published in 19 different local languages and scripts. This increases the complexity of the publishing operation and significantly increases costs through increased origination costs and smaller print run sizes. On the other hand, these costs might be less than the benefits gained from better school performance by young students. These benefits and costs should be carefully weighed. If the language policy continues, more thought must be given to how to make the transition from local languages toward English less difficult for both students and instructors.

Textbook Production and Distribution. Developing economies typically allocate a very small proportion of their budget to teaching resources such as books, maps, and visual aids. Industrial countries allocate 14 percent of primary school recurrent costs to classroom resources (books, teaching aids, furniture, etc.), whereas the average in Asia is 9 percent and in Africa 4 percent (Heyneman 1981). Ethiopia spends only 2.2 percent of its education budget on textbooks.

The Educational Materials Production and Distribution Agency (EMPDA) is responsible for the production and distribution of textbooks and other teaching materials for all primary and secondary educational institutions. There is some evidence that the true production costs of the EMPDA are not as low as they are reported to be. As "there is no system with EMPDA for assessing full costs of production" (USAID/Ethiopia 1994), it is quite possible that overhead, capital costs (hidden costs), and indirect subsidies (tax exemptions) are not fully accounted for. In fact, the enterprise imputes overhead and capital costs at a rate of 25 percent of the material and labor costs expended in production. Commercial enterprises, unlike the EMPDA, impute these costs at a rate ranging from 31 to 40 percent of their total production costs. If these more realistic rates were applied to the EMPDA, the unit cost of producing a textbook would rise as high as Birr 1.91. This is significant, when compared with the average unit costs of textbooks for primary, junior secondary, and senior secondary schools of Birr 0.76, Birr 0.70, and Birr 1.44, respectively. A system of competitive bidding for textbook production with private publishers could be established by leveling the playing field and removing EMPDA's subsidies, rent, and tax privileges.

PROGRAM IMPLICATIONS IN THE EDUCATION SECTOR

Demand analysis produces a bleak picture of education for the typical Ethiopian household in rural areas. Opportunity costs of schooling are high, and as a result most children do not attend school despite the positive attitudes toward schooling that were expressed by surveyed households. The children who do attend school are mostly overaged and ill prepared for the classroom. Dropout and repetition rates are high. Children are frequently taken out of school to work in the farm or home. The returns to schooling are perceived to be low although they are actually high based on estimates by the World Bank (1998).

In the short run, policies that minimize the opportunity costs of schooling are recommended:
- changes in the school calendar to provide breaks from classes that allow children to help in planting and harvesting;
- more schools closer to the communities even if they are smaller than the government's quality

standards for the size and number of classrooms;
- reduced time demands of schooling through, for example, use of double-shift class schedules when there are enough students to make this an efficient strategy;
- more relevant curriculum, including an upgraded and more flexible technical and vocational education curriculum capable of absorbing school leavers;
- improvements in and expansion of electricity and communications infrastructure to facilitate the increased use of mass media for "distance learning;"
- alternative teaching centers and methods for reaching pastoralist populations;
- cross-sectoral programs and activities with the goal of reaching more people with minimum demands on their time, for example, early childhood development.

In the long term, the general goal of education policies in Ethiopia should be to make the returns to schooling more known and visible to households. Economic growth is also likely to result in the expansion of the formal sector, which itself will serve as an incentive to acquire more education. As a more educated workforce becomes increasingly more capable of working with higher-level technologies, a cycle of economic growth is ensured.

Financial constraints underscore the need for increased private investment and participation in education. While the government has acknowledged the importance of involving the private sector in the provision of education services, a number of its policies discourage private investment:
- standards set for building and classroom size are often big and costly for smaller private investors;
- inadequate tax breaks and import tax exemptions;
- bureaucratic bottlenecks (PHRD Study Number 13, 1996);

- lack of government recognition of schools run by NGOs that are found in remote, rural, and typically undeserved areas;

The no-fee policy until Grade 10 in government schools may need to be reexamined in order to take into account two important realities. First, schools might experience substantial loss in incomes. Second, most households are willing to contribute to their children's education either in cash or in kind. Thus, fees could be reinstated, but fee exemptions should be granted to poor students.

The following issues, most of which are under consideration by the government, have implications for the efficiency of the education sector:

- Language policy has cost and efficiency implications. The unit production cost of textbooks based on EMPDA reports rises from Birr 1.45 to Birr 3.30 as print run is reduced from 60,000 to 1,500. Currently elementary school textbooks are to be published in 19 different local languages and different scripts. It is also likely that additional languages of instruction will be introduced within the next few years. This will increase the complexity of the publishing operation and increase costs still more. Moreover, if there are insufficient teachers in a particular region then teacher training costs will increase to ensure that enough teachers are trained in a specific local language. Benefits and costs of language policy need to be compared. If the language policy is to remain, then more thought needs to be given to how to efficiently deploy teachers and how to improve the transition from local language instruction to English for students who will proceed beyond primary schooling.

- Multiple shifts have the dual advantage of increasing enrollments and reducing per student cost. By organizing separate class sessions (morning and afternoon) and by having teachers share facilities, twice as many students can be accommodated, and savings can be realized on capital and recurrent costs. Substantial economies of scale in the use of land, physical facilities, and equipment can be achieved.

- Distance learning could be used as an alternative form of instruction for older children and for upgrading teacher skills.

- Multigrade teaching for schools with small class sizes needs to be considered, particularly in sparsely populated areas.

- Student-teacher ratios should be increased and a program for upgrading the skills and qualifications of existing teachers should be implemented.

8

IMPLICATIONS OF FINDINGS
ON THE PROPOSED HEALTH AND EDUCATION
SECTOR DEVELOPMENT PROGRAMS

The Federal Democratic Republic of Ethiopia presented its proposed Education and Health Sector Development Programs (ESDP and HSDP, respectively) at the Consultative Group Meeting of Donors in Addis Ababa in December 1996. These proposals reflect the strong commitment of the government to improve social services in Ethiopia. During the next five years, the ESDP will emphasize the expansion of primary education, quality improvements, and a more equitable distribution of opportunities in order to promote gender equality and address regional imbalances. The HSDP will emphasize the preventive and promotive aspects of health care while not neglecting essential curative services. The more specific goals of the two programs are outlined in Boxes 8.1 and 8.2.

The cost of the five-year ESDP is Birr 12,251 million (US$1.83 billion), of which Birr 3,374 million was unfunded (US$505.8 million). Assuming modest growth in the private sector, Birr 3,024 million (US$453 million) was sought as external assistance. The cost of the five-year HSDP is Birr 4,995 million (US$748 million) of which Birr 2,167 million (US$323 million) was unfunded.

In March 1997 a joint government and donor Sector Investment Program workshop was held in Debre Zeit, Ethiopia. The workshop was a continuation of the Consultative Group Meeting held in Addis in December 1996. Discussions took place regarding the strengths of the two programs,

---

Box 8.1. Goals of the Education Sector Development Program, 1997–2001

The new education policy adopted in 1994 focuses on the development of education over a 20-year program. From 1997 to 2001, the program has the following monitorable objectives:

- expand access by raising primary enrollments from 3.1 to 7 million, and achieve an average gross enrollment ratio of 50 percent for primary education;
- improve quality by extending the new curriculum to all levels of the system, increasing the number of certified primary teachers from 85 percent to 95 percent, and lower the textbook ratio at the primary level from 5:1 to 1:1;
- increase efficiency by the more effective use of teachers, with a 50:1 student- to-teacher ratio and raising the overall efficiency level, reflecting the number of dropouts and repeaters, from 60 percent to 80 percent;
- improve equity by achieving a gross enrollment ratio for primary education of at least 25 percent in underserved regions, raise the female participation share in primary schools from 38 percent to 45 percent, and increase the share of female teachers from 25 percent to 35 percent;
- increase financing for education by raising public expenditure on education to 4.6 percent of GDP, achieving a target of 5 percent of new school construction owned by nongovernment institutions, and introducing cost sharing at the tertiary level.

as well as donor concerns about certain program assumptions and strategies. The workshop was highly successful in generating support for the two programs. As a result, the funding gap for the HSDP was entirely covered while the funding gap for ESDP was reduced to approximately US$133 million. More important, the workshop set the stage for further dialogue and cooperation between the government and donors. Three joint multidonor missions for ESDP have taken place, while the third multidonor mission for HSDP is under preparation. In partnership with the FDRE, these missions have been successful in helping refine the technical components of both SDPs.

OVERALL ASSESSMENT

The two programs clearly reflect the government's commitment to improve the education and health sectors in Ethiopia. They also represent major attempt to involve all stakeholders, under the coordination and guidance of the government. There is general agreement that well-coordinated sector investment programs will reduce the workload of ministries and local government authorities concerned. The SDPs show a clear understanding of the problems in both sectors despite the supply-side focus of most of the proposed interventions. Their developmental objectives are sound and benefit from a good policy framework. In particular, the education program emphasizes primary education but calls for additional investments in all other levels of education. In health, the emphasis is on primary health care but with additional and more cost- effective investments in curative care as well.

In the discussions with the FDRE, the joint multidonor missions pointed out that the strengths of the programs could be enhanced if certain key issues are addressed. One major issue discussed was the insufficient attention given to demand-side analysis. In particular, will the pro-

---

> **Box 8.2. Goals of the Health Sector Development Program, 1997–2001**
>
> - emphasis on improved access to preventive health care services, increasing coverage from 45 percent to 70 percent by 2001
> - improved technical quality of preventive health care services
> - improved health systems management
> - improved financial sustainability of the health sector
> - greater private sector investment in the health sector
> - restructuring of the pharmaceutical sector
> - development of an information, education, and communication plan to communicate PHC messages to isolated areas
> - expansion in the supply and productivity of health personnel
> - strengthened local capacity in evaluation, research, and development planning

vision of more facilities be enough to increase enrollment rates and health facility utilization rates? The findings of the PHRD studies clearly indicate that additional factors would need to be taken into account in order to realize the targets set by the SDPs. Both programs are comprehensive and will require substantial resources and implementation capacity. Thus issues concerning the financial and implementation feasibility within the proposed five-year period were also discussed. Third, in view of these constraints, discussions also focused on what can realistically be done given available resources and existing opportunities? In particular, how can the private sector and communities be more actively engaged in sectoral planning and service provision?

ISSUES FOR EDUCATION AND HEALTH SECTOR DEVELOPMENT PROGRAMS

Demand Side Constraints

The findings of the household surveys unambiguously indicate that households have positive attitudes toward education and give a high premium to health. However, gross enrollment rates in Ethiopia are among the lowest in the world; use of health facilities is also very low. Further analysis suggests that many households are resource and time constrained. Thus they are often compelled to make tough decisions regarding whether to send their children to school or not and whether household members should seek medical treatment or not.

Education. Building more schools is not a sufficient condition for getting children to go to and stay in school. Majority of the households are poor and must make trade-offs between sending their children to school or asking them to stay and work at home and on the farm. Thus, aside from a longer-term strategy of raising household incomes, short- to medium-term strategies are needed to reduce the opportunity costs of schooling to get more school-aged children to attend school.

Locating schools closer to communities will minimize travel time to and from school. Other policies could also be implemented, such as changing the school calendar so that schooling can take place during nonpeak agricultural seasons. Moreover, the plan for double shifts (one in the morning and another in the afternoon) could be supported in order to give households some choice. Distance education could also be an option for older students who are attending higher grade levels.

Households need to be made aware of the benefits of primary education. Most households do not feel that it is worthwhile to send their children to school if they cannot complete secondary education. First, they need to be assured that there will be accessible and affordable secondary schools that their children can attend. Second, information campaigns are needed that will highlight the more practical benefits of education, especially at the primary level. Third, the policy

of conducting classes using regional languages in primary school needs to be re-evaluated. Its advantages include the ease experienced by young learners in adjusting to the formal school environment. Amharic and English are the preferred languages of instruction by a majority of households surveyed (Oxford-AAU Sub-sample Household Survey 1996), mainly because parents believe that knowing both languages will increase their children's prospects of finding jobs outside their own communities. On the other hand, if the policy will be maintained, then measures must be taken to make the transition from local languages to Amharic and English less difficult for students and teachers.

The average age of children entering Grade 1 in Ethiopia is 11 years. This is a serious problem that is not addressed in the ESDP. Children who enter school at such a late age may have difficulty with the mental rigors and demands of schooling if they have not received adequate stimulation prior to attending school. Their adjustment problems could lead to poor school performance. The probability of dropping out without gaining basic literacy also increases for older children who start late in school because girls tend to get married early in Ethiopia while older boys are often needed much more on the farm as they grow older.

Households must be encouraged to send their young children (6 to 10 years) to school where these are available. Although younger children are also needed to assist in household activities such as animal herding, they have lower opportunity costs to the household, compared with 11–18-year-olds. Earlier school attendance also has multiple benefits. First, it increases the chances of children's getting four years of primary schooling before they become more valuable on the farm. Second, it enables girls to obtain at least a basic education before they get married (35 percent of Ethiopian girls are married by 15 years; 70 percent are married by age 17). Third, it is likely to reduce fertility since educated girls are likely to marry late and/or are more likely to use contraceptives

Given that a significant proportion of the school-aged population is out of school and that a large majority of the population has never attended school, what measures will be taken in the ESDP to address their learning needs? Nonformal education was not given enough emphasis in the original ESDP proposal although the government has now incorporated this as a component of ESDP.

Health. Increasing use of health facilities and services is more than an access issue that can be addressed by building more health facilities. Clearly, minimizing the opportunity cost of households' time in seeking treatment is also important. Hence, building closer facilities and integrating services (for example, integrating interventions that address childhood illnesses with those that address mothers' reproductive health services and prenatal care) can help minimize the demands on households' time. Nonetheless, as can be gleaned from the results of the HICE-WMS and Oxford-AAU household surveys, cost considerations were the main reason cited by households for not seeking treatment. Thus, once again, longer-term income generating strategies must be adopted while in the short term well-targeted exemptions or subsidies must be given to indigent households. Third, aexpanding facilities without providing necessary inputs will not generate the desired demand for health services. Quality of care (measured by the increased availability of drugs, medical supplies and equipment, and well-trained and qualified staff) needs to be improved.

Financial and Organizational Sustainability

Financing is an important issue in both the health and education sectors in Ethiopia; it becomes even more so given the huge expenditure outlays required by the SDPs, especially since other sectors

need resources as well. Public health is substantially underfunded. Expenditure per capita at around US$1.50 is significantly lower than the Sub-Saharan African average of US$14 per capita and the amount estimated by the World Bank necessary to provide an essential package of primary and preventive services of US$12 per capita at 1993 prices. The health sector share of GDP is only around 3 percent. Thus, either GDP must increase substantially or a substantial reallocation of resources toward the health sector needs to take place. On the other hand, public expenditures on education as a proportion of GDP are greater than in several other SSA countries that have much higher enrollment rates. This suggests that the issue is more one of efficiency in use rather than the amount of resources flowing to the sector (Rosati and Mikael 1997). In order to address financial and capacity constraints, both sectors may benefit from a reassessment of SDP targets and expansion goals. Concrete steps to encourage private sector participation, community involvement, cost recovery, and measures to improve efficiency are essential.

Both SDPs assume a nominal annual GDP growth of 10 percent over the next 20 years. While this projection is in line with its current economic indicators, contingency plans are needed in the event of a macroeconomic shock or natural disaster such as a drought. In this regard, priorities and fallback options would be helpful. For example, expansion of the public health system as proposed by the HSDP would require growth in health personnel that is more than 10 times what presently exists in Ethiopia. This, in turn, translates into greater investment in training and an increased wage bill. Aside from new facilities, existing facilities need to be adequately staffed if quality is to be maintained.

Phasing of Expansion. In terms of the financial resources and level of effort required, the two largest components of the sector development programs are those related to the construction and renovation of facilities and human resource development. Both components need to be carefully reassessed in terms of financial, implementation, managerial, and informational capacity. Moreover, it is important to consider that together with these SDPs, another SDP will be implemented in the roads sector. This program will also require an enormous amount of resources. As the public expenditure review (1997) points out, the substantial increase in SDP-related expenditures could result in a decline in funding for non-SDP sectors, if additional revenues and/or grants generated are insufficient. In particular, there will be a Birr 14 billion reallocation from other sectors to finance incremental SDP-related expenditures. Recurrent budget implications are relatively marginal (although this might be due to underestimation of ongoing and new recurrent expenditures). Intersectoral capital expenditure effects are substantial, however, increasing the combined share of capital spending for the three SDPs from 35 percent to 86 percent. Thus, it might be more prudent to revise the implementation schedule over a longer but more reasonable time period. Phasing of both programs could be undertaken, for example, by linking capital investments with recurrent costs to ensure the quality and sustainability of operations. A slower pace in HSDP expansion could be considered, such that capital construction could be phased and take place only if recurrent costs can be financed and sustained. System expansion could also keep pace with attempts to strengthen complementary systems such as information, education, and communication; water; and sanitation, which must function properly to sustain the proposed health facilities and programs.

The Government has expressed its view, however, that its planned expenditures are very much in line with its sectoral priorities, which are the three SDPs and the water sector.

Private Participation. Government should not do it alone but should re-engage the private sector and mobilize communities. Both programs propose to re-engage the private sector in the provision of education and health services. Paying attention to the private sector in the health sector is particularly important from an equity point of view since majority of poor households go to drug vendors who are usually private operators. Based on the PHRD provider survey's results, easing licensing requirements might not be enough of an incentive for private investors. In particular, private investors in the education sector have voiced their concern about standard building specifications (such as size and minimum number of classrooms), and inadequate tax breaks and import exemptions. Moreover, most NGOs and other private-sector providers in the health sector reported bureaucratic constraints, restrictive regulations, and shortages of drugs and equipment. Finally, encouraging private participation also entails leveling the playing field for potential private sector investors. Genuine competition can be fostered only if subsidies and special tax breaks are removed from EPHARMECOR (in health) and EMPDA (in education). In order to encourage private entry into pharmaceuticals, public health institutions should be free to buy from private as well as public wholesalers. Assistance could also be given to rural drug vendors whose clients are predominantly poor. In the provision of education materials, subsidies could be disengaged from the process of production and reallocated to consumers so that households are able to purchase learning materials at lower cost.

Eliciting private sector participation in sectoral planning is likely to yield payoffs in terms of better coordination and quality of services. Actively and formally engaging the private sector means more than dealing with issues of registration, certification, and the design of incentives; it also necessitates a higher correlation between private sector investment and government objectives. This must be supported by a national regulatory framework outlining geographic service, coverage, and quality priorities on private sector expansion.

Financing Options. Cost-sharing efforts need to be maximized to the fullest possible extent. Households who are willing to pay for primary education should be encouraged to do so, by allowing and encouraging private investors to build and manage more schools. Children from households who cannot afford private schools can be accommodated in government schools. The same principle could be followed in the health sector, that is, better-off households can seek treatment at the private hospitals. It is important to keep in mind, however, that if cost recovery is not to result in a lower demand for health services, quality improvements must accompany increased fees for services.

Exemptions must be available for the poorest households. However, better targeting of subsidies is called for because health sector studies in Ethiopia suggest that the existing cost recovery system has been eroded partly due to a large proportion of exemptions. Thus the administrative costs of implementing an effective cost-recovery scheme that allows for exemptions must be budgeted for. This may imply a slower rate of expansion in the short run, but in the longer term, as revenues are realized, resources made available from cost recovery could allow further increases in quality and release budgetary resources for expansion. Communities can also be mobilized to assume some of the responsibilities for targeting and thereby minimize its administrative costs. Eligibility criteria (such as income) and administration guidelines would need to be developed.

Developing community insurance funds along the lines of the *iddir* (funeral insurance) and via cooperative-based schemes such as agricultural cooperatives needs to be explored. According to PHRD Study 2.a, rural households spend a portion of their income on *iddir*, which in some cases also includes health and disaster coverage. Government input would be required to promote the wider use of *iddir* and agricultural cooperatives for this purpose. Some policies and guidelines would also need to be developed regarding the management of these community insurance schemes and the extent to which government financial support is required to facilitate these efforts.

Community contributions are expected to cover as much as 10 percent of the total cost of capital construction and renovations in both ESDP and HSDP. The present ESRDF Program methodology could be applied to the SDPs. Such contributions will be maximized through increased community participation in the planning and implementation of projects. In the PHRD community assessment survey, 70 percent of the communities interviewed stated that they were not involved in the planning process of health facilities at the local level. About 43 percent of the communities have participated in local sanitation activities and the provision of free labor, material, and finance for the construction of health facilities. A small number of indigenous community institutions are already involved on a limited scale in the promotion of health and education services, while others have expressed a willingness to become involved. However, the majority of indigenous associations are not ready or equipped for participatory development of education and health services. Thus, assistance and training in this regard is needed. Once again, it must be emphasized that fostering community contributions requires maintenance or improvements in quality. Improvements at the facility level provide an indication of government commitment without which sustained mobilization of contributions from the community is unlikely.

Flexible Service Delivery

Regional governments were involved in the formulation of health and education sector programs. Allowances are currently being made for more flexibility to enable each region to proceed at its own pace and based on its own goals in line with the national policies. There is, however, some scope for more flexibility as long as the alternatives to be considered do not undermine quality. For example, much of the focus of the SDPs is on construction and renovation of facilities to conform to the government's quality standards. Strict specifications also exist on equipment and staffing profiles of different types of facilities. Regions and districts could be given greater flexibility to determine their capital requirements, equipment standards, and staff profiles according to their needs and available resources. Such a strategy, for example, would allow certain remote areas to reduce costs by having smaller schools (fewer classrooms) but more of them, in order to reach far-flung communities. Multigrade teaching in smaller schools could also be encouraged to efficiently use school resources in sparsely populated areas. Mobile schools and teachers could be further encouraged.

What other modalities of health service delivery can be used to take care of nomadic, pastoralist populations? Mobile clinics is one option but these would not be practical if travel is difficult because of poor roads. Perhaps, regions with low population density could also increase outreach/extension services through community health workers whenever appropriate. Can modern communications improve the delivery of health services? In such a rugged terrain as Ethiopia, is modern technology feasible or desirable, and what are the corresponding cost implications of technology adoption? Clearly options must be carefully weighed. The government plans to study additional options for cost-effective service delivery in both education and health.

The Social Sector Strategic Vision

To maximize benefits, the SDPs need to consider the timing and sequencing of interventions that promote synergy across components and across different stages of the human capital development life cycle. Each stage is crucial because each one builds upon the previous stage, and therefore it

may be more costly, and at times too late, to intervene only at later stages. Interventions related to health and nutrition at infancy and childhood via integrated programs can be linked to their impact on school attendance and performance. Investments in schooling, in turn, can be linked to their impact on reproductive health and family planning in early adulthood. In addition, investments made in reproductive health and family planning can reduce fertility rates and help relax the binding resource constraint that rapid population growth can impose on Ethiopia's economy. Good antenatal and maternal health care can minimize maternal mortality, birth complications, and the incidence of low birth weight in infants. Further investments in nutrition beyond childhood, into adolescence and adulthood, are also important from a productivity point of view. The rural surveys show that protein-energy malnutrition measured by low BMI (body mass index) affects 25 percent of the adult working population. The impact on agricultural productivity is likely to be high since agriculture in Ethiopia is based on manual labor.

Improvements in the social sectors must be coordinated with interventions undertaken in other sectors of the economy. For example, poverty reduction strategies can help alleviate the income constraint faced by households, which would allow them to look beyond how to meet their minimum daily subsistence requirements and perhaps allocate a greater proportion of their incomes to health care, better nutrition, and schooling. Improved infrastructure through better roads will improve access to schools and health facilities. The increased availability of safe water and proper sanitation facilities can help minimize the onslaught of communicable and preventable diseases. Finally, initiatives to enhance gender sensitivity and empower women may have positive consequences such as increased schooling for girls, and improved income-earning potential for women that could translate into better nutrition for households (other studies have shown that children's nutritional status is positively linked with mother's income) and better health care (PHRD Study Number 2.a has shown that the probability of seeking treatment is positively related with mother's level of education).

Monitoring and Evaluating Progress

Finally, appropriate monitoring and evaluation mechanisms are also needed for timely feedback to be given to and from planning and implementing agents to ensure that the SDPs are on track. Both process and impact indicators need to be d3eveloped aside from input indicators. Training of personnel in data information gathering, analysis, and information dissemination is important.

The issues presented in this chapter have been discussed with the government and almost all of them are being considered particularly in the context of the implementation of the education and health sector development programs. These programs present many challenges, but they also provide immense opportunities for improving Ethiopia's human capital.

ANNEX 1
LIST OF PHRD SOCIAL SECTOR STUDIES AND AUTHORS

Report No.

1a   Shara Weir and John Knight (1996), *Household Demand for Schooling (Rural Survey of Ethiopia)*, Centre for the Study of African Economies, Oxford University, U.K.

1b   KUAWAB Audit Services and Business Consultants (1996), *Household Demand for Schooling (National Survey)*, Addis Ababa, Ethiopia.

2a   Stefan Dercon (1996), *Household Demand for Health and Nutrition (Rural Survey)*, Centre for the Study of African Economis, Oxford University, U.K.

2b   KUAWAB Audit Services and Business Consultants (1996), *Household Demand for Health and Nutrition (National Survey)*, Addis Ababa, Ethiopia.

3   T. Geressu, A. Nurhussein, G. Lemecha, Y. Taddese, and B. Legesse (1996), *Burden of Disease (National and Regional)*, Ministry of Health, Addis Ababa, Ethiopia.

4   Zubeida Abdulahi (1996), *Demographic Analysis and Population Projections to Year 2020: Impact on Future Social Sectors*, B&M Development Consultants, Addis Ababa, Ethiopia.

5   KUAWAB Audit Services and Business Consultants (1996), *Cost and Financing of Education*, Addis Ababa, Ethiopia.

6   KUAWAB Audit Services and Business Consultants (1996), *Cost and Financing of Health, Nutrition, and Population Services*, Addis Ababa, Ethiopia.

7   Tadele Tedela and Mohammed Mussa (1996), *Cost-Effectiveness and Program Evaluation of Major Health Interventions*, Addis Ababa, Ethiopia.

8   D. Dufera, F. Melesse, H. Shiferaw, and S. Woldemariam (1996), *Cost-Effectiveness and Program Evaluation of Major Interventions in Education*, Institute of Educational Research (IER), Addis Ababa University, Ethiopia.

Report No.

9a   Pramila Krishnan (1996), *Private and Social Returns to Schooling (Using the 1990 Survey)*, Centre for the Study of African Economies (CSAE), Oxford University, United Kingdom.

9b   Wolday Amha (1996), *Private and Social Returns to Schooling (Using Own Survey Data)*, Addis Ababa, Ethiopia.

10   T. Teferra, M. Gleselassie, Z. Fekadu, and A. Ahmed (1996), *Access to and Supply of Education Facilities and Services*, Institute of Educational Research (IER), Addis Ababa University, Ethiopia.

11   Tadele Mengesha and Negussie Taffa (1996), *Access to and Supply of Health, Nutrition, and Population Facilities and Services*, Addis Ababa, Ethiopia.

12   Hailemikael Liqu (1996), *Community Consultation and Participatory Development*, Addis Ababa, Ethiopia.

14   Kassa Kinde and Halegiorgis Kenso (1996), *Demand and Supply of Health Manpower: Alternative Scenarios*, Addis Ababa, Ethiopia.

15   Daniel Desta and Desalehn Chalchisa (1996), *Demand and Supply of Education Manpower: Alternative Scenarios*, Institute of Educational Research (IER), Addis Ababa University, Ethiopia.

16   Hailu Sime (1996), *Survey of Educational Institutions*, Policy and Human Resource Development Project Office, Addis Ababa, Ethiopia.

17   Gabremaskal Habtemariam (1996), *Survey of Health and Me..* Human Resource Development Project Office, Addis Ababa, Ethiopia.

Additional Studies Funded by the PHRD Grant

PHRD Project Office. 1996. *Social Sector Review: Education Sector Synthesis*. Addis Ababa.

PHRD Project Office. 1996. *Social Sector Review: Health Sector Synthesis*. Addis Ababa.

K. Subbarao and K. Mehra. 1996. *Improving Nutrition in Ethiopia*. Washington, D.C.: World Bank.

ANNEX 2
POPULATION PROJECTIONS

Ethiopia's population growth is projected up to 2020 based on two different data sources: the 1994 National Population and Housing Census and the 1990 National Family and Fertility Survey. Alternative projections are referred to as the Census and the Survey alternatives, respectively. In both cases, assumptions are made about two important trends: changes in the total fertility rate (TFR) and the rate of decrease in mortality. In addition, the net international migration for the country is assumed to be zero. The population projections were prepared using the DEMPROJ program (Stover 1990).

The census data have used adjusted fertility rate of 5.8 and 5.4 according to Arriaga and Rele methods, respectively. However, owing to the fact that the information on current fertility refers to a relatively short time duration and is strongly affected by temporary fluctuations in fertility behavior of a population, a TFR of 6.1 has been taken as a plausible estimate for the Census alternative. Mortality is expected to improve at the rate of 0.3 years per year throughout the projection period. This slow rate of improvement is assumed to occur after compensating for the impact of additional deaths that are expected to occur as a result of AIDS.

Three variations on Census projections were used. For the medium variant, the fertility level is assumed to reach replacement within 50 years. This variant is expected to indicate the most plausible trend, based on past experiences and

the governmental and nongovernmental programs envisaged for the future. For a high variant, fertility is assumed to remain stable throughout the projection period. For the low variant, fertility is assumed to reach replacement level within 40 years. This variant is considered optimistic unless

Table A2.1 Population Projections: Census Alternative, 1995-2020

Year	Low Variant	Medium Variant	High Variant
1995	53,277	53,276	53,277
1996	54,589	54,610	54,656
1997	55,978	56,019	56,111
1998	57,425	57,493	57,646
1999	58,918	59,024	59,263
2000	60,441	60,603	60,965
2001	62,001	62,234	62,750
2002	63,611	63,926	64,616
2003	65,256	65,669	66,566
2004	66,918	67,454	68,602
2005	68,584	69,274	70,729
2006	70,266	71,133	72,946
2007	71,975	73,047	75,252
2008	73,691	74,994	77,644
2009	75,391	76,953	80,124
2010	77,055	78,903	82,689
2011	78,689	80,866	85,337
2012	80,307	82,844	88,070
2013	81,900	84,823	90,890
2014	83,459	86,786	93,801
2015	84,976	88,712	96,806
2016	86,457	90,618	99,904
2017	87,908	92,511	103,092
2018	89,320	94,375	106,374
2019	90,683	96,193	109,754
2020	91,992	97,945	113,234

Source: PHRD Study Number 4, 1996.

population control is given massive resources and the highest governmental priority.

The Survey projections use a TFR of 7.7 (CSA 1993: 137). For the medium variant of this projection, the fertility level is assumed to reach replacement within 60 years beginning in 1990. For the high variant of projection, fertility is assumed to remain stable throughout the projection period. For the low variant, fertility is assumed to reach replacement within 50 years. In these projections, mortality is expected to improve at the rate of 0.5 years per year throughout the projection period in the absence of AIDS. However, the effects of the AIDS epidemic were also factored in during the preparation of projections.

The results of these projections have strong implications on resource requirements and future prospects of the health conditions in Ethiopia. As has been mentioned, the medium variant projection indicates the most plausible trend the population size will follow if the current governmental and nongovernmental programs continue as planned. The implications of the projected population sizes are here analyzed using the medium variant of projected population sizes. Using this projected population size, three different scenarios of expansion of services are utilized in the assessment. Table A2.1 provides what is considered the most realistic population projections using the Census data. Table A2.2 presents population projections based on the Survey-based fertility estimates.

Some caution is required in the interpretation of these projections. Calculations for the Census alternative are based on preliminary, unadjusted census data, which is currently available

Table A2.2   Population Projections: Survey Alternative, 1995-2020

Year	Low Variant	Medium Variant	High Variant
1995	53,277	53,276	53,277
1996	54,953	55,000	55,068
1997	56,679	56,764	56,909
1998	58,449	58,569	58,809
1999	60,255	60,416	60,778
2000	62,091	62,304	62,826
2001	63,960	64,233	64,945
2002	65,868	66,203	67,132
2003	67,808	68,215	69,392
2004	69,772	70,267	71,738
2005	71,752	72,359	74,179
2006	73,760	74,500	76,705
2007	75,797	76,686	79,313
2008	77,852	78,910	82,012
2009	79,912	81,166	84,814
2010	81,965	83,441	87,730
2011	84,018	85,747	90,742
2012	86,079	88,085	93,844
2013	88,138	90,447	97,061
2014	90,185	92,829	100,421
2015	92,208	95,219	103,953
2016	94,216	97,632	107,636
2017	96,214	100,063	111,454
2018	98,194	102,509	115,434
2019	100,145	104,961	119,603
2020	102,055	107,415	123,988

Source: PHRD Study Number 4, 1996.

from the 1994 census. The baseline TFR estimate used in the Census alternative is derived in part from a subjective analysis of its consistency with a range of related information. In addition, assumptions on life expectancy do not fully account for likely age-specific variation, owing to the likely impact of HIV/AIDS, for example. While these concerns represent potential shortcomings in the analysis, the projections produced are useful in the development of the various policy scenarios described in Section 2.4.

ANNEX 3
STATISTICAL APPENDIX

Table A3.1   Number of Pupils Enrolled in Government Primary Schools by Region

Table A3.2   Number of Pupils Enrolled in Junior Secondary Schools by Region

Table A3.3   Pupils Enrolled in Senior Secondary Schools

Table A3.4   Distribution of Schools by Region and Level, 1993/94 and 1994/95

Table A3.5   Gross Enrollment Ratios by Level and by Region, 1994/95

Table A3.6   Dropout Rates by Rural/Urban Residence and Sex

Table A3.7   Age at Entry Into Primary School Grade 1, by Rural/Urban Residence

Table A3.8   Flow Rates: Promotion, Repetition, and Dropout Rates in Primary
                 Schools, 1994/95

Table A3.9   Gross Enrollment Ratio by Per Capita Expenditure Group, National Level

Table A3.10   Gross Enrollment by Gender of the Household Head

Table A3.11   Enrollment, Teachers, Pupil/Teacher Ratios for Some Years by Level
                 and Provider

Table A3.12   Educational Facilities by Level of Education, 1992/93–1994/95

Table A3.13   Government Education Budget Compared with Distribution
                 of Enrollment, 1993/94 Budget with 1994/95 Enrollment

Table A3.14   Government Recurrent Education Budget By Level of Schooling
                 and by Region 1987, 1994/95 G.C.

Table A3.15   Total Capital Education Expenditures by Schooling Level, Nonformal
                 and Administrative Nature, 1978–1988, 1985/86–1995/96 G.C.

Table A3.16   Recurrent Health Budget by Activity, 1993/94–1995/96

Table A3.17   Recurrent Health Budget by Programs and Facilities, 1993/94–1995/96

Table A3.18   Capital Health Budget Allocation by Sources and Year

Table A3.19   Regional Distribution of Health Facilities by Type of Facility and
                 Ownership, 1994/95

Table A3.20   Physical Condition of Health Institutions by Type

Table A3.21   Health Facilities Reporting Availability of Selected Equipment and Transport
                 Facility by Type, 1995

Table A3.1   Number of Pupils Enrolled in Government Primary Schools by Region

Region	1992/93 Total	Percent Female	1993/94 Total	Percent Female	1994/95 Total	Percent Female
Tigray	257,131	40.3	290,834	40.1	286,423	42.3
Afar	5,000	44.9	10,038	35.8	10,899	38.2
Amhara	331,663	48.1	311,857	45.9	391,119	45.0
Oromiya	570,124	38.2	715,351*	34.6	623,891	29.9
Somali	9,903	34.3	47,436	33.0	57,213	30.9
Benshangul Gumuz	2,708	20.9	30,411*	32.7	34,598	26.4
SNNP	53,077	30.1	539,030	29.4	609,657	29.1
Gambella	6,142	35.8	11,864	34.2	16,981	34.9
Harari	12,022	49.9	10,326	47.4	12,200	43.3
Addis Ababa	254,299	51.3	265,828	49.8	263,575	51.6
Dire Dawa	15,970	47.9	12,960	49.4	17,730	49.6
Total	1,518,039	42.8	2,245,935	38.1	232,4286	36.5

Source: PHRD Study Number 10 (1996) based on 1993/94 Educational Statistics, MOE.

TableA3.2   Number of Pupils Enrolled in Junior Secondary Schools by Region

Region	1992/93 Total	Percent Female	1993/94 Total	Percent Female	1994/95 Total	Percent Female
Tigray	13,867	43.5	13,666	41.3	17,961	40.9
Afar	895	41.2	521	36.9	1,895	42.1
Amhara	68,470	49.6	123,746	48.2	64,791	48.5
Oromiya	108,355	45.2	111,589	44.9	113,425	43.2
Somali	1,565	35.9	1,304	39.6	1,336	35.9
Benshangul Gumuz	335	15.2	1,698	38.3	1,515	34.9
SNNP	7,272	43.4	53,390	35.3	71,068	33.1
Gambella	546	29.3	1,001	30.6	1,375	18.0
Harari	3,420	31.0	2,707	54.2	2,847	52.4
Addis Ababa	93,688	54.4	95,966	53.4	87,645	53.7
Dire Dawa	4,331	49.3	3,126	48.7	4,509	53.1
Total	302,744	48.7	408,714	46.8	368,367	43.8

Source: PHRD Study Number 10 (1996) based on 1993/94 Educational Statistics, MOE.

Table A3.3   Pupils Enrolled in Senior Secondary Schools

Region	1992/93		1993/94		1994/95	
	Total	Percent Female	Total	Percent Female	Total	Percent Female
Tigray	10,904	44.8	13,689	43.9	13,939	40.3
Afar	850	40.6	1,338	43.7	1,402	42.4
Amhara	76,020	45.6	78,795	48.2	77,927	45.9
Oromiya	103,307	43.2	102,794	42.3	130,617	41.9
Somali	1,820	39.1	1,773	37.1	1,659	26.3
Benshangul/Gumuz	—	—	1,549	39.1	1,057	32.6
SNNP	6,656	43.1	41,676	37.5	53,778	36.5
Gambella	360	33.1	642	30.1	871	24.0
Harari	2,022	40.1	4,207	44.6	—	—
Addis Ababa	114,027	50.6	109,728	49.3	115,441	50.7
Dire Dawa	5,336	43.4	5,162	42.7	5,608	45.8
Total	321,302	46.4	361,353	45.2	360,118	49.6

Source: PHRD Study Number 10 (1996) based on 1993/94 Educational Statistics, MOE.

Table A3.4.   Distribution of Schools by Region and Level, 1993/94 and 1994/95

Region	1993/94						1994/95					
	Primary		Junior Secondary		Senior Secondary		Primary		Junior Secondary		Senior Secondary	
	Government	Nongovernment	Government	Nongovernment	Government	Nongovernment	Government	Nongovernment	Government	Nongovernment	Government	Nongovernment
Tigray	543	23	37	5	17	3	556	25	40	6	18	3
Afar	59	—	10	—	3	—	68	—	12	—	3	—
Amhara	2,419	10	217	4	73	—	2,493	10	226	3	76	—
Oromiya	3,224	156	422	26	99	6	3,438	163	437	31	102	7
Somali	—	—	—	—	—	—	159	1	6	1	3	—
Benshangul/ Gumuz	168	3	11	1	3	—	195	—	14	—	5	—
SNNP	1,621	118	219	19	53	1	1,728	95	238	18	61	2
Gambella	48	—	5	—	2	—	65	2	5	5	4	—
Hareri	27	6	7	5	2	—	27	6	7	—	2	—
Addis Ababa	61	155	53	115	23	15	60	159	53	116	23	19
Dire Dawa	26	7	6	5	2	1	17	9	7	5	1	1
Total	8,196	478	987	180	277	26	8,806	470	1,045	185	298	32

Source: PHRD Education Synthesis Document (1996) based on Annual Education Statistics (MOE, 1995 and 1996).

Table A3.5   Gross Enrollment Ratios by Level and by Region, 1994/95

Region	Grades 1–6			Grades 1–8			Grades 9–12		
	Male	Female	Total	Male	Female	Total	Male	Female	Total
Tigray	60.0	45.9	53.1	49.0	38.0	43.7	5.5	3.4	4.4
Afar	10.9	7.2	9.1	10.0	6.8	8.4	1.9	1.1	1.5
Amhara	20.7	18.0	19.3	18.9	16.8	17.9	5.5	4.8	5.2
Oromiya	30.2	15.6	23.1	27.2	14.9	21.2	6.5	4.7	5.6
Somali	19.9	8.2	14.3	16.2	6.6	11.6	0.8	0.2	0.5
Benshangul-Gumuz	57.6	23.3	41.1	49.3	20.2	35.4	3.1	1.7	2.4
SNNPR	44.4	19.2	32.2	39.5	17.4	28.8	6.6	3.5	5.1
Gambella	74.5	44.7	60.6	67.8	38.2	53.9	8.2	2.3	5.3
Harari	57.6	50.8	54.4	55.3	51.4	53.4	35.9	27.6	31.6
Addis Ababa	85.9	87.4	86.7	84.4	85.3	84.9	45.6	37.2	40.8
Dire Dawa	45.5	40.7	43.1	42.8	39.1	41.0	21.6	17.2	19.4
Total	35.7	22.1	29.0	31.7	20.4	26.2	7.5	5.7	6.6

Source: PHRD Study Number 1.b, 1996.

Table A3.6   Dropout Rates by Rural/Urban Residence and Sex

Urban/Rural and Gender	Percentage of Students Who Dropped Out After Attending				
	Grades 1-3	Grades 4-6	Grades 7-8	Grades 9-10	Grades 11-12
Rural					
Male	31.18	18.90	25.33	13.03	22.01
Female	29.58	10.94	22.08	21.49	32.74
Total	30.72	16.64	24.23	16.03	24.08
Urban					
Male	9.46	7.14	14.44	16.97	10.40
Female	10.84	13.86	11.96	19.14	11.11
Total	10.17	10.63	13.07	18.10	10.78
Urban and Rural					
Male	23.55	12.52	17.98	14.23	13.45
Female	18.61	13.17	13.66	19.24	12.56
Total	21.65	12.80	15.82	16.65	13.02

Source: PHRD Study Number 1.b, 1996.

Table A3.7   Age at Entry into Primary School Grade 1, by Rural/ Urban Residence

Residence and Gender	Average Age at Entry in Grade 1	Percentage of Students Currently Enrolled in Grade One			
		7 Years	8 Years	9 Years	10 Years and Above
Rural					
Male	11.74	7.70	8.89	10.11	73.30
Female	11.50	9.18	9.30	13.60	76.92
Total	11.67	8.15	9.01	11.18	71.66
Urban					
Male	9.45	21.97	24.18	15.76	38.09
Female	9.49	19.66	26.42	15.32	38.60
Total	9.47	20.77	25.34	15.53	38.36
Urban and Rural					
Male	11.20	11.04	12.46	11.43	65.07
Female	10.64	13.76	16.64	14.34	55.35
Total	10.99	12.01	14.01	12.51	61.46

Source: PHRD Study Number 1.b, 1996.

Table A3.8   Flow Rates: Promotion, Repetition, and Dropout Rates in Primary Schools, 1994/ 95

	Flow Rates	Grades						Total
		1	2	3	4	5	6	
Boys	Enrollment 1993/94	590,775	251,788	194,975	156,129	128,828	120,621	1,443,116
	Enrollment 1994/95	714,492	322,939	222,059	183,173	141,525	130,247	1,714,435
	Repeaters 1994/95	73,048	16,217	9,120	10,977	6,644	11,975	127,981
	Promotion Rate	0.5192	0.8457	0.8832	0.8639	0.9181	0.8929	
	Repetition Rate	0.1236	0.0644	0.0468	0.0703	0.0516	0.0993	
	Dropout Rate	0.3572	0.0899	0.0701	0.0658	0.0304	0.0078	
Girls	Enrollment 1993/94	329,074	152,122	118,935	103,305	90,527	94,299	888,262
	Enrollment 1994/95	325,405	149,148	116,316	101,007	88,465	92,737	873,078
	Repeaters 1994/95	53,164	13,320	7,791	10,788	6,907	16,816	108,786
	Promotion Rate	0.4128	0.7134	0.7586	0.7895	0.8387	0.8000	
	Repetition Rate	0.1616	0.0876	0.0655	0.1044	0.0763	0.1783	
	Dropout Rate	0.4257	0.1990	0.1759	0.1061	0.0850	0.0217	
Total	Enrollment 1993/94	919,849	403,910	313,910	259,434	219,355	214,920	2,331,378
	Enrollment 1994/95	1,039,897	472,087	338,375	284,180	229,990	222,984	2,587,513
	Repeaters 1994/95	126,212	29,537	16,911	21,765	13,551	28,791	236,767
	Promotion Rate	0.4811	0.7959	0.8360	0.8343	0.8853	0.8000	
	Repetition Rate	0.1372	0.0731	0.0539	0.0839	0.0618	0.1340	
	Dropout Rate	0.3817	0.1310	0.1102	0.0818	0.0529	0.0660	

Source: PHRD Education Synthesis Document (1996) based on Education Statistics (MOE 1996).

Table A3.9   Gross Enrollment Ratio by Per Capita Expenditure Group, National Level

Residence Schooling Level	Per Capita Expenditure Group			
	0-50	51-100	101-200	201 +
Urban and Rural				
Primary				
Male	.26	.33	.42	.49
Female	.15	.23	.31	.55
Total	.21	.28	.37	.52
Junior Secondary				
Male	.20	.15	.34	.46
Female	.10	.16	.23	.37
Total	.15	.16	.28	.40
Senior Secondary				
Male	.05	.08	.13	.23
Female	.05	.07	.11	.22
Total	.05	.07	.12	.22
Higher Education				
Male	—	—	.01	.03
Female	—	—	.01	.01
Total	—	—	.01	.02
Urban and Rural Total				
Male	.17	.19	.24	.30
Female	.10	.14	.18	.26
Total	.13	.16	.21	.28

Source: PHRD Study Number 1.b, 1996.

Table A3.10   Gross Enrollment by Gender of the Household Head

Residence Schooling Level	Gender of Household Head		
	Male	Female	Total
Urban			
Primary			
Male	.89	.86	.88
Female	.90	1.00	.94
Total	.90	.93	.91
Junior Secondary			
Male	.77	.99	.84
Female	.66	.62	.64
Total	.71	.76	.73
Senior Secondary			
Male	.43	.47	.44
Female	.33	.34	.34
Total	.38	.38	.38
Higher Education			
Male	.04	.02	.03
Female	.02	.01	.01
Total	.03	.01	.02
Urban Total			
Male	.57	.60	.58
Female	.50	.52	.51
Total	.53	.55	.54
Rural			
Primary			
Male	.24	.25	.24
Female	.11	.10	.11
Total	.18	.17	.18
Junior Secondary			
Male	.08	.12	.09
Female	.04	.04	.04
Total	.06	.08	.06
Senior Secondary			
Male	.02	.04	.02
Female	.01	.01	.01
Total	.02	.03	.02
Higher Education			
Male	—	—	—
Female	—	—	—
Total	—	—	—
Rural Total			
Male	.13	.14	.13
Female	.06	.06	.06
Total	.09	.10	.09

Source: PHRD Study Number 1.b, 1996.

Table A3.11   Enrollment, Teachers, and Pupil /Teacher Ratios for Some Years by Level and Provider

Year	Provider	Primary		Junior Secondary		Senior Secondary		Pupil/Teacher Ratio		
		Student	Teacher	Student	Teacher	Student	Teacher	Primary	Junior	Senior
1973/74	Government	644,998	13,043	84,601	2,506	74,662	2,482	50:1	34:1	30:1
	Nongovernment	214,833	5,601	17,148	713	6,634	473	38:1	24:1	14:1
1992/93	Government -	1,638,897	65,091	292,849	9,632	358,072	10,897	25:1	30:1	33:1
	Nongovernment	216,997	4,652	55,954	1,164	5,614	277	47:1	48:1	20:1
1993/94	Government	2,041,115	70,636	302,787	9,390	349,960	10,647	29:1	32:1	33:1
	Nongovernment	242,523	5,100	54,164	1,221	7,234	340	48:1	45:1	21:1
1994/95	Government	2,474,462	77,857	322,042	10,241	360,678	10,846	32:1	31:1	33:1
	Nongovernment	247,730	5,256	54,188	1,303	10,238	389	47:1	42:1	26:1

Source: PHRD Education Synthesis Report (1996) based on Education Statistics (MOE 1994, 1995, 1996).

Table A3.12   Educational Facilities by Level of Education, 1992/93–1994/95

Year	KG	Primary (Grades 1–6)			Junior Secondary (Grades 7–8)			Senior Secondary (Grades 9–12)			TTIs	Colleges	Universities
		Government	Nongovernment	Total	Government	Nongovernment	Total	Government	Nongovernment	Total			
1992/93	550	7,722	398	8,120	944	155	1,099	257	22	279	12	15	2
1993/94	652	8,196	478	8,674	987	180	1,167	277	26	303	12	17	2
1994/95	678	8,806	470	9,276	1,045	185	1,230	298	32	330	13	17	2

Source: PHRD Education Synthesis Report (1996) based on Annual Education Statistics (MOE 1994, 1995, and 1996).

Table A3.13 Government Education Budget Compared with Distribution of Enrollment, 1994/95 (1987 E.C) budget with 1994/95 (1987) Enrollment

Region	Number and Percent of Enrolled Student			Recurrent Budget Student (in Birr)	Capital Budget			Recurrent and Capital Budget	
	Number	Percent	Recurrent Budget (in '000 Birr)		in '000 Birr	Per Enrolled Student (in Birr)		in '000 Birr	Per Enrolled Student
National	3,175,047	100.0	885,302	279	411,574	130		1,296,876	409
Central			111,405	6,236	121,844	6,820		233,249	13,056[a]
MOE			20,927	—	49,101	—		70,028	—
Tertiary	17,865	0.6	90,478	5,064	72,743	4,071		163,221	9,135
Regional	3,157,182	99.4	773,897	245	289,730	92		1,063,627	337
Tigray	309,049	9.7	42,087	136	46,375	150		88,462	286
Afar	16,033	0.5	15,950	995	17,411	1,085		33,361	2,080
Amhara	624,146	19.7	173,607	278	51,614	83		225,221	361
Oromiya	1,008,914	31.8	273,078	271	50,844	50		323,922	321
Somalia	62,581	2.0	20,312	325	24,019	384		44,331	709
B. Shangul/Gumuz	39,316	1.2	13,281	338	23,267	592		36,548	930
SNNPR	756,024	23.8	136,615	181	46,654	62		183,269	243
Gambella	19,945	0.6	7,405	371	12,944	649		20,349	1,020
Harari	16,258	0.5	6,765	416	1,807	111		8,572	527
Addis Ababa	283,164	8.9	78,737	278	11,172	39		89,909	317
Dire Dawa	21,752	0.7	6,060	279	3,623	167		9,683	446

a. Includes overhead of MOE. When the MOE overhead is reduced, allocation per student enrolled in tertiary level is reduced to Birr 9,135. Overhead expenditure spent at MOE level should be shared by all students at all levels.
Source: PHRD Study Number 5, 1996.

Table A3.14 Government Recurrent Education Budget by Level of Schooling and by Region 1987, 1994/95 G.C, (in '000 Birr)

Region	Primary	Junior Secondary	Senior Secondary	Technical and Vocational Training	Teacher Training (Primary School)	Higher Education	Nonformal Education	Education Administration and Others	Total
National	489,659	112,341	104,946	7,941	11,701	90,478	2,779	65,453	885,302
Central	—	—	—	—	—	90,478[a]	2,143	18,783	111,405
Regional	489,659	112,341	104,946	7,941	11,701	—	636	46,669	773,896
Tigray	26,192	4,857	4,380	576	1,292	—	79	4,708	42,087
Afar	10,219	2,289	2,369	—	—	—	—	1,071	15,949
Amhara	119,829	21,951	19,490	807	3,066	—	166	8,295	173,607
Oromiya	179,786	41,006	34,416	985	4,501	—	224	12,157	273,078
Somalia	13,335	2,883	2,543	—	—	—	—	1,549	20,311
B. Shangul/Gumuz	9,099	1,612	1,158	—	—	—	—	1,410	13,280
SNNPR	87,801	19,802	13,707	712	2,334	—	—	12,256	136,614
Gambella	4,438	803	551	—	505	—	—	1,105	7,405
Harari	4,213	1,002	1,021	—	—	—	—	527	6,765
Addis Ababa	31,801	15,127	24,098	4,360	—	—	165	3,183	78,737
Dire Dawa	2,942	1,005	1,208	498	—	—	—	404	6,059

a. Institutions of higher education are responsible to the Central Government regardless of where they are. Other schools are responsible to the regions in which they are located.
Source: PHRD Study Number 5, 1996.

Table A3.15 Total Capital Education Expenditure by Schooling Level, Nonformal and Administrative
Nature, 1978-1988, 1985/86-1995/96 G.C (in '000 Birr)

G.C	Eth.C	Primary	Secondary	Teacher Training	Tertiary	Curriculum and other Services	Nonformal[a]	Others[b]	Total
1985/86	1978	9,948	12,142	3,498	7,659	6,175	285	—	39,709
1986/87	1979	9,190	6,604	4,236	13,265	5,340	867	75	39,579
1987/88	1980	12,020	4,016	3,554	12,735	9,288	236	—	41,851
1988/89	1981	10,897	3,247	2,835	27,597	14,202	293	—	59,074
1989/90	1982	5,399	3,640	522	14,258	13,108	2,445	—	39,375
1990/91	1983	8,869	8,400	2,822	7,409	13,548	1,545	—	42,594
1991/92	1984	6,598	6,368	1,214	10,392	11,518	2,089	—	38,181
1992/93	1985[c]	27,298	48,114	14,913	23,636	45,682	1,250	—	160,894
1993/94	1986[c]	98,727	124,745	9,576	39,029	44,775	—	—	316,853
1994/95	1987[c]	157,773	126,186	9,841	72,743	45,028	—	—	411,573
1995/96	1988[c]	159,137	83,619	19,118	109,104	22,904	—	—	393,885

a. Non-formal includes literacy programs and radio based distance education.
b. Includes kindergarten.
c. Budgeted, the rest are actual figures.
— No budget maintained for it
Source: MOF and MEDAC.

Table A3.16 Recurrent Health Budget by Activity, 1993/94-1995/96 (in 000 Birr)

Activities	1993/94		1994/95		1995/96	
	Amount	Percent	Amount	Percent	Amount	Percent
Personnel Service	168,007	55.8	179,541	52.0	191,541	53.0
Nonpersonnel Service	27,141	9.0	33,789	9.8	32,888	9.1
Material Supplies	90,501	30.1	105,339	30.5	110,137	30.5
Grants and Transfers	7,293	2.4	18,941	5.5	19,700	5.5
Purchase of Equipment and Motor Vehicles	7,977	2.7	7,881	2.3	7,085	2.0
Total	300,920	100.0	345,492	100.0	361,353	100.0

Source: PHRD Study Number 6, 1996.

Table A3.17   Recurrent Health Budget by Programs and Facilities, 1993/94–1995/96

Facilities and Programs	1993/94 Amount	1993/94 Percent	1994/95 Amount	1994/95 Percent	1995/96 Amount	1995/96 Percent
Administrative and General Services	33,313,700	11.1	50,153,500	14.5	60,855,500	16.9
Hospitals	131,979,100	43.9	136,311,100	39.5	139,505,400	38.6
Health Stations and Centers	93,300,600	31.0	108,932,800	31.5	113,328,000	31.4
Training	11,878,900	3.9	14,357,700	4.2	15,697,700	4.3
Research Institutes	3,248,700	1.1	4,180,500	1.2	6,652,700	1.8
Malaria Control	24,500,000	8.1	28,445,000	8.2	23,635,500	6.5
Tuberculosis Control	1,577,500	0.5	1,776,700	0.5	1,082,500	0.3
Others	1,122,400	0.4	796,000	0.2	—	—
Health Education Material Production and Distribution Agency			538,500	0.2	595,600	0.2
Total	300,920,900	100.0	345,491,800	100.0	361,352,900	100.0

Source: PHRD Study Number 6, 1996.

Table A3.18   Capital Health Budget Allocation by Sources and Year (in '000 Birr)

GC	EC	Total Allocation	Allocation by Sources Government	Loan	Assistance	Allocation by Sources in Percent Government	Loan	Assistance
1986/87	1979	47,373	36,913	489	9,970	77	1	21
1687/88	1980	54,519	29,148	7,252	18,118	53	13	33
1688/89	1981	65,989	36,442	3,068	26,479	55	4	40
1989/90	1982	63,657	30,480	13,360	19,816	47	21	31
1990/91	1983	48,914	21,969	10,215	16,729	44	20	34
1991/92	1984	63,014	21,003	22,036	19,974	33	35	31
1992/93	1985	84,302	45,012	13,452	25,838	53	30	16
1993/94	1986	197,885	85,473	29,151	83,260	43	14	42
1994/95	1987	234,098	148,058	58,242	27,797	63	24	11
1995/96	1988	237,860	141,968	71,216	24,676	59	29	10

Source: PHRD Study Number 6 (1996) based on data from Revised Budget, 1986/87-1991/92 E.C, and MOF 1992/93-1995/96, Negarit Gazetta, Proclamation Nos. 27/1992, 81/1994, 109/1995, and 128/1995.

Table A3.19   Regional Distribution of Health Facilities by Type of Facility and Ownership, 1994/95

Type of Facility and Ownership

Region	Hospital				Health Center			Health Station			
	1	3	4	T	1	4	T	1	3	4	T
Tigray	12[a]	—	—	12	14[a]	—	14	136	—	5	141
Afar	2	—	—	2	4	—	4	31[a]	2	1	34
Amhara	11[a]	—	—	11	44	1	45[a]	427	—	17	444
Oromia	22[a]	—	3	25	56[a]	7	63	728[a]	9	108	845
Somali	3	—	—	3	7	—	7	66	—	—	66
Benishangul	2	—	—	2	4	—	4	65	—	4	69
SNNPR	7	—	2	9	31	3	34	381	—	43	424
Dire Dawa	2[a]	—	1	3	1	—	1	6	1	11	18
Gambella	1	—	—	1	1	2	3	29[a]	2	3	34
Harari	5[a]	—	—	5	—	—	—	5	—	—	5
Addis Ababa	8	1	1	10	16	—	16	9	231	150	390
Nationally Administered	6	—	—	6	—	—	—	—	—	—	—
Total	81	1	7	89	178	13	191	1,883	245	342	2,470

Region	Pharmacy					Drug Shop					RDV				Health Post	Private Clinic
	1	2	3	4	T	1	2	3	4	T	2	3	4	T	T	Total
Tigray	—	—	9	—	9	—	—	6	—	6	—	162	1	163	272	14
Afar	—	—	1	—	1	—	—	2	—	2	—	42	—	42	—	—
Amhara	4	4	11	—	19	—	—	23	—	23	17	210	—	227	281	48
Oromia	—	11	18	5	34	—	—	66	—	66	2	447	4	453	333	—
Somali	—	—	3	—	3	—	—	1	—	1	—	5	—	5	—	—
Benishangul	1[a]	—	—	—	1	—	—	1	—	1	—	39	—	39	—	—
SNNPR	3[a]	5	2	—	10	—	—	10	—	10	2	379	—	381	256	—
Dire Dawa	—	—	4	1	5	—	1	2	—	3	—	19	—	19	3	1
Gambella	—	—	—	—	—	—	—	—	—	—	—	5	—	5	—	—
Harari	—	2	3	—	5	—	—	1	—	1	—	5	—	5	—	3
Addis Ababa	—	9	62	1	72[b]	—	—	39	—	39	—	13	—	13	21	43[a]
Nationally Administered	—	—	—	—	—	—	—	—	—	—	—	—	—	—	—	—
Total	8	31	113	7	159	—	1	151	—	152	21	1,326	5	1,352	1,175	196

a. Number of private clinics in Region 14 could include the 231 shown under private health stations.

b. Total number of RDV in region 4 does not include those in Bale Zone.

Notes: The number of health stations will increase to 2,551 when 45 health stations in region 3 under construction are included.

1 = Governmental (MOH); 2 = Public; 3 = Private; 4 = NGO.

Source: PHRD Study Number 11, 1996.

Table A3.20   Physical Condition of Health Institutions by Type

Condition of Health Facility	Type of Health Facility			
	Hospitals (n=17)	Health Centers (n=18)	Health Station (n=38)	Total (n=73)
Excellent	17.6	11.1	15.8	15.1
Minor Repair	35.3	55.6	36.8	41.1
Major Repair	29.4	22.2	31.6	28.8
Replacement	17.6	11.1	15.8	15.1
Total	23.3	24.7	52.1	100.0

Source: PHRD Study Number 17, 1996.

Table A3.21   Health Facilities Reporting Availability of Selected Equipment and Transport Facilities by Type, 1995

Type of Equipment	Hospital (n=14) (Percent)	Health Center (n=16) (Percent)	Health Stations (n=33) (Percent)
Baby Scale	86	94	64
Adult Scale	86	94	64
Examination Bed	79	75	67
Delivery Bed	86	81	45
Oto/Opthalmoscope	79	75	n.a.
Autoclave/Sterilizer	86	69	67
Vacuum Extractor	n.a.	62	n.a.
Ultra Sound	14	n.a.	n.a.
E.C.G. Machine	64	n.a.	n.a.
X-ray Machine	86	n.a.	n.a.
Microscope	79	81	n.a.
Laboratory Incubator	57	n.a.	n.a.
Refrigerator	100	87	67
Washing machine	43	n.a.	n.a.
Ambulance	21	n.a.	n.a.
Other Vehicle	50	69	n.a.
Motorcycle	...	75	24
Bicycle	...	50	21

Source: PHRD Study Number 17 (Survey of medical and health care institutions), 1996.

BIBLIOGRAPHY

Abdulhamid, B.K. 1994. *Economic Impact of AIDS and Its Implication on Health Care Service System in Ethiopia.* Addis Ababa.

Ainsworth, M., K. Beegle, and A. Nyamete. 1995. *The Impact of Female Schooling on Fertility and Contraceptive Use: A Study of Fourteen Sub-Saharan Countries.* Washington, D.C.: World Bank.

Alderman, Harold and Marito Garcia. 1994. "Food Security and Health Security: Explaining the Levels of Nutritional Status in Pakistan." *Economic Development and Cultural Change.* 42 (3): 485-507.

Amha, W. 1996. "Private and Social Returns to Schooling. PHRD Study Number 9.b." Addis Ababa, Ethiopia

Anand, Sudhir and Martin Ravallion. 1993. "Human Development in Poor Countries: On the Role of Private Incomes and Public Services." *Journal of Economic Perspective.* 7 (1): 133-150.

Aredo, D. 1989. "Labor Force Utilization in Traditional Agriculture: Estimates of Surplus in a Village in the Central Highlands of Ethiopia." *Ethiopian Journal of Development Research* 2 (2).

Asmerom, K. 1994. *Demographic-Macroeconomic Impact of AIDS in Ethiopia.* Addis Ababa.

Baryoh, A. 1994. *Socioeconomic Impact of HIV/AIDS on Women and Children in Ethiopia.* Addis Ababa.

B&M Development Consultants. 1996. "Demographic Analysis and Population Projections to Year 2020: Impact on Future Social Sectors." PHRD Study Number 4. Addis Ababa, Ethiopia.

European Commission. publication date unknown. "Ethiopia: Food Security Analysis." mimeo.

Central Statistical Authority. 1993. *Report on the National Rural Nutrition Survey, Core Module.* Statistical Bulletin 113. Addis Ababa, Ethiopia

_____. 1992. *Report on the National Rural Nutrition Survey, Core Module.* Statistical Bulletin 113. Addis Ababa, Ethiopia.

_____. 1985. *Report on the Rural Nutrition Survey.* Volume 1. *Statistical Bulletin* 47. Addis Ababa.

Chen, Shaohu, Gaurav Datt, and Martin Ravallion. 1994. *Is Poverty Increasing in the Developing World?* Washington, D.C: Policy Research Department, The World Bank.

Colclough, C., and K. Lewin. 1993. *Educating All the Children: Strategies to Primary Schooling in the South.* Oxford: Clarendon Press.

Cotlear, D. 1989. "Effects of Education on Farm Productivity". *Journal of Development Planning* 19: 73-99.

CSAE (Center for the Study of African Economies), Oxford University. 1996. *Ethiopia*

Social Sector Review (PER II). Report prepared for the Ministry of Finance, Government of Ethiopia. Funded and Coordinated by the European Commission.

Dercon, Stefan, Pramila Krishnan, and Abdulhamid Bedri Kello. 1994. *Poverty in Rural Ethiopia 1989-94*. Draft Report. Oxford: Center for the Study of African Economies, Oxford University.

Dercon, S. 1996. *Household Demand for Health and Nutrition (Rural Survey)* PHRD Study Number 2.a. Oxford: Center for the Study of African Economies, Oxford University.

Desta, D., and D. Chalchisa. 1996. *Demand and Supply of Education Manpower: Alternative Scenarios*. PHRD Study Number 15. Addis Ababa: Institute of Educational Research (IER), Addis Ababa University.

Destefano, J., K. Tietjen, C. Bonner, B. Wilder, S. Hoben. 1993. *Education Sector Country Strategy Assessment*. Draft. Addis Ababa: U.S. Agency for International Development/Ethiopia.

Dufera, D, F. Melesse, H. Shiferaw, and S. Woldemariam. (IER). 1996. *Cost-effectiveness and Program Evaluation of Major Interventions in Education*. Addis Ababa: Institute of Educational Research (IER), Addis Ababa University.

Farell, J., and E. Schiefelbern. 1974. *Expanding the Scope of Educational planning: The Experience of Chile*. Interchange 5 (2): 18-30.

Federal Democratic Republic of Ethiopia. 1997. *Government Financing of Education and Health Sector Programs*. Presented at the Sector Investment Program Meeting (March, 1997). Debre Zeit, Ethiopia.

_____. 1996a. *Education Sector Development Program*. Prepared for the Consultative Group Meeting of December 10-12, 1996. Addis Ababa, Ethiopia.

_____. 1996b. *Health Sector Development Program*. Prepared for the Consultative Group Meeting of December 10-12, 1996. Addis Ababa, Ethiopia.

_____. 1996c. "Food Security Strategy." Prepared for the Consultative Group Meeting of December 10-12, 1996. Addis Ababa, Ethiopia.

Gargiulo, C. 1996. *Ethiopian Education: Minimum Quality Standards and a Policy Modeling Approach*. Presentation made at the World Bank.

Geressu, T., A. Nurhuseein, G. Lemecha, Y. Tadesse, and B. Legesse. 1996. *Burden of Disease(National and Regional)*. PHRD Study Number 3. Addis Ababa: Ministry of Health.

Glewwe, P., and H. Jacoby. 1995. "An Economic Analysis of Delayed Primary School Enrollment in a Low Income Country: The Role of Early Childhood Nutrition." *Review of Economics and Statistics:* 156-169.

Habtemariam, G. (1996). *Survey of Health and Medical Institutions*. PHRD Report No. 17. Addis Ababa: Policy and Human Resource Development Project Office.

Heyneman, S. 1981. *Textbook Availability and Other Determinants of Student Learning in Uganda*. Comparative Education Review 24.

Indevelop. 1996. *A Review of the Ethiopian Health Sector and Development Program*.

Institute of Educational Research (IER). 1996. *Access to and Supply of Education Facilities and Services*. PHRD Study Number 10. Addis Ababa: Addis Ababa University.

Kassie, Workneh, and Helmut Kloos. 1993. "Modern Health Services." In *The Ecology of Health and Disease in Ethiopia.*, ed. by H. Kloos and Zein Ahmed Zein. Oxford: Westview Press.

Kinde, K., and H. Kenso. 1996. *Demand and Supply of Health Manpower: Alternative Scenarios*. PHRD Study Number 14. Addis Ababa.

Krishnan, P. 1996. *Private and Social Returns to Schooling*. PHRD Study Number 9.a. Oxford: Center for the Study of African Economies (CSAE), Oxford University.

KUAWAB Audit Services and Business Consultants. 1996a. *Household Demand for Schooling*. PHRD Study Number 1.B. Addis Ababa, Ethiopia.

_____. 1996b. *Household Demand for Health and Nutrition (National Survey)*. PHRD Study No. 2.b. Addis, Ababa.

_____. 1996c. *Cost and Financing of Education*. PHRD Study Number 5. Addis Ababa.

_____. 1996d. *Cost and Financing of Health, Nutrition, and Population Services*. PHRD Study Number 6. Addis Ababa.

Liqu, H. 1996. *Community Consultation and Participatory Development*. PHRD Study Number 12. Addis Ababa.

Lockheed, Jamison, and Lau. 1980. "Farmer Education and Farm Efficiency: A Survey. World Bank Staff Working Paper." World Bank, Washington, D.C.

Macro International, Inc. 1992. *Africa Demographic Health Survey 1992*. Maryland.

Makuria, G. and L. Mengiste. 1996. *The Role of NGOs and Private Sector in Social Service Deliver., Ethiopia*. PHRD Study Number 13. Addis Ababa.

Mekonnen, T., and S. Ghebre. 1995. *Household Consumption and Expenditure*. Draft presented at the Workshop on the Preliminary Report of the First Round of the Ethiopian Rural Household Survey. AAU and Oxford U. Workshop.

Mengesha, T. and N. Taffa. 1996. *Access to and Supply of Health, Nutrition, and Population Facilities and Services*. PHRD Study Number 11. Addis Ababa.

Ministry of Education, 1994, 1995, and 1996. *Annual Education Statistics*. Addis Ababa.

Ministry of Health. 1994. *Health and Health-Related Indicators, October 1994*. Planning and Programming Department. Addis Ababa.

Office of the Prime Minister. 1993. *National Population Policy of Ethiopia*. Addis Ababa.

Pelletier, D. L., K. Deneke, Y. Kidane, B. Haile and F. Negussie. 1995. "The Food-First Bias and Nutrition Policy: Lessons from Ethiopia." *Food Policy* 20 (4): 279-298.

PHRD Project Office. 1996a. *Social Sector Review: Education Sector Synthesis*. Addis Ababa.

PHRD Project Office. 1996b. *Social Sector Review: Health Sector Synthesis*. Addis Ababa.

Rosati, F. and L. Mikael. 1997. *Public Expenditure Review: Increasing Non-Government Financing Sources in Education and Health Care Delivery*. Draft Report. Addis Ababa: Italian Cooperation and USAID/Ethiopia.

Rosenzweig, M. 1995. "Why Are There Returns to Schooling?" *American Economic Review (Papers and Proceedings)* 85: 153-58.

Sime, H. 1996. *Survey of Educational Institutions*. PHRD Study Number 16. Addis Ababa.

Social Services and Administration, Office of the Prime Minister. 1994. *Ethiopia Human Resources Development Strategy for Health: Report for the National Task Force on Human Resources Development for Health*. Addis Ababa.

Subbarao, K., and K. Mehra. 1996. *Improving Nutrition in Ethiopia.* Washington, D.C.: World Bank.

Taddese, M., S. Ghebre, P. Bevan, S. Dercon, and P. Krishnan. 1995. *Food Consumption Habits, Expenditures, Vulnerability, and Poverty.* Paper presented during the Workshop on the Preliminary Report of the First Round of the Ethiopian Rural Household Survey. July 18-20, 1995. Addis Ababa.

Tedela, T., and M. Mussa. 1996. *Cost-Effectiveness and Program Evaluation of Major Health Interventions.* PHRD Study Number 7. Addis Ababa.

Teka, Gabre E. 1993. "Water Supply and Sanitation." In *The Ecology of Health and Disease in Ethiopia.,* ed. *by* Kloos, H. and Zein Ahmed Zein. Oxford: Westview Press.

Transitional Government of Ethiopia/United Nations Children's Fund (TGE/UNICEF). 1993. *Children and Women in Ethiopia: A Situation Report.* Addis Ababa.

TGE. 1993. *Health Policy of the Transitional Government of Ethiopia.* Addis Ababa.

UNESCO, 1993 and 1994. *Statistical Yearbook.*

United Nations Fund for Population Activities (UNFPA). 1995. *Mid-Term Review Report: UNFPA Third Country Program (1993-1997).* Addis Ababa.

United Nations (Administrative Committee on Coordination/Subcommittee on Nutrition). 1994. *Update on the Nutrition Situation, 1994.* Prepared in collaboration with International Food Policy Research Institute. Washington, D.C.

Webb, Patrick, Joachim von Braun, and Yisehac Yohannes. 1992. *Famine in Ethiopia: Policy Implications of Coping Failure at National and Household Levels.* Research Report 92. Washington, D.C.: International Food Policy Research Institute.

Webb, Patrick, Edgar Richardson, Senait Seyoum and Yisehac Yohannes. 1994. *Vulnerability Mapping and Geographical Targeting: An Exploratory Methodology Applied to Ethiopia.* Washington, D.C.: International Food Policy Research Institute.

Weir, S., and J. Knight. 1996. *Household Demand for Schooling (Rural Survey).* PHRD Study Number 1.A. Oxford: Center for the Study of African Economies (CSAE).

World Bank. 1998. "Education Sector Development Program: Project Appraisal Document." draft. Washington, D.C.

World Bank. 1997a. *World Development Report 1997.* New York: Oxford University Press.

_____. 1997b. *Ethiopia: Public Expenditure Review.* Washington, D.C.

_____. 1996. *World Development Report 1996.* Washington, D.C.

_____. 1996a. *Africa Development Indicators.* Washington, D.C.

_____. 1996b. *Health Policy in Eastern Africa: A Structured Approach to Resource Allocation.* Population and Human Resources Division, Eastern Africa Department, Africa Region. April 24. Washington D.C. (Draft Report).

_____. 1996c. *Approach Paper for the Health, Nutrition, and Population Sector.* Washington, D.C.

_____. 1995a. "Country Assistance Strategy for Ethiopia." World Bank, Washington, D.C.

_____. 1995b. *World Development Report: Workers in an Integrating World.* Oxford University Press, New York.

_____. 1994a. *Better Health in Africa: Experience and Lessons Learned.* Washington, D.C.

_____. 1994b. *Ethiopia: Public Expenditure Policy for Transition.* Country Operations Division, East Africa Department, Washington, D.C.

_____. 1993a. *Eritrea: Options and Strategies for Growth* . Washington, D.C.

_____. 1993b. *Ethiopia: Toward Poverty Alleviation and a Social Action Program.* Report No. 11306-ET. Washington, D.C.

_____. 1993c. *World Development Report 1993.* New York: Oxford University Press.

_____. 1987. *Sector Review Ethiopia: A Study of Health Financing Issues and Options.* Washington, D.C.

Distributors of World Bank Publications

Prices and credit terms vary from country to country. Consult your local distributor before placing an order.

ARGENTINA
Oficina del Libro Internacional
Av. Cordoba 1877
1120 Buenos Aires
Tel: (54 1) 815-8354
Fax: (54 1) 815-8156
E-mail: olilibro@satlink.com

AUSTRALIA, FIJI, PAPUA NEW GUINEA, SOLOMON ISLANDS, VANUATU, AND SAMOA
D.A. Information Services
648 Whitehorse Road
Mitcham 3132
Victoria
Tel: (61) 3 9210 7777
Fax: (61) 3 9210 7788
E-mail: service@dadirect.com.au

AUSTRIA
Gerold and Co.
Weihburggasse 26
A-1011 Wien
Tel: (43 1) 512-47-31-0
Fax: (43 1) 512-47-31-29

BANGLADESH
Micro Industries Development Assistance Society (MIDAS)
House 5, Road 16
Dhanmondi R/Area
Dhaka 1209
Tel: (880 2) 326427
Fax: (880 2) 811188

BELGIUM
Jean De Lannoy
Av. du Roi 202
1060 Brussels
Tel: (32 2) 538-5169
Fax: (32 2) 538-0841

BRAZIL
Publicações Tecnicas Internacionais Ltda.
Rua Peixoto Gomide, 209
01409 Sao Paulo, SP.
Tel: (55 11) 259-6644
Fax: (55 11) 258-6990
E-mail: postmaster@pti.uol.br

CANADA
Renouf Publishing Co. Ltd.
5369 Canotek Road
Ottawa, Ontario K1J 9J3
Tel: (613) 745-2665
Fax: (613) 745-7660
E-mail: order.dept@renoufbooks.com

CHINA
China Financial & Economic Publishing House
8, Da Fo Si Dong Jie
Beijing
Tel: (86 10) 6333-8257
Fax: (86 10) 6401-7365

China Book Import Centre
P.O. Box 2825
Beijing

COLOMBIA
Infoenlace Ltda.
Carrera 6 No. 51-21
Apartado Aereo 34270
Santafé de Bogotá, D.C.
Tel: (57 1) 285-2798
Fax: (57 1) 285-2798

COTE D'IVOIRE
Center d'Edition et de Diffusion Africaines (CEDA)
04 B.P. 541
Abidjan 04
Tel: (225) 24 6510;24 6511
Fax: (225) 25 0567

CYPRUS
Center for Applied Research
Cyprus College
6, Diogenes Street, Engomi
P.O. Box 2006
Nicosia
Tel: (357 2) 44-1730
Fax: (357 2) 46   ??1

CZECH REPUBLIC
USIS, NIS Prodejna
Havelkova 22
130 00 Prague 3
Tel: (420 2) 2423 1486
Fax: (420 2) 2423 1114

DENMARK
SamfundsLitteratur
Rosenoerns Allé 11
DK-1970 Frederiksberg C
Tel: (45 31) 351942
Fax: (45 31) 357822

ECUADOR
Libri Mundi
Libreria Internacional
P.O. Box 17-01-3029
Juan Leon Mera 851
Quito
Tel: (593 2) 521-606; (593 2) 544-185
Fax: (593 2) 504-209
E-mail: librimu1@librimundi.com.ec

CODEU
Ruiz de Castilla 763, Edif. Expocolor
Primer piso, Of. #2
Quito
Tel/Fax: (593 2) 507-383; 253-091
E-mail: codeu@impsat.net.ec

EGYPT, ARAB REPUBLIC OF
Al Ahram Distribution Agency
Al Galaa Street
Cairo
Tel: (20 2) 578-6083
Fax: (20 2) 578-6833

The Middle East Observer
41, Sherif Street
Cairo
Tel: (20 2) 393-9732
Fax: (20 2) 393-9732

FINLAND
Akateeminen Kirjakauppa
P.O. Box 128
FIN-00101 Helsinki
Tel: (358 0) 121 4418
Fax: (358 0) 121-4435
E-mail: akatilaus@stockmann.fi

FRANCE
World Bank Publications
66, avenue d'Iéna
75116 Paris
Tel: (33 1) 40-69-30-56/57
Fax: (33 1) 40-69-30-68

GERMANY
UNO-Verlag
Poppelsdorfer Allee 55
53115 Bonn
Tel: (49 228) 949020
Fax: (49 228) 217492
E-mail: unoverlag@aol.com

GHANA
Epp Books Services
P.O. Box 44
TUC
Accra

GREECE
Papasotiriou S.A.
35, Stournara Str.
106 82 Athens
Tel: (30 1) 364-1826
Fax: (30 1) 364-8254

HAITI
Culture Diffusion
5, Rue Capois
C.P. 257
Port-au-Prince
Tel: (509) 23 9260
Fax: (509) 23 4858

HONG KONG, CHINA; MACAO
Asia 2000 Ltd.
Sales & Circulation Department
Seabird House, unit 1101-02
22-28 Wyndham Street, Central
Hong Kong
Tel: (852) 2530-1409
Fax: (852) 2526-1107
E-mail: sales@asia2000.com.hk

HUNGARY
Euro Info Service
Margitszgeti Europa Haz
H-1138 Budapest
Tel: (36 1) 350 80 24, 350 80 25
Fax: (36 1) 350 90 32
E-mail: euroinfo@mail.matav.hu

INDIA
Allied Publishers Ltd.
751 Mount Road
Madras - 600 002
Tel: (91 44) 852-3938
Fax: (91 44) 852-0649

INDONESIA
Pt. Indira Limited
Jalan Borobudur 20
P.O. Box 181
Jakarta 10320
Tel: (62 21) 390-4290
Fax: (62 21) 390-4289

IRAN
Ketab Sara Co. Publishers
Khaled Eslamboli Ave., 6th Street
Delafrooz Alley No. 8
P.O. Box 15745-733
Tehran 15117
Tel: (98 21) 8717819; 8716104
Fax: (98 21) 8712479
E-mail: ketab-sara@neda.net.ir

Kowkab Publishers
P.O. Box 19575-511
Tehran
Tel: (98 21) 258-3723
Fax: (98 21) 258-3723

IRELAND
Government Supplies Agency
Oifig an tSoláthair
4-5 Harcourt Road
Dublin 2
Tel: (353 1) 661-3111
Fax: (353 1) 475-2670

ISRAEL
Yozmot Literature Ltd.
P.O. Box 56055
3 Yohanan Hasandlar Street
Tel Aviv 61560
Tel: (972 3) 5285-397
Fax: (972 3) 5285-397

R.O.Y. International
PO Box 13056
Tel Aviv 61130
Tel: (972 3) 5461423
Fax: (972 3) 5461442
E-mail: royil@netvision.net.il

Palestinian Authority/Middle East
Index Information Services
P.O.B. 19502 Jerusalem
Tel: (972 2) 6271219
Fax: (972 2) 6271634

ITALY
Licosa Commissionaria Sansoni SPA
Via Duca Di Calabria, 1/1
Casella Postale 552
50125 Firenze
Tel: (55) 645-415
Fax: (55) 641-257
E-mail: licosa@ftbcc.it

JAMAICA
Ian Randle Publishers Ltd.
206 Old Hope Road, Kingston 6
Tel: 876-927-2085
Fax: 876-977-0243
E-mail: irpl@colis.com

JAPAN
Eastern Book Service
3-13 Hongo 3-chome, Bunkyo-ku
Tokyo 113
Tel: (81 3) 3818-0861
Fax: (81 3) 3818-0864
E-mail: orders@svt-ebs.co.jp

KENYA
Africa Book Service (E.A.) Ltd.
Quaran House, Mfangano Street
P.O. Box 45245
Nairobi
Tel: (254 2) 223 641
Fax: (254 2) 330 272

KOREA, REPUBLIC OF
Daejon Trading Co. Ltd.
P.O. Box 34, Youida, 706 Seoun Bldg
44-6 Youido-Dong, Yeongchengpo-Ku
Seoul
Tel: (82 2) 785-1631/4
Fax: (82 2) 784-0315

LEBANON
Librairie du Liban
P.O. Box 11-9232
Beirut
Tel: (961 9) 217 944
Fax: (961 9) 217 434

MALAYSIA
University of Malaya Cooperative Bookshop, Limited
P.O. Box 1127
Jalan Pantai Baru
59700 Kuala Lumpur
Tel: (60 3) 756-5000
Fax: (60 3) 755-4424
E-mail: umkoop@tm.net.my

MEXICO
INFOTEC
Av. San Fernando No. 37
Col. Toriello Guerra
14050 Mexico, D.F.

Tel: (52 5) 624-2800
Fax: (52 5) 624-2822
E-mail: infotec@rtn.net.mx

Mundi-Prensa Mexico S.A. de C.V.
c/Rio Panuco, 141-Colonia Cuauhtemoc
06500 Mexico, D.F.
Tel: (52 5) 533-5658
Fax: (52 5) 514-6799

NEPAL
Everest Media International Services (P) Ltd.
GPO Box 5443
Kathmandu
Tel: (977 1) 472 152
Fax: (977 1) 224 431

NETHERLANDS
De Lindeboom/InOr-Publikaties
P.O. Box 202, 7480 AE Haaksbergen
Tel: (31 53) 574-0004
Fax: (31 53) 572-9296
E-mail: lindeboo@worldonline.nl

NEW ZEALAND
EBSCO NZ Ltd.
Private Mail Bag 99914
New Market
Auckland
Tel: (64 9) 524-8119
Fax: (64 9) 524-8067

NIGERIA
University Press Limited
Three Crowns Building Jericho
Private Mail Bag 5095
Ibadan
Tel: (234 22) 41-1356
Fax: (234 22) 41-2056

NORWAY
NIC Info A/S
Book Department, Postboks 6512 Etterstad
N-0606 Oslo
Tel: (47 22) 97-4500
Fax: (47 22) 97-4545

PAKISTAN
Mirza Book Agency
65, Shahrah-e-Quaid-e-Azam
Lahore 54000
Tel: (92 42) 735 3601
Fax: (92 42) 576 3714

Oxford University Press
5 Bangalore Town
Sharae Faisal
PO Box 13033
Karachi-75350
Tel: (92 21) 446307
Fax: (92 21) 4547640
E-mail: ouppak@TheOffice.net

Pak Book Corporation
Aziz Chambers 21, Queen's Road
Lahore
Tel: (92 42) 636 3222; 636 0885
Fax: (92 42) 636 2328
E-mail: pbc@brain.net.pk

PERU
Editorial Desarrollo SA
Apartado 3824, Lima 1
Tel: (51 14) 285380
Fax: (51 14) 286628

PHILIPPINES
International Booksource Center Inc.
1127-A Antipolo St, Barangay, Venezuela
Makati City
Tel: (63 2) 896 6501; 6505; 6507
Fax: (63 2) 896 1741

POLAND
International Publishing Service
Ul. Piekna 31/37
00-677 Warzawa
Tel: (48 2) 628-6089
Fax: (48 2) 621-7255
E-mail: books%ips@ikp.atm.com.pl

PORTUGAL
Livraria Portugal
Apartado 2681, Rua Do Carmo 70-74
1200 Lisbon
Tel: (1) 347-4982
Fax: (1) 347-0264

ROMANIA
Compani De Librarii Bucuresti S.A.
Str. Lipscani no. 26, sector 3
Bucharest
Tel: (40 1) 613 9645
Fax: (40 1) 312 4000

RUSSIAN FEDERATION
Isdatelstvo <Ves Mir>
9a, Kolpachniy Pereulok
Moscow 101831
Tel: (7 095) 917 87 49
Fax: (7 095) 917 92 59

SINGAPORE; TAIWAN, CHINA; MYANMAR; BRUNEI
Ashgate Publishing Asia Pacific Pte. Ltd.
41 Kallang Pudding Road #04-03
Golden Wheel Building
Singapore 349316
Tel: (65) 741-5166
Fax: (65) 742-9356
E-mail: ashgate@asianconnect.com

SLOVENIA
Gospodarski Vestnik Publishing Group
Dunajska cesta 5
1000 Ljubljana
Tel: (386 61) 133 83 47; 132 12 30
Fax: (386 61) 133 80 30
E-mail: repansekj@gvestnik.si

SOUTH AFRICA, BOTSWANA
For single titles:
Oxford University Press Southern Africa
Vasco Boulevard, Goodwood
P.O. Box 12119, N1 City 7463
Cape Town
Tel: (27 21) 595 4400
Fax: (27 21) 595 4430
E-mail: oxford@oup.co.za

For subscription orders:
International Subscription Service
P.O. Box 41095
Craighall
Johannesburg 2024
Tel: (27 11) 880-1448
Fax: (27 11) 880-6248
E-mail: iss@is.co.za

SPAIN
Mundi-Prensa Libros, S.A.
Castello 37
28001 Madrid
Tel: (34 1) 431-3399
Fax: (34 1) 575-3998
E-mail: libreria@mundiprensa.es

Mundi-Prensa Barcelona
Consell de Cent, 391
08009 Barcelona
Tel: (34 3) 488-3492
Fax: (34 3) 487-7659
E-mail: barcelona@mundiprensa.es

SRI LANKA, THE MALDIVES
Lake House Bookshop
100, Sir Chittampalam Gardiner Mawatha
Colombo 2
Tel: (94 1) 32105

Fax: (94 1) 432104
E-mail: LHL@sri.lanka.net

SWEDEN
Wennergren-Williams AB
P.O. Box 1305
S-171 25 Solna
Tel: (46 8) 705-97-50
Fax: (46 8) 27-00-71
E-mail: mail@wwi.se

SWITZERLAND
Librairie Payot Service Institutionnel
Côtes-de-Montbenon 30
1002 Lausanne
Tel: (41 21) 341-3229
Fax: (41 21) 341-3235

ADECO Van Diemen EditionsTechniques
Ch. de Lacuez 41
CH1807 Blonay
Tel: (41 21) 943 2673
Fax: (41 21) 943 3605

THAILAND
Central Books Distribution
306 Silom Road
Bangkok 10500
Tel: (66 2) 235-5400
Fax: (66 2) 237-8321

TRINIDAD & TOBAGO AND THE CARRIBBEAN
Systematics Studies Ltd.
St. Augustine Shopping Center
Eastern Main Road, St. Augustine
Trinidad & Tobago, West Indies
Tel: (868) 645-8466
Fax: (868) 645-8467
E-mail: tobe@trinidad.net

UGANDA
Gustro Ltd.
PO Box 9997, Madhvani Building
Plot 16/4 Jinja Rd.
Kampala
Tel: (256 41) 251 467
Fax: (256 41) 251 468
E-mail: gus@swiftuganda.com

UNITED KINGDOM
Microinfo Ltd.
P.O. Box 3, Alton, Hampshire GU34 2PG
England
Tel: (44 1420) 86848
Fax: (44 1420) 89889
E-mail: wbank@ukminfo.demon.co.uk

The Stationery Office
51 Nine Elms Lane
London SW8 5DR
Tel: (44 171) 873-8400
Fax: (44 171) 873-8242

VENEZUELA
Tecni-Ciencia Libros, S.A.
Centro Cuidad Comercial Tamanco
Nivel C2, Caracas
Tel: (58 2) 959 5547; 5035; 0016
Fax: (58 2) 959 5636

ZAMBIA
University Bookshop, University of Zambia
Great East Road Campus
P.O. Box 32379
Lusaka
Tel: (260 1) 252 576
Fax: (260 1) 253 952

ZIMBABWE
Academic and Baobab Books (Pvt.) Ltd.
4 Conald Road, Graniteside
P.O. Box 567
Harare
Tel: 263 4 755035
Fax: 263 4 781913